VOICES FROM THE BRIDGE

To Mary and Claire

VOICES
FROM THE
BRIDGE

Recollections of Members
of the Honourable Company
of Master Mariners

David Smith and John Johnson-Allen

SEAFARER BOOKS

© David Smith and John Johnson-Allen 2010

Published in the UK by Seafarer Books Ltd
102 Redwald Road · Rendlesham · Suffolk IP12 2TE

www.seafarerbooks.com

ISBN 978-1-906266-16-5 paperback

A CIP record for this book is available from the British Library

Line drawings © Peter Adams

Photographs, all provided by contributors, are copyright and used
in this book with the permission of the copyright-holders.

Design, typesetting
Louis Mackay / www.louismackaydesign.co.uk

Editing: Hugh Brazier

Text set digitally in Proforma

Printed in Finland by WS Bookwell

Contents

The Merchant Navy has served Britain throughout five centuries. Those five centuries saw the growth of the British Empire and the start of the industrial revolution, and by the end of the reign of Queen Victoria around half the world's seagoing trade was conducted in ships that flew the Red Ensign. Fifty years later, after two World Wars, a fifth of all merchant ships were still registered in the United Kingdom.

The advent of mass air travel, the development of containerisation, and the globalisation of the shipping industry resulted in an unprecedented, and largely unforeseen, decline in the size of the British Merchant Navy. Today just one or two per cent of the world's merchant ships fly the 'red duster'.

The authors of this book travelled round Britain recording the memories of retired Master Mariners, nearly all of whom are members of the Honourable Company of Master Mariners. Here, in the words of some of those who sailed as Apprentices, Mates and Masters, is the story, not only of the day-to-day routine, hard work and inevitable drudgery, but also of the dangers, excitement and humour of life in the Merchant Navy in the middle of the last century. Although much less than one lifetime ago, it is a way of life that is now no more, having disappeared as a result of the changes within the shipping industry during the 1970s and 1980s.

This is a book of memories: memories of men who 'went down to the sea in ships'; memories of a vanished way of life. As Patron of the Wellington Trust, and a Past Master of the Honourable Company of Master Mariners, I am delighted to have been asked to write this foreword, and that the proceeds from this book will go to the Wellington Trust, to support the education of the nation on our Merchant Navy heritage and its protection.

Anne

IN MEMORIAM

Professor David Smith
1931–2010
Master Mariner
Liveryman of the Honourable Company of Master Mariners
Fellow of the Royal College of Radiologists

David was the kindest of co-writers to one embarking on
his first book. It was a privilege and a delight to work with him.
Laughter was so often a part of the collaboration.

J J-A

Introduction

The idea for this book came almost simultaneously to each of the two authors. John Johnson-Allen was studying for an MA in maritime history, while David Smith had just completed a guide to the Honourable Company of Master Mariners and its floating headquarters, the *Wellington*. Both realised what a collective wealth there was in the memories of the membership of the Company, and that once lost this would be gone for ever. A way of life had started to vanish in the 1960s with the advent of containerisation and flags of convenience. It has now almost disappeared. Rather than work separately, they decided to cooperate, and this book is the result.

The Honourable Company of Master Mariners is a Livery Company of the City of London. There are nearly eight hundred members, most of whom are Master Mariners, and their homes are to be found not only throughout the United Kingdom but also around the world.

The book is based on both recorded interviews and written accounts. The interviews were transcribed and then, in association with the contributor, edited for continuity and to smooth out some of the infelicities that are an inevitable part of the spoken word. Every effort has been made to retain the flavour of the original contributions.

Given the nature of the membership of the Honourable Company, the book reflects a view of what life was like as seen from the bridge of a ship of the merchant navy in the middle of the twentieth century. This is the story of the deck officer, from the time that he made the decision to go to sea until he eventually rose to command, and then how he fared when he decided to come ashore or 'swallow the anchor'.

Goods have been carried by sea for thousands of years, and until just a few years ago the method of loading and discharging ships remained much the same. The galley and the longboat gave way to the galleon, which in turn was replaced by the clipper ship, only for sail to be superseded by steam. But the slave stowing amphorae in a hundred-ton cargo vessel in the Mediterranean two thousand years ago would have felt at home watching stevedores in London or Liverpool docks stowing crates and cartons in the hold of a six-thousand-ton steamship. The process was both labour-intensive and time-consuming. It would take over a hundred stevedores some four to five weeks to discharge and then to load the eight thousand tons of general cargo carried by a typical cargo liner in the 1950s. Nowadays a handful of gantry drivers can discharge and load eight thousand containers each carrying up to ten tons of cargo in less than forty-eight hours.

The quick turn-round in port, combined with a faster steaming speed, means that one container ship with a total crew of perhaps twenty replaces some twenty-five conventional cargo ships, each with a crew of fifty or more. Over a thousand seafarers replaced by just twenty.

In the 1950s passenger liners were criss-crossing the seas. Today, the children and grandchildren of those passengers all travel by air. A 400,000-ton very large crude carrier (VLCC) carries as much oil as thirty of the largest tankers afloat in the years following the Second World War. These changes took just twenty to thirty years, within the span of a single generation.

Also, in the 1950s it became common practice for merchant ships to be registered in tax havens such as Liberia and Panama – the so-called 'flags of convenience'. In the latter part of the nineteenth century around one half of the world's merchant ship tonnage flew the Red Ensign. By the middle of the twentieth century this had fallen to some twenty per cent, and at the start of the twenty-first century only one per cent of the world's merchant fleet was registered in the United Kingdom.

This, told in their own words, is the story of the last generation of British merchant-navy deck officers to experience life at sea in the days before 'globalisation'.

I · Then and now

In 1948 the United Kingdom was recovering from war, much energy was being exerted in re-establishing markets for our exports, ship owners were rebuilding their fleets, and life at sea was settling down into a pattern not too dissimilar from what it had been pre-war.

The merchant navy was still an integral, and significant, part of our economy. But – and here the literal and the metaphorical blend into one – a sea change was just over the horizon. In the immediate post-war period ships were being registered in countries such as Panama and Liberia, a practice known as 'flagging out' or sailing under a flag of convenience. This trend was to become ever more popular with ship owners and managers, and increasingly ships were being manned by foreign, often multinational, crews as costs were cut in the pursuit of profit. The move to containerisation would result in much larger ships, and the conventional docks in ports such as London, Glasgow and Liverpool would become redundant, while the growth of air travel, epitomised by the introduction of the Boeing 747 in the 1960s, resulted in passenger liners being replaced by cruise ships. Advances in electronics led to revolutionary developments in control mechanisms that in turn led to smaller crews. By 1980, in barely more than one generation, a whole way of life had largely vanished.

By 1948 the British merchant navy had recovered its pre-war position in terms of tonnage, to 17.9 million tons. The largest ship was the *Queen Mary*, with a gross registered tonnage of 81,237, whilst among the smallest was the *Crescence*, a coaster with a gross tonnage of 255 tons. At that time (1948) there were over 131,000 British seafarers.

Although there was some blurring at the edges, it was at that time possible to divide the ships of the merchant navy into five main classes: passenger liners, cargo liners, tramp ships, tankers and coasters. There was also the government-owned Royal Fleet Auxiliary, which provided logistical support for the Royal Navy, a fleet of chartered troopships, and a number of specialised vessels such as cross-channel ferries, survey vessels and deep-sea tugs.

The passenger liner companies all had their home ports. For example, Southampton was the home of the Cunard and Union Castle Lines, Liverpool of Canadian Pacific and Elder Dempster Lines, London of the Peninsular and Orient (P&O), and Glasgow of the Donaldson Line. These companies owned fleets of cargo liners as well. Both passenger and cargo liners sailed on scheduled voyages to well-defined destinations. Most passenger ships carried some cargo, and many of the cargo vessels carried up to twelve passengers. (If more than twelve passengers were carried, then the crew had to include a doctor.) Outward bound the holds would contain a general cargo, whilst on the homeward voyage the holds would be filled with agricultural products and the raw materials for our factories. The regular pattern of the voyages, with leave on return to the United Kingdom, gave at least the possibility of some semblance of normality to family life. Unquestionably, a degree of elitism pervaded these companies.

There were a number of companies that ran cargo liner services, but had no passenger ships. An example is the Ellerman and Papayanni Line, which ran a regular service to Spain, Portugal and the Mediterranean.

Tramps were the workhorses of the sea, chartered on an ad hoc basis to carry bulk cargoes. The owners, or their agents, arranged the charters, which could be between ports anywhere in the world. The crew signed on for a period not exceeding two years, and there was no guarantee that the vessel would return to the United Kingdom during this period. The availability of cargoes fluctuated, as did the rates for carriage, and some tramp companies had an (often well-deserved) reputation for being tight-fisted. Well-known tramp ship companies included Bank Line, Sir William Reardon Smith and Runcimans. The Baltic Exchange in London was the UK centre for arranging charters and cargoes.

Tankers, as the name implies, carried bulk liquids. The majority of tankers belonged to one of the major oil companies, Shell, BP and Esso, and were employed carrying crude oil or its refined products. The vessels traded between the oil terminals in the producer countries and refineries in Europe and North America. Independent tanker operators included Common Bros and also the Athel Line, which specialised in carrying molasses.

The coastal and short-sea traders formed yet another class of vessels. A large number of small and varied vessels traded around the coast of the British Isles and nearer Continent, often using small ports that were inaccessible to larger ships. So long as they did not venture beyond the Elbe to the north and Brest to the south the deck officers did not have to possess foreign-going certificates of competency, while those Masters and Mates who sailed in coastal cargo ships did not have to have any certificate at all until 1970 when, as a result of a major inquiry into the shipping industry, various wide-ranging changes took place. The manning scale was very different on the smaller vessels, and in many cases just a Master and a Mate took watch and watch about whilst at sea. There was undoubtedly a degree of snobbery in the attitude of many foreign-going deck officers towards their coastal colleagues but, nevertheless, a considerable number of deck officers with foreign-going certificates joined the coastal trade.

The ships of the Royal Fleet Auxiliary could easily be mistaken for those of the Royal Navy: painted grey, with military helicopters landing and taking off from their afterdecks. They were, and still are, a fleet of support ships that keep the fighting ships fed, watered and fuelled whilst at sea. Although government-owned, they are nevertheless part of the merchant navy and the crews remain civilians, although all are now Naval reservists.

There was also a fleet of troopships carrying service personnel between the United Kingdom and military bases overseas. These were all ex-passenger ships on government charter from the liner companies, who still managed them. A typical voyage would entail picking up a consignment of troops and any accompanying families from Liverpool or Southampton and then calling at Port Said, Aden, Colombo, Singapore and finally Hong Kong. The officers and the accompanying families were accommodated in the erstwhile passenger cabins, but the ratings were allocated bunks in what had once been the cargo holds. This accommodation was poorly ventilated, and many a soldier, sailor and airman must have had unpleasant memories of life aboard – especially in bad weather and in the tropics.

There were also a significant number of vessels that did not fit into any of these categories. Cross-channel ferries were small and, compared to today, relatively few in number. In addition there were, and still are, the survey vessels that are necessary for keeping the channels marked, and the deep-sea tugs needed for long distance towage.

Not much more than half a century later the scene is almost unrecognisable – except, perhaps surprisingly, for the coastal trade. Cruise ships have replaced the passenger liners, container ships have replaced the cargo liners, bulk carriers of 150,000 tons or more have largely taken the place of the tramps, VLCCs can now transport up to 400,000 tons of oil, and service personnel now travel by air. Crew sizes have diminished on virtually all ships, and some of the largest container ships have a crew of less than twenty. Very few of these ships fly the Red Ensign. In the year 2000 there were under 28,000 British seafarers, a fall in numbers of nearly eighty per cent in half a century.

2 · Pre-sea training

In the period covered by this book it was usual for aspiring deck officers to undergo a period of pre-sea training before starting their apprenticeship.

This may have been at one of the three training establishments recognised as 'public' schools: HMS *Conway*, HMS *Worcester* and the Nautical College, Pangbourne. Boys entered these schools at the age of thirteen or fourteen, having passed the Common Entrance examination, and had a general as well as a nautical education. After three years most of the boys opted for a life at sea, some electing for the Royal Navy whilst others joined the merchant navy. There was also the one-year residential course at the School of Navigation, Warsash, Southampton. Nautical schools, often with hostels attached, that offered pre-sea training were also found in all the major seaports, and additionally there was the short-lived and all-but-forgotten London Nautical Training School.

What they all had in common, whether the course lasted three months or three years, was an introduction to seamanship and navigation, together with some signalling and boat work. Even after the shortest of courses, the apprentice joining his first ship would know port from starboard and be able to tie a bowline! The longer courses effectively covered the syllabus for the Second Mate's certificate, and included subjects such as ship construction and meteorology. The value of these longer courses was recognised by the Board of Trade, who gave some remission of the sea-time needed before a candidate was allowed to sit for his ticket, as the Certificates of Competency were almost universally known among seamen. This meant that a cadet who had successfully completed the course at the *Conway* or the *Worcester* only had to do a three-year apprenticeship instead of the full four years, while the year-long course at Warsash earned six months remission of sea-time.

The original HMS *Conway* dates back to 1857, when an ex-naval vessel was loaned by the Admiralty, moored off Rock Ferry in the River

Mersey, and used to train boys who wished to become officers in the mercantile marine, as the merchant navy was usually known at that time. The original vessel soon proved too small, and it was replaced twice. In 1941, when Liverpool was being targeted by German bombers, HMS *Conway* was moved to the safety of new moorings in the Menai Strait. Anthony Braithwaite recalls the circumstances that led to him choosing to go to sea, and his time aboard HMS *Conway*:

❢ I was very interested in ships and the sea. I was well acquainted with the River Thames – my father had tugs and barges – and on a Saturday morning, even before the war when I was seven years of age, I was told to go with a friend on a Saturday morning with a pack of sandwiches and spend the whole day going up and down the river in one of the company tugs. So Father, perhaps to discourage me from going to sea, decided that I had better have a taste of it, and so he arranged with a friend of his who owned the Everard fleet at Greenhithe to go away in 1945 in a ship called the *Ability*. It had a crew of twelve, and I spent the summer moving between Bellamy's wharf, Rotherhithe and Hamburg with grain. It was very interesting to see Hamburg at that time, which was in ruins and the people starving coming down to the ship's side and trying to sell anything they had to get some money to buy food, and so I did this for several summers. I steered the ship and made myself useful, they only had a crew of twelve, I was kept pretty busy. I kept watches and that was very interesting.

So at the age of sixteen a decision was made as to whether I should go to the *Worcester* at Greenhithe or the *Conway* at Bangor, and my mother thought that it would be better if I was to go further away from home, so off I went and joined the *Conway*. A very daunting thing, you have a self-measurement chart which you take to a tailor and he measures you up and you send this off and then a great big parcel arrives with a uniform and a cap, and you have to dress up in this and go off and catch a train from Euston. My parents took me there and found another set of parents with another similarly attired *Conway* cadet starting his first day. So we went off together and remained life-long friends.

The *Conway* was a nineteenth-century wooden wall and she

had been employed in the Crimea,[1] and it was a very tough sort of life. We all slept in hammocks that were very comfortable. In the morning we would lash up and stow the hammocks into hammock racks and go and have meals at tables and when we had finished the meals the tables would be put up into the ceiling, the deckhead, and the decks would be turned into classrooms. Partitions would come down. The masters lived ashore. They came off in the morning in the ship's boats and we always longed for rough weather when the masters couldn't get out and we had a day off from lessons. We soon made friends and there was tremendous camaraderie and everything was done by bugle calls. The food generally was dreadful and there was rationing on at the time and when we went ashore for sports days we would be able to buy something to supplement our diet.

It was a school and it had three terms a year. We always looked forward very much to the end of term and at the bugle call that called us in the morning there would be a shout of 'Six days to the end of term', 'Five days to the end of term', and on the day that we left the entire band would go onto the upper deck and play and so you knew it was time to go home. But my two years on the *Conway* were among some of the happiest times of my life. ❥

Peter Richards-Jones's pre-sea training was at the London Nautical Training School (LNTS). Here he recalls the circumstances that led to his going to sea. He refers to the Royal Research Ship *Discovery*, which carried Captain Scott to the Antarctic and is now berthed at Dundee – but which at that time was moored in the Thames alongside the embankment opposite Somerset House. The *Exmouth* was a purpose-built training ship that was moored off Grays in Essex. She was one of a number of training ships and schools set up as a result of the Industrial Schools Act of 1866. These were intended to provide both education and training for poor boys, many of whom ended up in the Services. The improvements in education in the twentieth century meant that

---

1. As HMS *Nile.*

they were becoming redundant and, following the repeal of the Poor Law Act in 1929, the London County Council (LCC) took over the responsibility for running the *Exmouth* from the London Metropolitan Asylums Board. Relaunched as the London Nautical Training School, the school was evacuated to Lydney in Gloucestershire for much of the war. In 1947 it became an LCC boarding school in Suffolk, and all nautical training was abandoned in 1951.

After the war the *Exmouth* was bought by the Thames Nautical Training College (HMS Worcester) and renamed HMS *Worcester*. As the *Exmouth* she accommodated 700 boys; as the *Worcester* she accommodated 180 cadets.

❻ During the war, about 1941/42, I was very interested in the sea so I became a sea scout on the *Discovery*, and I used to cycle from Dulwich up to the Embankment every Sunday and go on board. We used to climb about in the lower rigging, mainly the older boys, and one day, before we set off in the rowing boats on the Thames with our sandwiches, I elected to go up and look at the crow's nest. I got up there but I couldn't get down, and everybody was shouting at me 'Come on down', and I was there waving to them and saying 'I can't', and they thought I was waving them goodbye and they all got into the boats and went off. Four hours later when they all got back I was still stuck up there in the crow's nest and two of the older boys had to come up and guide me down. I couldn't have been more than twelve and could you imagine that happening today? The health and safety regulations and things like that. Absolute nonsense, isn't it? So that is how I began to look at the sea, and of course there was no education in the war. Even if you were evacuated it was all in bits and pieces, two half-days per week, you didn't get an uninterrupted line of education and I failed the Eleven-plus, so when I was thirteen I eventually passed the Junior Tech which meant that I could either go to Brixton School of Building and become something there, on the drawing board or whatever, or I could go to the London Nautical Training School which had just started up and which the LCC wanted to pretend was a kind of public school for London children, to offset the Pangbournes and Worcesters and that sort of thing. And so poorer boys from London, and I was one of them, went to this wretched school, which resulted, when I was sixteen, in going to sea and I joined my first ship on 27 April 1946.

The London Nautical Training School (LNTS) found its origin in the TS *Exmouth*, which, for whatever reason, folded in the early days of the war. The LCC thought it a good idea to change the remnants to a neo-public school. So, with the small residue of *Exmouth* boys and a batch of scholarship boys – of which I was one – the LNTS was formed (had my father been aware of its history, I would not have been allowed to go). I was just thirteen years.

We were billeted among the people of Lydney, Gloucestershire, and had to walk a couple of miles for breakfast in the outbuildings of the Feathers Hotel where we had all our meals. The school itself was situated in an empty church school. When other schools had holidays, we were sent to lift potatoes for Lord Bledisloe, at sixpence a day, my part of the war effort.

Around 1944/45 the school moved to the estate of Lord Haig at Bray Court, Bray, Maidenhead, a well-appointed mansion. Generally speaking the lads went into the RN as artificers and some went to the RMSM.[2] I played the euphonium in the brass band. But my father (then in the army) spoke to the school and the authorities at length and was the instigator of boys going into the merchant navy as apprentices. I was the first to take that road,[3] and remember well showing off my new uniform to the other lads at school the day before departing (on the headmaster's instructions).

I wasn't sorry to leave as she was a tough school – second-hand patched boots, the war was still on and clothes still rationed. The school moved some time later to Woolverstone, where the nautical side petered out. ❥

---

2. Royal Marines School of Music.
3. This is disputed by another contributor. The authors do not wish to become embroiled.

Warsash, at least in the aftermath of the war, was very much modelled on military training and was proud of its reputation for discipline and 'character building'. It even went so far as to send the parents of prospective entrants a conspectus rather than the more usual prospectus. Great store was placed on shiny toecaps and neatly folded blankets. Much of the time seemed to be spent polishing the floor (or rather the deck) in the living quarters. A glass-like surface was required, and the situation was reached where this was covered with newspapers except for those times when it was being polished or inspected. In many ways life for a new cadet was not all that dissimilar from that of the National Serviceman, except that one was taught seamanship and navigation rather than how to strip a Bren gun. Once in a while someone would run away – and in all probability Captain Wakeford, the Director, was secretly delighted when this happened since it would have enhanced the school's reputation for toughness. Stuart Bradley recalls his decision to go to sea and his time at Warsash:

❢ There is a long history of sailors in my family. In fact I have four Master's certificates in my possession – mine, my father's, my grandfather's and my great grandfather's. We think that we probably go back much further than that. They were a seafaring family from Whitby, although my father during his career in the thirties spent a lot of time running in and out of South Wales ports. My grandfather on my mother's side worked in Cardiff docks and my father married his daughter and I was born and brought up in Wales. And I am afraid that I am the last of my family that are going to sea – my son certainly hasn't been interested in it, neither have other relatives.

I have always had a pretty good feel for seafaring – part of the culture – part of the language in the family. Indeed in the suburbs of Cardiff when I was in my prep school that was a fairly common sort of thing. There were a lot of boys who came from families with a long pedigree of seafarers. Sometimes tragically. In my form in Westbourne House Preparatory School for Boys in the war there were five boys who lost their fathers. Mine was the only one who survived. He ended up a prisoner of war. The other four were drowned – that's rather a lot when you think about it in a class of fifteen. So it was that sort of background where it all started, I never thought of doing anything else except going to sea. Partly because my father was an exotic character, in that he went away and came back and had that aura that all sailors have – a degree of mystique that was hugely attractive to a young boy. He was different from our near neighbours' fathers. I always knew what I wanted to do, and though I think he did his best to put me off, because he obviously did know a lot more about it than I did, he failed.

So I did go to sea. I went to Warsash in 1952 – on my sixteenth birthday, actually. And that year was the most formative year of my life, I guess, I think probably in common with a lot of other cadets. You grew up quickly. You also, in my case as for others too, came into contact with people from a completely different background, and you had to measure yourself against them in a fairly uncompromising regime. But it was something that I absolutely loved. (a) I loved the subject matter, and (b) I had a huge respect for the people who were teaching us. Frankly, this was probably the result of my father's strong belief that there were two classes of people on this earth – one was sailors, and then the rest.

At Warsash I made friends that I still have today, and I suppose it knocked some of the spots off me. I always thought that by going to Warsash I had a head start because I knew about it, but they soon brought me down to earth, and of course I thought it was absolutely brilliantly run. It was magnificently structured. The concept was good – you had three intense terms. You went there as a relatively immature young man and you came away as a mature young man. They instilled a sense of purpose. It was much more focused than I perceive to be the case with other pre-sea training schools. This was the time of Captain Wakeford, who was a remarkable man, no question. My father knew him and that probably didn't do me any favours, but I had a great respect for him. Partly because my father was Commodore of South America Saint Line and they took a lot of Warsash cadets because they thought they were the best trained. Maybe he was slightly prejudiced but they tended to be more of a grammar school background than probably some of the others, and my father always thought his best cadets came from there.

It was quite interesting – when I was in my final term at Warsash you were required to name three shipping companies that you wished to be considered for, and I put down Royal Mail because I knew they had short trips to South America, the New Zealand Shipping Company because I rather liked the idea of going to this exotic place, perversely as that was a long trip, and Port Line because I liked the colour of the funnel. But your choice had to be endorsed by one's parents. When this came up my father was actually on his ship in Buenos Aires and so my mother cabled him with my choice and he sent back a cable to Wakeford who passed it on to me which read 'Stuart will join the P&O Steam Navigation Company if he is good enough', and of course I did. I mean, that tells you two things: (a) I was in awe of my father and (b) I had utter faith in his judgement.

And we didn't meet again for another three years, because he was at sea and I was at sea with P&O going out to the Far East and he going back and forth to South America. We didn't meet until I was just about to take my Second Mate's certificate and I said 'Why did you want me to go into the P&O?' and he said 'Because they have the best pension scheme.' That was his priority, reliability and that they treated their sailors well. He had been at sea during the Depression, when people were being laid off left, right and centre, and that was his criterion – not the fact that they had fancy liners and, if you like, they were an elite company. What did interest him was the way they treated people. And he was right. Although my year at Warsash had been formative, it was the years at P&O that really 'maketh the man'.

Warsash was the first time, as a boy of sixteen, that I was treated as an adult, and that was the general approach at Warsash. You were not talked down to. You were talked to as man-to-man. They made you feel that you were capable of handling life as a mature individual. Not merely because of attitude but for the respect that they gave you for doing things on your own. There was a great deal of initiative required to complete your course successfully in Warsash. And the fact that you rubbed shoulders with people from all over the place. It was there that I first met someone from the subcontinent of

India, and I learnt a lot of what Indians thought of us at that time that was completely new to me. It broadened your horizons, also made me realise that, if you are to succeed in this life, you have not just got to be dedicated, efficient and all that, but also have got to have a wider aura, you have to be more rounded, so that you have friends. You do have to have an ability to mix with people. This is particularly true of sailors. It would be very difficult to be a loner, and I think that came out at Warsash. Warsash set you up physically as well of course. It was over in a flash, and they always used to say at Warsash that going to sea is going to be easy after this. I don't necessarily fully agree with that, but from the point of view of the rigour, I think that it was probably right. 9

In the first half of the nineteenth century British maritime trade was growing very rapidly, and the shortage of adequately trained Masters and Mates had become apparent. So in 1853 the Department of Science and Art laid down the framework for a more structured approach to nautical education, and as a result during the following decade navigation schools were set up in Poplar in London, in Liverpool, in Hull, in Plymouth and in Glasgow, and it was not long before further nautical schools were established in other major ports.

Oliver Signorini attended the one-year course at Aberdeen in the early 1950s:

6 I am an Aberdonian, and my pre-sea training was carried out at Robert Gordon's Navigation School, Aberdeen. I was very fortunate because it meant that I could live at home while completing the course, not like many of the boys who came from far and wide and had to find local accommodation or stay with relatives or at the Mission to Seamen in Mearns Street.

The year's course split into four quarterly periods, and we had four lecturers at the college at that time, headed up by the College Principal, Captain Cameron. The course was an introduction to seafaring and we were taught the basics of seamanship, navigation and signals. We had a boatshed down on the River Dee where we were trained in dinghies, basic sailing techniques and rowing. We had college quarterly examinations to see how we were progressing, and towards the end of the fourth quarter we had to individually try and seek out a shipping company that we could be indentured to. Of course at that time there were many companies but somehow it was not easy to get into the better ones. I was offered an apprenticeship with the famous Ben Line of Leith but unfortunately became ill and lost that opportunity. I was one of those that ended up on the tramp ships, which were not as salubrious as a liner company or even a vessel on regular runs. However, it was generally understood that the experience gleaned from serving on this category of vessel was second to none, and I enjoyed it.

My school class was made up of about fifteen boys, and we all got on socially very well, and our lecturers were actually very good. In addition to normal classroom work we had facilities on the roof of the building where we were introduced to basic astronomy, the magnetic compass and associated nautical equipment.

At the end of the twelve-month course of training I had to go down to Newcastle with my father for an interview with a shipping company called Stag Line. We went down by train and attended at the offices of Joseph Robinson and Son, the owners of the company, where I met David Robinson who interviewed me prior to becoming an apprentice. The amusing thing about that was that my father expected to come into the room with me, but was greeted by David very politely saying, 'No, it is your son I want to see and not you, so would you please sit outside and have a cup of coffee.' I was in there with him for perhaps three-quarters of an hour at least, but was accepted and thereby became indentured as a Deck Apprentice for four years and joined my first ship, called the MV *Zinnia*, in September 1953. ❥

3 • Apprentice

The first stage of the aspiring officer's seagoing career was normally the apprenticeship. The relatively few exceptions were those who went to sea as ordinary seamen and then, after time as ABs, enrolled for a period at a nautical college before sitting for the Second Mate's certificate.

The would-be apprentice would attend for interview at the shipping company of his choice and then, if successful, he and a parent (or guardian) would sign an indenture.

The apprentice's indenture was a time-honoured document with its roots firmly in the Middle Ages. In the earlier part of the twentieth century a premium would have been paid by his parents or guardian for the apprentice to be bound to the company, although by the 1960s this had become a nominal sum. The young man became bound apprentice to the company for a period of four years, the company in turn covenanting 'to teach the Apprentice or cause him to be taught navigation seamanship and the business of a seaman and Ship's Officer'.

Although the broad framework of the four-year apprenticeship remained the same, each individual company, and there were over a hundred of them in the middle of the twentieth century, had its own variations on the training that was provided. While, sadly, a number of companies exploited their apprentices, treating them as little more than cheap labour, the better companies ensured that each apprentice had experience working as a seaman on deck, spent time on the bridge with the watch-keeping officers, and had adequate time for study to prepare for the examination for the Second Mate's certificate at the end of the four years.

For those boys who had had no pre-sea training, and at just sixteen they *were* still boys, leaving home and entering the insular adult world of a merchant ship was usually an experience that was etched deeply into their memories. In many cases it would be a year or more before they next came back to the United Kingdom and, in the days before airmail, let alone e-mail, letters from home might be few and far between.

In 1951 Terence Jewell, a Plymouth lad, signed indentures with the Hain Steamship Company on his sixteenth birthday, and immediately joined the *Tregothnan*.

Hain's had started in the 1830s as a family concern at St Ives in Cornwall with just two small schooners. During the second half of the nineteenth century the family made the transition to steam, and by the end of the century they were firmly established as a tramp-ship company. The company was acquired by P&O in 1917, but continued to be managed as an autonomous company with a tradition of recruiting from the West Country.

Terence Jewell recalls some memories of his apprenticeship. The pastoral care sounds rather draconian by today's standards, but these lads were starting early on a life beset with temptation, and the Master knew only too well that the dockside bars in Marseille were rather different from the beachside cafés in St Tropez.

❻ We were three apprentices. I was the junior, obviously, at just sixteen. It was the Commodore's ship. We had three bunks in the main cabin, we had a study, we had our own toilet, bathroom and shower. We were very well appointed. It went downhill after that on other ships.

We were trading on a P&O charter. We would go outward, the usual P&O trip which was Marseille, Genoa, Port Said, the Canal, Singapore, Australia starting at Cairns all the way down the Barrier Reef as far as Perth. Discharge there and then we would wait for the wool sales, and we took the first cargo of wool to Japan after the war. That was about 1951. Waited anything about six to eight weeks, alongside. That was the charter, we loaded Perth, Melbourne, Sydney, Brisbane and then we would head up to Hong Kong and then around the Japanese coast discharging wool. We would then load steel, flat steel, back via Borneo where we picked up teak logs, back down to Australia, discharge, right round the coast again as far as

Perth and then reload for the UK. Perth, Melbourne, Sydney, Brisbane and then home.

I remember that first trip. Sat on the wall in Marseille of a dockside pub while walking back to the ship, and all the officers were there except the duty officer and the engineers, and the Master comes by in his blue serge suit and homburg hat and sees me sat there, and he taps me on the shoulder and says, 'See me in my cabin at 0900 hours tomorrow, boy.' Next morning he said, 'You were in a house of ill repute. For that you can have your indentures cancelled. I shall be writing to your father. You are now gated for six months. You will not go ashore. You will not get any pocket money.' Six months I was gated and he wrote to my old man and he said if he did it again he would cancel my indentures. That's it. And it was the standard that you got. I wasn't even drinking – the others were. I don't even know if I had been in a house of ill repute. I didn't get a chance to find out!

We were doing the MNTB[4] syllabus. Not very much of it though. That is why I took three goes for Second Mate's. The support from the Master and Mates was very good. Every so often they would say 'come on', and see if you were doing enough studying. So most mornings we did the four-to-eight watch, obviously, came off watch and if we weren't then working with the Bosun we proceeded to the smoke room with our books and spent the morning studying. And then, of course, in the afternoon we were expected on the bridge with the Second Mate for the afternoon sights, so it got us into a good routine very early on.

I had a couple of bad trips when I was eighteen to nineteen when I had to keep the four-to-eight watch, work all morning, probably most of the afternoon, and then go back on watch. And in my day, to earn sufficient money to come ashore and study I used to do night watchman. Wouldn't be allowed nowadays. I used to paint over the ship's side at night on my own, on a stage, up and down a pilot ladder. We were a fortnight in one port in Australia and I painted the offshore side from end

---

4. Merchant Navy Training Board.

to end, cutting in the white line, the ship's name and the draft. I used to get a bob an hour for that, come off at seven in the morning and be asleep before the winches started, as there was one just outside my cabin. And I used to sleep straight through. Wake up at about four o'clock and get tea and at seven o'clock I was back on watch again. It was a busy life. I got paid a shilling an hour extra for all that. Fourteen shillings every night – old money. That was twelve bob for twelve hours and two bob for being night watchman. You wouldn't be allowed to do it now. Rig your own stage, put it over the side, get yourself up and down with the paints. Put it this way – I was totally self-sufficient, and by the time I was a Second Mate, or even a Third Mate, I could run the deck watch without any problems.

As the senior apprentice I always steered the vessel from the fairway buoy to the harbour entrance and berth. If we were transiting the Canal I was always steering from the fairway buoy at one end to the fairway buoy at the other. I would do anything from fourteen to sixteen hours on the wheel. If you don't know how to steer, boy, you can't teach anyone else. So it was always 'Apprentice on the wheel' and I would be up there. The fact was I got to know the pilot quite well and he said, 'Tell me when she is not steering.' It was the same in Sydney Harbour. He was a Preference Pilot and he would say 'Hello, you on the wheel again?' and I would say 'I'm always on the bloody wheel.' He would say, 'Dead Slow Ahead – you know the way. Tell me when she is not steering and you need more power,' and I used to steer up Sydney Harbour and when we got off the berth he would say 'Brilliant'.

I had a superb four years. I really did. You're tickling the memory up now. It was a good apprenticeship. The great pity is they don't do it these days. I accept it has been a great loss when they started MAR release.[5] Your apprentices only doing two years at sea. That I think is one of the worst things they ever did. Less sea time and next thing they had Second Mate's before they were ready to go back to sea. They hadn't really learnt their trade. Sixteen to twenty or seventeen to twenty-one

5. Mid-apprenticeship release.

was a very important formative period. The more I look back on it the more I think it was correct. I really do. And the same with the engineers. The Sixth Engineer or the Fifth Engineer – he had done his four-year apprenticeship in the shipyard, and then they did their time on board and then went for their Second Engineer's ticket and they were fully briefed and fully trained. The system was excellent. I think the current system fails people. I think that is why we are having more accidents at sea.

I did – let me see now – I did four voyages in four years. The average voyage was about a year for those ships on a fixed charter. When you were doing the P&O trips, Bank Line sub-charters, those were all eleven or twelve months. Two trips of one year. Then a six weeks to Montreal, then round the coast as well. Four trips in four years.

There is one last story. We were on the way to Galveston on a ship where I was senior apprentice. The Master called me to his cabin and told me that the Second Mate had appendicitis. He wanted me to help because we would have to operate on him. I was surprised because why had he asked me, not the Mate or the Third Mate? Well, the problem was that the Mate had a drink problem and his hands shook and the Third Mate was squeamish, so I was the next best option. The Captain told me that we would have to put ice packs on the Second Mate's stomach to keep the temperature down while we sorted out what do. He decided that I should be the anaesthetist. I told him that I had never done anything like that but he told me not to worry as it was only a case of holding the ether pad over his nose and mouth and dripping the ether on to it from time to time. We then went to look for the scalpels. They were in the first aid kit which had not been used for a long time, so the scalpels were rusty. The Captain said not to worry because they could be sharpened up and cleaned in the engine room by the engineers and then sterilised with the ether. We then had to contact the International Radio centre in Italy who assisted with this sort of medical emergency. However by this time we had managed to arrive in Galveston, so the Second Mate was rushed ashore to hospital and operated on within the hour. We were told that it was only just in time, the appendix was about to burst and the ice packs had been of great assistance. It had been a close-run thing. **9**

Memories of one's first voyage to sea as an apprentice often remain vivid even after those of subsequent voyages begin to fade. David Smith records some memories from his first voyage aboard the *Santander* in 1948. She was a six-thousand-ton cargo liner belonging to the Pacific Steam Navigation Company and was on their regular run between Liverpool and the west coast of South America via the Panama Canal. Like many cargo liners, she carried twelve passengers. The Pacific Steam Navigation Company was founded in 1838 to trade on the coasts of Chile and Peru. It was not long before it extended its routes to include Ecuador and the Pacific coast of Colombia. In 1867 a regular service was introduced between Liverpool and the west coast of South America.

Almost inevitably, many of the memories recalled in this book centre around time at sea, the navigation, the unexpected, the personalities. However, all these were ancillary to the safe carriage and delivery of cargo and passengers. The *Santander* was carrying a general cargo on the outward voyage. A general cargo was just that, a bit of everything: bricks, pipes, cases of beer and spirits, cars and lorries, machinery, bales and wooden cases, cartons and sacks. All this had been loaded so that the cargo bound for the early ports was not blocked off by that destined for discharge towards the end of the outward voyage. As well as this, the cargo destined for each port of call had been evenly distributed between the five holds, as this both facilitated a quicker discharge and kept the ship on an even keel. The cargo plan was crucial to a successful discharge. Copies had to be available for the Master Stevedore at each of the ports, and aboard the *Santander*, in those days before photocopiers, fax machines and e-mail, these copies were made by the apprentices.

6 We sailed just as it was getting light on the morning of 26 September 1948. The time for sailing was dictated by the tide, as it was only possible to enter or leave the docks for an hour or so either side of high water. I was on duty at the stern of the ship where I was manning the telephone. I relayed orders such as 'Cast off, aft' from the bridge to the Second Officer, and passed back information such as 'All clear, aft' to let the bridge know that the hawsers were clear of the screw.

There were no farewells. Just a few stolid faces watched our departure as we moved out of the lock into the river. Then a few minutes later we let go the tugs and headed down the Mersey towards the open sea. Once clear of the bar at the entrance to the Mersey we steered a westerly course to the pilot station off Point Lynas. Around noon the pilot was dropped and we rounded Anglesey and steamed south into the Irish Sea. For one seventeen-year-old, a dream had come true.

That first morning I found myself on day work while the other three apprentices kept bridge watches. I was introduced to 'sooji', an unpleasantly aggressive washing powder that was ladled liberally into the bottom of a bucket that was then filled with cold water, the resultant mixture being used to clean the white paintwork. It was applied with a large wad of cotton waste and then washed off with cold water – clean this time. This was not too unpleasant when the paintwork was below shoulder level, but above that height and when working overhead a cold stream of sooji ran down one's sleeve and one's clothes gradually got wetter and wetter.

Once we were clear of the shipping lanes and well out to sea I was joined on day work by two of the other apprentices, while the senior apprentice stayed on watch with the Chief Officer. It was an odd hybrid life, half officer, half seaman. We worked on deck during the day doing much the same jobs as the seamen, but ate in the saloon with the officers and the twelve passengers.

When at sea, our first task every morning was to scrub down the wooden decks of the midships superstructure, and then to set out the deck chairs ready for the passengers. This was before breakfast, so we had to change out of our dungarees into uniform before going down into the saloon. Then as soon as breakfast was eaten, back into working gear until lunchtime. Once the ship was clean, a process taking several days, the next job was overhauling all the metal blocks on the derricks. These would all see extensive use during the next two months and each block had to be stripped down, greased and reassembled. A morning of this and one's hands were black with grease. It was quite a job to get clean and into uniform for lunch in the saloon, and we envied the seamen who just had to wash their hands before eating in their mess. While we had lunch and dinner, they had dinner and tea! In these less formal days it is hard to credit that even for breakfast we had to wear stiff collars as part of our uniform. The board-like starched white collars were attached to the shirt by collar studs. I soon found out that the other, more experienced, apprentices had stratagems available for simplifying this hurried mealtime clothes change. After washing they would put on a 'dickie'. This consisted of just the front part of a shirt with tapes that tied behind the back to hold it in place. A wipe-clean celluloid collar meant a lot less washing and ironing, for we had to do our own laundry when we were at sea. Dirty clothes were boiled in a bucket, rinsed and then hung out to dry on a line between two derricks. Whites were rinsed with blue-bag and starched before ironing.

The meals were traditional, but the cooking was good and the helpings generous. Twelve fare-paying passengers meant that standards were not allowed to fall. It was certainly a contrast from life ashore in England, where food rationing was still in force. A typical breakfast might be grapefruit or prunes, porridge or cereal, a fish dish such as kipper or smoked haddock, bacon and eggs, toast and marmalade, and tea or coffee. We apprentices had our own table, which, like the rest, had hinged wooden rails (fiddles) on the sides that were rotated up to make a rim, and these, helped by wetting the tablecloth, ensured that it was only in exceptionally rough weather that plates and glasses would shoot off the table.

One of the more extraordinary jobs that fell to us apprentices was the preparation of copies of the cargo plan. When we sailed from Liverpool, a master copy of the cargo plan was given to the Chief Officer. Copies of this had to be available at each port of discharge, and further copies were needed

A P P R E N T I C E S
LIST OF OUTFIT REQUIRED

1. Burberry Style, Single Breasted Raincoat, Blue. £11.5.0
   (R.N. pattern without belt).
1. Uniform Suit, Cloth (R.N. pattern) for shoregoing use. £13.15.0
1. Uniform Suit, (R.N. pattern) for ship use, Battle-dress type. £5.5.0
1. White Mess Jacket. £1.16.6
- 1. Black Cummerbund. 15/9d.
1. White Uniform Cap, Badge and Band - best quality for shore use £2.19.5
1. White Uniform Cap, Badge and Band - cheap quality for ship use.
2. Uniform Black Ties. to buy 6/11
1. Black Bow Tie. 6/-
6. Stiff White Collars. £1.1.0
2. White Wing Collars. 7/-
1. Pair Uniform Brown Gloves (R.N. pattern). 19/11
1. Pair Uniform Shoes (R.N. pattern) no toe caps and no protectors. £2.12.6.
2. Set Shoulder Straps with 3 buttons across. 11/6 ea.
3. White Uniform Shirts. 29/6 ea.
1. White Duck Uniform (R.N. pattern). £2.12.6
2. Pairs White Shorts (R.N. pattern). 22/6 ea
2. White Shirts (R.N. pattern). 21/-
2. Pairs White Stockings (R.N. pattern). 7/9 ea.
2. Pairs White Socks. 5/-
1. Pair White Canvas Shoes. cleaner £2.1.2.
2. Blue Boiler Suits. £4.5.0
2. Pairs Dungaree Trousers, Blue. 19/3 ea.
1. Oilskin and Southwester. £3.7.0
1. Pair Working Shoes (no protectors) Black. own Black
1. Pair Rubber Sea Boots (Thigh length, not hip) and stockings. 58/11 w 43/6d.
2. Blue Working Shirts. 17/6 ea.
2. Pairs Blue Working Shorts. 22/6 ea.
1. Pair Dark Grey Flannel Trousers.
1. Pair White Gym Shoes. 19/11
2. White Gym Singlets.
2. Pairs White Gym Shorts. to buy 8/6d.
1. Pair Swimming Trunks 15/- ea.
3. Suits of Pyjamas.
3. Suits Underwear. Pants relaced Vests to buy 5/6 ea 2
4. Pairs Black Socks. 5/-
12. White Handkerchiefs. 3 @ 2/-
1. Pair Braces.
1. Clothes Brush; 1 Nail Brush; 1 Hair Brush and Comb.
   Shoe Cleaning Gear for Black and White Shoes.
2. Tooth Brushes and Tooth Paste or Powder.
1. Housewife. Nail Scissors 9/6
1. Plain strong leather Belt and Green River Sheath Knife.
1. Canvas Sea Bag with lock and key. 23/6   8/6   13/11
1. Cabin Trunk.

Storm cap 13/11
Best 5/11   Apprentices wear the Company's Cap Badge and Buttons
                 their distinctive marks being - Three Company's
                 Buttons across Cuffs.

Note   Civilian Clothing (Lounge Suits, Caps etc.) must not
        form part of Apprentices' Outfit.

Grey socks
own Black shoes

The required uniform for an apprentice to the British and Commonwealth
Lines, annotated with prices by Christopher Laycock's mother.

Subjects and Duties	Requires further experience			Considered Competent	
Seamanship	Officer's Initials	Date	Remarks	Officer's Initials	Date
CARGO GEAR 19. Rig, top and lower derricks	*(init)*	7/1/66	Command practical experience	*(init)*	9.1.68
20. Drive winches/capstans/ cranes (name types)	*(init)*	20/1/67	Wind.	*(init)*	20/1/67
ROPES AND WIRES 21. Make slings and preventer guys	*(init)*	4/1/67	Slings		
22. Sling a stage and rig a boat-swain's chair	*(init)*	5.10.68	*illegible*		
23. Break out new coils of ropes and wire, and make fast painters, boat ropes and messengers	*(init)*	18/9/66		*(init)*	13.2.68
24. *Rig and lower stays, aerials and whistle lanyards	*(init)*	3/1/67		*(init)*	9.1.68
25. Stopper ropes and wires.	*(init)*	1/9/66		*(init)*	12.11.67
26. Run, heave and turn up mooring and towing lines	*(init)*	1/9/66		*(init)*	10.2.68
27. Place and use fenders and fit rat guards.	*(init)*	1/9/66		*(init)*	3/5/67
28. Assist with stowage and care of mooring ropes and wires	*(init)*	1/9/66		*(init)*	22.12.67
BLOCKS AND TACKLES 29. Overhaul cargo blocks and running gear	*(init)*	3/12/66		*(init)*	17.8.67
30. Reeve topping lifts					
31. Reeve guy falls	*(init)*	5.11.68			
32. Reeve three-fold and other purchases					
WINDLASS, ANCHORS AND CABLES Assist in :— 33. Operating windlass, engaging and disengaging gears and brake	T.S.A.	14/14/69			
34. Preparing for anchoring	31/12/66 *(init)*			*(init)*	10.2.68
35. Letting go and weighing anchor	23/1/67 18.2.68 *(init)*				
36. Securing anchors and cables and using bow stoppers or compressors	*(init)*	17/9/66		*(init)*	15.1.68

8

A page from Christopher Laycock's Merchant Navy Training Board Logbook. He was serving with the British and Commonwealth Lines, but not all shipping companies were so meticulous in their approach to the training of apprentices.

so that we all knew what was destined for where. We would be given a large outline plan of the ship and a pile of different coloured crayons of a special waxy consistency, rather like hard, thin candles. We would reproduce the master plan on this outline using a different colour for each port. We would then be given a roll of something that in colour and texture resembled nothing so much as the skin with accompanying layer of fat that is cut away from a joint of boiled bacon. When unrolled this was about three feet long and half as wide. Our carefully coloured cargo plan was then placed face down on the jelly-like surface and a roller was vigorously applied so that the surface of the roll absorbed our waxy writing. Our sub-master was then removed and replaced by another blank outline. More rolling and the wax writing was transferred from the roll to the blank. This was repeated, but each time the copy became fainter. With some very hard rolling one would be lucky to get some five or six copies.

This was inefficient and labour-intensive, but it didn't take up more than a small part of that outward voyage. And remember that Britain was still grey and austere in 1948. We had many new experiences, and I'm sure they made a greater impression than might be the case today. Watching flying fish skimming over the surface of the sea; seeing porpoises playing in the bow wave; and above all, later in the voyage, at anchor off Talcahuana in Chile, the wonder of seeing penguins swimming in the clear waters of the Pacific. **9**

A very few shipping companies had one or more of the ships in their fleet dedicated to cadet training. On these cargo ships there were no deck hands, the seamen being replaced by the cadets. The training was outstanding, and it engendered a very special *esprit de corps* among the cadets who sailed on them. The *Otaio* was the cadet training ship of the New Zealand Shipping Company (NZSC), a company that was founded in 1873 and based in Christchurch, New Zealand, but which by 1881 had passed into UK ownership. This was a time when the British Empire was at its apogee, and ships were in demand to carry both emigrants and manufactured goods outward bound from the UK, and to return laden with agricultural products and other raw materials. The New Zealand Shipping Company introduced its first refrigerated compartments on its ships as early as 1881, making it possible for New Zealand beef and lamb to be sold on the UK domestic market, which in turn led to great hardship for British farmers. By 1916 the NZSC had become part of the P&O group, but it continued to trade as a separate entity until 1973, when all the ships were transferred to the parent company. Michael Keat recalls his apprenticeship:

❢ I joined the *Otaio* as an apprentice in October 1958 straight from school, with no pre-sea training at all. I finished my O-levels in July, got the results in August, and two months later went off to sea. I was just sixteen years and two months old. It was a nominal four-year apprenticeship, but with various remissions for being on the training ship, it was nearer three. There were six direct-entry 'trippers' and I think about five pre-sea 'trippers' who joined at that time. We joined in the Royal Albert Dock graving dock, which was a bit frightening. Ships in dry dock have a strange, sort of detached atmosphere. When all the other apprentices came back from leave, we sailed, round the world, west to east, on our first voyage. All my friends and family at home were very impressed with that, but somehow we didn't think too much of it.

I don't remember having to do quite a lot of hard manual work as well as school work as being a problem. Everything was so different from school and home life that we just accepted it. All the other apprentices, who had done at least one voyage already, of course looked down on us 'trippers'. We of course did the same eventually, after our first voyage was completed.

The daily routines varied between school work and deck work. There were no ABs on the ship, so all the deck work was done by the apprentices. There were three cycles involving school work, deck work and watch keeping. School work was either early morning and evening, morning, or afternoon. Early-morning school was usually practical seamanship under a specialist seamanship instructor who was either a bosun or senior AB. He taught us knots and splices, canvas sewing, etc. Morning or afternoon school was in the classroom with the 'Schoolie'. He was usually a senior Second Mate who was signed on in addition to the watch-keeping officers. The school work was a bit difficult for us direct-entry apprentices, as the class was mixed pre-sea and direct entry. The pre-sea guys knew a lot more than us, at least for the first voyage. The pre-sea guys were usually from *Worcester* or Warsash. There were some from Pangbourne and *Conway*, but not many. After my

Account of wages for Michael Keat, when an apprentice aboard *Otaio*, for a voyage lasting 5 months and 20 days.

first couple of voyages, the school work was changed to correspondence course work, with some lectures from Schoolie. I think this was the MN Training Board.

We started watch keeping on our first voyage. Helmsman, lookout or stand-by – no automatic pilot in those days. Four hours on, four off. We would have a week on watches, then two or three weeks' day work and school work. The worst part of watch keeping for me was helmsman, second wheel on the twelve-to-four. This meant being on the wheel from 0200 until 0400. Every 30 seconds the wheelhouse clock, behind the helmsman's head, would 'click' just to remind you how slowly time was passing. Lookout on the fo'c'sle for two hours was boring and sometimes very cold and wet, but at least you could shout at people, no one would hear you. Sometimes you saw a ship, and could ring the bell. Senior apprentices on watch were called 'Junior Officers' or JOs. They kept the full four hours on the bridge, shadowing the officer of the watch. He took sights, compass errors, etc. This was the most valuable training we got I think. It made navigation papers in the Mate's and Master's exams quite easy. I served as Third Officer some years later, on the *Otaio*. I made sure the JOs got experience of daytime sights of the moon and Venus whenever possible. Even horizontal sextant angles when on anchor watch. The training we received was first class, and set us up well for Mate's and Master's.

There were quite a few opportunities for sport, particularly when on the Australian or NZ coast. At sea we had compulsory PT before turn-to in the early morning, but quite a few played other sports, such as deck tennis, deck cricket, deck hockey. There was some boxing, which I did on my first voyage, but never after that. It wasn't well supervised, we had no gum shields, and sometimes it got too brutal. The company supplied quite a lot of equipment, and employed a Physical Training Instructor. The usefulness of the PTI varied from very little to none. On the coast we used the two whalers and two fourteen-foot dinghies quite a lot. The whalers were used for pulling races, and at the weekends, for sailing. Teams could be made up for any sporting challenge we received. Football, rugby, hockey, cricket, even small-bore rifle shooting. We very rarely won, but it usually meant an afternoon ashore, which was worth it. Some of the rugby matches were a bit more serious. We played various NZ high schools, lost most but won a few. We were usually older and a bit bigger, but they were more fit. As I remember, we only had about twenty lads who had ever played rugby, but we still managed to put up a team.

We had some good parties on the coast. For some reason, they were called 'jags', I have never known why. They were supervised by an officer, but he was usually taken care of, one way or another! There was an official Ship's Dance every voyage, usually in the last port on the coast. This was paid for by the company, and usually included a local band, a buffet supper, etc. If the weather suited, these were held on deck. We would finish loading either number four or five holds a day or two early. These holds had flush-fitting pontoons in the main deck. With all the cargo gear unrigged, and the decks scrubbed, awnings rigged, and lights, flags, etc. decorating the area, it was quite a 'do'.

We had cadets' mess room and pantry, with a full-time pantry man and pantry boy, who served the food and did the washing up. We had to serve the tables ourselves. This was the job of the 'trippers', of course. They were known as 'peggies', I have no idea why. The 'peggies' also had to keep the accommodation clean, and do linen changes, etc. Duty officers' rounds were made every evening when the bathrooms, toilets, alleyways and cabins were inspected. Twice a week the Captain also inspected the accommodation. Suitable 'rewards' were won for best or worst cabin. The best were allowed a lie-in on the following Sunday, until 0745. The worst, of which there could be many, were given extra work on deck, usually sandpapering and varnishing the whalers and dinghies.

Our only involvement with cargo work, until you became a JO, was looking after the gear. Apart from routine maintenance, one of six duty watches was always available to repair or replace cargo gear. If the wharfies were in a bad mood, they would stop work for every light bulb that blew or every wire that had a snag. We could be called out at any time to repair the gear. If you were duty watch, you could not go ashore, you had to clean the accommodation every evening, for rounds, and do just about anything that was needed, unpaid of course. 9

Michael Keat has other memories that stand out from the background. Fortunately, poignant ones such as this are relatively uncommon:

6 Many memories stay with you, some good, some bad. One memory stronger than most was the death of one of our apprentices. His name was Stuart-Jones. He was one, or maybe two, voyages junior to me. His nickname was inevitably Hyphen. He was killed falling from the bridge front down to number three hatch. He had been cleaning the bridge front windows, and was climbing back over the dodgers, holding on to the awning wire that ran round the bridge wing. As he climbed over, the bottle-screw on the awning wire unwound and parted. There was no mousing on the bottle-screw to prevent this.

There was a very solemn burial service that afternoon, in the middle of the Pacific. The ship was stopped. We all turned out in No. 10s (formal tropical uniform). The ship's piano was manhandled up onto the deck. Hyphen was sewn in canvas by the seamanship instructor. I can remember him sitting on number six hatch with a new bolt of canvas, sewing for some hours. Waxing every yarn before using it, and working his way through a bottle of Scotch after he had finished. 9

John Williams was among the last of those who served the traditional four-year apprenticeship. His fourteen years at sea were all spent with Bibby Line. They were years of transition in the British merchant navy and many long-established shipping companies did not survive these years of change. For many years Bibby Line had had a regular service of passenger/cargo liners running out to Ceylon and Burma, but this trade had been in decline since those countries gained independence. They had also managed a number of troopships for the Government. By the time that the young John Williams joined it, Bibby Line had made the decision to diversify and was developing a fleet of large bulk carriers. He has recorded some memories of his apprenticeship:

6 I travelled with Dad to Birkenhead on 26 November 1964 to join my first ship, the MV *Yorkshire*. She was laid at the Bibby Line shed in West Float and was preparing to load a cargo for South Africa. We arrived at 8 pm and the ship was very quiet and much larger than I thought. I had of course read all about the ship and knew that she was one of three general cargo ships built in Sunderland in 1958 and designed for worldwide trading. This was Bibby Line's first venture away from the liner service and came about after the government ended the trooping contract in 1956. The compensation paid to the company was invested, and very wisely it turned out to be.

The quartermaster on gangway watch showed me my cabin and told my father and me to go and report to the Captain. Captain Albert Edward Young, DSO, looked like a ship's master despite being several inches shorter than his newest recruit. He offered us tea and asked what family connections we had used to get me into Bibby Line! He spoke to me in a most friendly manner and assured my father that not only would I receive the very best training but that my welfare was paramount. After we left the Master's cabin, Dad said 'A fine man, you are in good hands.' I never did tell Dad that Captain Young not only never spoke to me again, but that after four months at sea he even asked somebody who I was!

Dad left me that evening to return to Staffordshire, parting with some words of advice. 'When you are in port there is life beyond the first pub outside the dock gate,' and, 'Don't do anything you would not tell your mother about.' In the years that followed I heeded the first of his pieces of advice and in doing so was able to completely ignore the second.

The following morning I met my fellow cadets, Fletcher, Kumarasingh and Nyunt. Fletcher, a chain-smoking twenty-year-old, was the senior cadet and soon to sit his Second Mate's examinations. Ranjan Kumarasingh was from a prosperous Colombo family and part of the Bibby Line training programme for Asian cadets. Nyunt, a Burmese, was from the same training programme, and the plan was that once they had obtained their Second Mate's certificate and completed one year as Third Officer they would return to the national fleet. Ranjy was my cabin mate, and although we got along reasonably well we were never friends. He came from a high-caste family and had an arrogance and air of superiority that is difficult to describe. Nyunt was an oddball and I do not think we exchanged more than a dozen words throughout the whole voyage. He was lazy and made sure that he did the minimum amount of work. It came as no surprise when he failed his Second Mate's exams and returned to Rangoon unqualified.

The trade winds, blowing hard from the south-east, did not trouble the ship as we steamed towards South Africa. It was summer in the southern hemisphere and the passage around the Cape of Good Hope was smooth and very pleasant. I have no recollection of Christmas 1964 being anything special, and this perhaps reflects the formal atmosphere on *Yorkshire* and the lack of fun amongst the officers and cadets. But I do remember Boxing Day because I awoke as we entered the port of Durban for the first of many times in my sea career.

In those days, cargo work was conducted at a leisurely pace with only occasional night work. This allowed those not on watch to go ashore in the evenings. Forgetting all my father's advice I found myself in the Smugglers Inn, a seedy dock-side drinking house full of sailors. I drank cane spirit, got very drunk and walked back to the ship – a dangerous thing to do as South Africa was even then a violent country. The following night I encouraged Ranjy to come with me and in doing so saw South Africa's apartheid laws at first hand. Ranjy was told to leave, as 'coloureds aren't allowed in here.' I am ashamed now to admit that I did not think too much of this incident. It was, after all, the law of the land and in my immature mind perfectly accept-able. Even Ranjy did not seem too perturbed as we returned to the ship and the comfort of our own bar.

Before leaving Durban for Beira, the main port of Portuguese East Africa, we began loading for the return trip to Britain, including coal, apparently an anthracite that was important for our steel industry. The remainder of our cargo was discharged in Beira and we sailed south for Lourenço Marques to com-plete the loading. LM was an exciting place to be in the sixties and, free of the restrictions of South Africa, was a haven for those who wished to have fun. The bars and night clubs were full of South Africans and the local radio station broadcast pop music in the same way that Radio Luxembourg transmitted to its British audience. The Portuguese, whilst keeping themselves apart from the native population, did not enforce their ideas and the atmosphere was relaxed and informal.

The voyage back to the UK was without incident and after almost four months away we docked again in Liverpool. Approaching the British Isles, I was aware of the 'channels', a state of excitement that all sailors feel as they approach home. It was my first return, and on the passage I had reflected deeply about my experience and about the future. The trip had not been enjoyable, as my shipmates were unfriendly and uncaring. This was a new experience to me. Nobody had called me by my first name for four months and I really did feel that if I had fallen overboard nobody would have noticed, let alone cared. I wondered if I had chosen the right career and began to think of the consequences if I decided not to return to sea. But I had enjoyed the adventure of travel and seeing new places – a privilege enjoyed by few people in the days before mass travel. I was also aware of the financial investment my parents had made and the support they had given to me in my determination to go to sea. As a child, my father had never allowed me to give things up without very good reason and I knew that I just had to make another effort. Also, I knew that the work was within my capability and that my earlier fears were unfounded. My correspondence-course results were good and I was coping with the deck work.

My next voyage, still on the *Yorkshire*, was taking a general cargo outward bound from Liverpool to Quebec. There we learned that we were to pick up a cargo in the Gulf of Mexico for Southern Africa. The trip, down the eastern seaboard of the USA, was at about the time of the next Gemini launch from Cape Canaveral and it looked as if we would pass through the Florida Strait at the right time. But the launch was delayed and our voyage plan adjusted to allow for the passage of Hurricane Betsy. Betsy became known as the $1 billion hurricane as, for the first time, the cost of the damage exceeded that milestone amount. It had other characteristics too, as it defied the normal pattern of a hurricane by turning back on itself. It went through the Bahamas and out into the Atlantic Ocean, and Captain Cooper decided to stay well north of the predicted path by stopping the vessel before approaching the Florida Strait. But the hurricane doubled back and went into the Gulf of Mexico, crossed the Louisiana coast and struck New Orleans with winds well in excess of 100 mph. There was massive flooding, and by the time of our arrival at the mouth of the Mississippi three days later the waters had hardly subsided. It was a remarkable sight that has lived with me, and I decided then to buy a camera as soon as possible as nobody at home would believe what I had seen. Houses floating down the river, large cargo ships adrift and one, a Lykes Liner still under construction, had been 'launched' by the winds from her slipway. In New Orleans, the buildings were badly damaged and I shopped in Woolworths where there was business as usual but no roof! The wonderful jazz bands played on in the Basin Street and Canal Street clubs, but were open to the skies – an extraordinary experience. It really did show the resilience of the American people, who, after all the damage and serious loss of life just seemed to get on as if this was a normal event. The flooding from the river caused the US government to build the levees which proved hopelessly inadequate almost forty years later when Hurricane Katrina arrived.

I also saw a darker side of American life on that first visit to the USA. My only previous experience of racism was in Durban when Ranjy was asked to leave the Smugglers Inn. In South Africa the racial separation was overt, with even park benches marked 'whites only' or 'blacks only'. There was none of that in New Orleans but racial segregation existed and it was unpleasant. The attitude of the white population towards the blacks was hostile and the language of hatred was evident. I never, in all the years I visited South Africa, heard a white person talk about an African in such a manner.

In 1966 I joined *Staffordshire*, a cargo passenger liner on the Rangoon service. The days of the Rangoon liner service were drawing to a close, and with the money earned from the premature end of the trooping contract the company had already invested in three general cargo ships and two more were due to be delivered. Bibby Line had had a regular service between Britain and Colombo and Rangoon for almost a hundred years but the closure of the Suez Canal in 1956 and the independence of Ceylon and Burma signalled the end of this tradition. The service had been shared with Henderson Bros, another Liverpool company, for some time but the Burma Five Star Line, the national carrier of Burma, entered the trade and reduced the volume for the two British companies. Together with a lack of passengers, who could now travel more cheaply by air, the service was no longer viable and the vessels were sold. The last of the larger passenger ships, the *Leicestershire*, was sold in 1964. As a replacement, the company purchased two twelve-passenger cargo ships from Prince Line and renamed them *Staffordshire* and *Gloucestershire*. They were old ships, built in 1950 to a pre-war design and not in the best of condition. But they were good enough to last a couple of years, allowing the company to meet its commitments before withdrawing completely in 1968.

Shortly before sailing Neil, the senior cadet, and I were detailed to inspect the crew quarters and report on any bicycles or live chickens that might be aboard. This strange order had a history, for the Indian crew were adept at commandeering bicycles that were left unattended in and around the dock estate. It was no coincidence that the number of missing bicycles reported to the local police rose when Bibby's ships were in port. The bicycles were somehow packed into baggage and taken back to Calcutta, where the new owner would assume a greater status as a result of his illicit acquisition. We did not find any bicycles but there were plenty of chickens that the crew intended to fatten up during the voyage and eat at the appropriate time. After an assurance from the Serang that we were welcome to join the crew for one of their feasts, Neil decided to report that the crew quarters were 'chicken free'. It was a decision that was to pay dividends later in the voyage.

Our first discharge port was Port Sudan, the main harbour in Sudan and a regular call for Bibby Line vessels. Also in the harbour at anchor was the *Chindwara*, the cadet ship owned by the British India Line. As long-established British shipping companies, BI and Bibby Line had much in common. Both also recruited Indian crew through Mackinnon Mackenzie in Calcutta. The Indian crew when asked always told us that BI was a better company, something I believed until a cadet from BI told me that their crew preferred Bibby Line!

On our first night ashore we met up with *Chindwara*'s cadets and Neil took an instant dislike to them. Perhaps it was that one was an old *Conway* cadet he didn't like, but whatever it was it became enough for Neil to hatch a plan to embarrass them. The following evening, after a few beers in a local bar we paid a boatman to row out into the harbour carrying us, two pots of white paint and a couple of brushes. The paint and brushes were lowered from the ship but only after we had persuaded our gangway watchman to turn a blind eye. The consequences of our boat trip were not evident until the following morning when we were awoken by the Chief Officer and told to come and inspect our handiwork. In very large letters along the hull of the *Chindwara*, from midships to the bow, was painted FOR SALE. The C/O had been advised by the gangway watchman that Neil and I were back on board and in bed by 2200 so it could not possibly have been us. The C/O did not believe this story for one minute, but our loyalty to the Indian crew by not disclosing their chickens in Birkenhead had paid off.

It was during this voyage that I visited the Commonwealth War Cemetery, something my father had suggested when he knew I was to visit Rangoon. Like many of his generation, Dad spoke little about World War II, preferring to concentrate on the future and the opportunities that were now available for his children. After a year in London during the Blitz, he had served as a senior NCO in the Royal Signals and for some of this time had been attached to infantry units fighting in the Burmese jungle. I know he had lost colleagues, and perhaps for this reason he wanted me to visit the cemetery.

I am not unduly sentimental or reflective but the sight of those graves, many of them members of Dad's regiment, had a profound effect. Nearly all were young men, and it made me immensely proud of my father and all the men and women of the Commonwealth who had fought on our behalf. My father only sacrificed a few years of his young adult life but many were killed or badly injured fighting for our future. We owe them all a great deal.

In recalling my apprenticeship I feel I must pay tribute to the work of the seamen's missions. These missions, run by various Christian churches, are a legacy of the time when seamen were the lowest form of our society and in need of spiritual salvation and guidance. In recent years their relevance has been questioned but, despite the general move in the developed world to a more secular life, they do have a function and in my view do it very well. Not only do they continue to give spiritual care for those who need it, and in many cases this is not just for Christians but those of other faiths, but they also provide more basic facilities. These include a meeting place with snooker tables, a bar and a place to call home. My personal experience was a positive one and the Mission was the first stop when going to a new port. The padres, most of whom were very much down-to-earth characters, were able to tell us about the place we were visiting and the best places to go to. They realised that young men, teenagers particularly, did not want to spend all their time sightseeing and were able to tell us about the nightlife. Importantly, they also knew where not to go, and as seamen are often the victims of crime and deceit, local impartial knowledge is vital. I must admit that their advice was not always taken but my general view was that the missions and their staff were an important part of seafaring life. 9

Anthony Braithwaite served his apprenticeship with Port Line, which was formed, although not yet with that name, in 1914 when four smaller companies serving the Australian and New Zealand routes came together to form the Commonwealth and Dominion Line. Two years later Cunard took over the new company and renamed it Cunard Line Australasian Services – Commonwealth and Dominion Line.

However, this was nearly always abbreviated to Port Line because the names of all the ships began with Port, and in 1937 this became the official name of the company. The company ceased to exist in 1982 when the last two ships were transferred to the Brocklebank Line.

In the first of two vignettes Anthony Braithwaite recalls how the hierarchical structure aboard merchant ships at that time could lead to great loneliness:

❛ I joined Port Line, which was a wholly owned subsidiary of the Cunard Steamship Company and had thirty ships in the Europe to Australia trade. I was very fortunate in that my first ship was the recently reconverted HMS *Niarana* which became the MV *Port Victor* and after a voyage there I was appointed to the *Port Vindex* which had been HMS *Vindex* during the war. Halfway through that voyage I was called up on deck, we were in Sydney discharging cargo, and I was told that I was being transferred to the *Port Campbell*, which was a coal burner on almost her last voyage at sea. This was so that the apprentice there, who was a New Zealander who subsequently became Hydrographer of the New Zealand Navy, could go across with the *Port Vindex* to New Zealand and have some leave. So it was a wonderful thing for me to be on a triple-expansion coal-fired vessel. There were very few about at that time with thirty firemen shovelling coal into the engine, but there was only one other apprentice aboard and he was studying for his certificate. He got his certificate, moved up to the officers' quarter and as a matter of principle didn't speak to apprentices. It was the loneliest time I have ever been in a ship. I was neither one thing nor the other. I had no friends, nobody to speak to. Later on in my life when I had authority over these matters I made certain that no apprentice was *ever* by himself in a ship. ❜

In the second he recalls how two stowaways were found on a voyage between Durban and Cape Town:

❛ When I was an apprentice in the *Port Campbell*, we were coming home via the Cape of Good Hope and we stopped at Durban and left Durban for Cape Town, Las Palmas and Liverpool. We were always on the lookout for stowaways, and throughout my whole career this is the only time I remember.

The Chief Steward said to me in the morning, 'There are two black men sitting on the after bollards like first-class passengers', so I went down, spoke to them, took them up to the bridge, and they were given a locker[6] to live in and a bucket to use as a toilet. They were well fed and people were giving them cigarettes and chatting to them. When we got to Cape Town the police came down with a paddy wagon in some numbers, came aboard, 'Where are they?' and they were produced, and to our horror they were picked up neck and crop and flung down the gangway. It was my first taste of South African brutality in the apartheid days. **9**

Unfortunately, not every shipping company ensured that its apprentices were treated properly. Ramsey McLaren joined his first ship in 1942, and recalls his time as an apprentice:

6 When I joined my first ship, I was treated like a piece of dirt by the Captain, who was a horrible old Scot. He would not allow us to eat in the saloon. We could eat in the pantry or we could eat in the fo'c'sle. I said I did not come to sea to eat in the fo'c'sle, so I chose to eat in the pantry. We had a lousy little room with two bunks in it and a wardrobe for our clothes. I had a beautiful uniform that had cost my father a lot of money and that was it. This awful Scot treated us like dirt. I studied as much as I could. I had no support from the Mates. I didn't stay with the ship because I could not have done. I asked for a transfer and was sent to another ship called the *Huntsman*. We had our own mess room, we had a tablecloth, we had cutlery, we had china, in a ship of the same company and we were treated as young cadets, as cadets expect to be treated, until Captain Ferguson from my first ship joined the ship. In less than three minutes we were back to crew standards. 'What's this?' he said, 'tablecloths for apprentices, cutlery, knives and forks? You will live as the crew. Steward, stop this, get them mess kits. They can stand in the galley and wait for their food.'

---

6. Aboard ship a locker means a storeroom.

In three minutes our lifestyle was destroyed. However, one of my friends jumped ship. I said, 'Eric, you are going to destroy yourself,' but he did it with two others and the police brought them back to the ship, which was near Southend. I said 'Eric, you will destroy your career by doing this, you can't win against this man,' so we suffered him and eventually I was transferred to a ship called the *Riverton* with a most delightful man as the Captain who had been a prisoner-of-war in Germany. Life on that ship was totally different, it was like being a young officer and Captain Morrison just wanted you to study and to do the right thing. We ate in the saloon. This was very, very special and Morrison was such a gentleman that we could not believe it. He had been held in the merchant-navy prisoner-of-war camp where he organised a school for young officers who wanted schooling because everyone there was a merchant seaman. The Third Mate had done all his studies with this Captain, and although he hadn't much seafaring experience he was allowed to take his Second Mate's tickel. **9**

Peter Adams was one of the relatively small number of merchant-navy officers who 'came up through the hawse pipe'. Serving as a seaman on deck, with no pre-sea training and none of the instruction, and indeed encouragement, that was normally given to apprentices, meant that the examination for the Second Mate's certificate became a very formidable hurdle indeed. The *Indefatigable* was founded in 1844 as a training ship for poor and destitute boys. Originally moored off Rock Ferry in the Mersey, it was evacuated to Anglesey in 1941 and became shore-based. By this time it was firmly established as a preliminary training establishment for the lower deck of both the Royal and Merchant Navies. It finally closed in 1995.

F T Everard and Sons Ltd were based at Greenhithe on the Thames and were owners of sailing barges, tugs, coasters and short sea traders. The hulls of the latter were painted bright yellow, and the owners did not like it that these ships were almost universally known as the 'Yellow Perils'.

Peter Adams recalls his early years at sea:

❻ I grew up in Nottingham and had planned to go to art school, but my father wasn't encouraging. He was an engineering commander in the Fleet Air Arm and he didn't think that artists were worth educating, and so in a fit of pique I said that I wanted to go to sea, so he sent me off to the TS *Indefatigable* in Anglesey. He didn't know much about nautical training for the merchant navy. I lasted about six weeks there, and I came home after six weeks as I had contracted impetigo from the grotty sheets there. After the August holiday, as I had said that I wasn't going to go back to the *Indefatigable* I found myself a job as Mate on a river barge which ran up and down the River Trent between Nottingham and the port of Hull, which got me around ships. I was on her for about four months and then we were in Hull one day and the Thames spritsail sailing barge *Will Everard* was alongside and she was still working on the Hull to King's Lynn grain trade. They wanted a Third Hand so I shipped aboard there, but they couldn't afford a Third Hand really because they were paid on shares and the English grain trade was not very good, so after about six weeks they were hinting that I should look for something else.

Very fortunately, again in Hull, I managed to get myself a job as an ordinary seaman on a small coastal cargo ship owned by a small company at the mouth of the River Trent. This was called the *Jackonia*, a small 350-ton inter-war motor ship, trading between UK ports and the Continent. All this company's ships were named after a member of the Wharton family who owned the company. So we pottered about on that for about four or five months, trading around north-west Europe within the home trade limits until I got myself a Seaman's Discharge Book and got on to the Shipping Federation, and then spent about five or six more years deep sea as an AB until I went up for my Second Mate's certificate.

The *Jackonia* was under the size where the board of trade required you to have a formal Discharge Book although you did get a paper discharge. Although she was small it was good training although it was hard work. Then I went to King Edward VII training college here in London for my Second Mate's certificate, which was in 1966. Although I couldn't pass all the parts at once I did manage to pass my orals and my signals which enabled me to sail as uncertificated Second Mate on coastal tankers up to about three thousand tons. I worked for Shell-Mex and BP. At that time their coastal ships, which just traded round the UK taking products from the refinery to the tank farms were combined with BP and Shell and were run as a separate organisation, so I had a rather nice job there and was doing about three months on board and a month ashore and every time I came ashore and went back to King Edward's to have another go at my written exams. Finally, after four shots, I managed to get it. **9**

Peter Richards-Jones served his apprenticeship on just one ship, the *Samaustral.* She was a Liberty ship belonging to J & C Harrison's, a London based tramp-ship company, and she was the flagship of the company. A total of 2,710 Liberty ships, all of the same design, were built in the United States of America during the war using industrial manufacturing methods. Sections weighing 250 tons were prefabricated off-site and then transported to the dockyard, where they were welded together. By the time the process had been perfected, on average it only took six weeks to build each ship. The record, from the laying of the keel to launching, was four days and fifteen hours! Many, including the *Samaustral,* were transferred to British owner-ship under the lend–lease scheme. These Liberty ships, each with a displacement of 14,245 tons, played a vital role during the Battle of the Atlantic as they replaced much of the tonnage that was being sunk by German U-boats. On one voyage Peter Richards-Jones was on watch at night with the Third Officer as the ship steamed up the Red Sea. He recalls:

6 Now it was pretty hot, in fact it was a stinking hot night, and what the deck crowd had done was to take out a huge hatch cover tarpaulin, throw it over the derricks, which were lowered of course, and make a huge tent of it. Then they brought out their bunks, which were made of steel piping, and put them underneath on the hatch and so they slept on deck. Lucky them, for as cadets we couldn't do that. We weren't allowed to and had to stick it out in the heat of the steel cabins that we had down aft.

I was on the bridge, a very dark night, hardly a star in the sky. It was misty, and something came into the wheelhouse and started flying around, buzzing around, and after chasing it for a bit we found it, we got a glass and put this creature under the glass and we looked at it and I said to the Third Mate – I can remember saying – 'It looks like a grasshopper with those long legs. Do you think it could be a locust because they look like that,' and I thought, 'No, it can't be a locust, it's too far from land and it looks so ugly' – you could see right through its body in parts – and he said, 'Oh, I don't know,' and we were discussing what it could be when all of a sudden we heard a spattering noise from the wheelhouse and rushed out to realise that a lot more had come in.

So we started to lift the windows – very, very rapidly indeed I might add. They were the old train type windows that slid up and down on a leather strap with holes in the strap to fasten it and we rushed around sliding the doors closed because these flying things were all over the place. Talk about tough men, we didn't even like to stamp upon the damned things, and they were flying around all over and jumping about. It was terrible. And then they hit the wheelhouse in a big cloud. They were dreadful, they were spattering on the windows, they were spattering on the side doors, all over the place. It was terrible.

But that wasn't the real story. The real story was that this cloud of locusts had descended on the ship and who were outside in the open but the crowd, all the deck crowd and the engineering crowd, and I have never heard grown men scream like women in my life before. To be suddenly woken up, awakened, by this huge swarm, these things crawling all over you and jumping all over you. You know, I am not joking, it was not just one or two hitting them, there were thousands. The next day we were shovelling them up and throwing them over the side, their dead bodies. They were a foot deep, so you can imagine what it was like when they landed on these men. They couldn't breathe. Gosh, we heard them screaming but we weren't going down to investigate. We were shut up in our little wheelhouse, and we thought, 'Oh blow that, we are not going down there.' 9

Peter Elphick also served his apprenticeship with J & C Harrison's. This company had a poor reputation for the quality of its food, but one particular voyage remains in his memory because of its macabre ending:

6 We had very strict victualling superintendents who wouldn't allow more than a certain amount of expenditure. Twice, during my time with them, we ran out of food. I was a cadet the first time when we ran out of food and we were on the way down to the west coast of Africa somewhere, so we had to call into Las Palmas which wasn't too much of a deviation. The second time it happened was a different story. We were on a great circle route from the Far East to Vancouver picking up a cargo of grain and we had to divert three days to Honolulu, because we ran out of food in the middle of the North Pacific. There were two tins of fruit left, and the story behind that is that the Chief Steward had been so scared to order, that he had failed to take the length of the trip into consideration and also he was a boozer. Anyway we got to Vancouver eventually from Honolulu but it was a big deviation and we were all worried about the Chief Steward, the fact he was a boozer and not a very efficient Chief Steward. He was getting more and more worried all the way home. We went back through the Panama Canal taking on bunkers in one or two places, on our way to Southampton.

Lo and behold, as soon as the ship got alongside, all the London delegation came down – the marine superintendent, the engineering superintendent, the victualling superintendent all wanted to see this Chief Steward. They wanted him called, so the Captain sent for me, and said, 'Elphick, go and find the Chief Steward, we want to see him up here.' So I went to find him, without success. I went to see the cook to see if the cook knew where he was but nobody could find him, so we thought he might have gone ashore. A few of us went to the First and Last, the pub just outside the gate. He wasn't there, and he hadn't been there, so we came back and reported. We hunted for the guy for two days but couldn't find him, then on the third day, and it shows you how bad the food was on Harrison's, the cook had not been to the main refrigerator for three days, but when he opened the refrigerator there was the Chief Steward hanging by his neck stiff as anything, with a box under his feet which of course he had kicked away, cigarette ends all around it and an empty whisky bottle.

As soon as we discovered that we reported it, obviously, and then we searched his room and we opened his wardrobe door and a cascade of empty bottles came out, why he had saved them I don't know. If you like that sort of thing then the best thing to do is to throw them over the side. My most vivid memory from those days is seeing his body because it was stiff and the only way we could get him ashore was in a cargo net and his legs were sticking through the cargo net. He had a red jumper on and I can remember that, seeing him going over the side. The point was the food was so bad and the Chief Steward was never given a chance to do the job properly. **9**

Ian Tew served his apprenticeship with the British India Steam Navigation Company. This company was founded in 1856 as the Calcutta and Burmah Steam Navigation Company to carry mail from Calcutta to Rangoon. It expanded rapidly into the Indian coastal trade, and was renamed the British India Steam Navigation Company in 1862. When the Suez Canal was opened in 1869 a regular service between the UK and the Orient was initiated, but trading between India, East Africa and the Persian Gulf remained important. The ships on this trade carried deck, or unberthed passengers. In the early days many of these passengers were indentured labourers, while others were pilgrims on hajj.

His second ship was the *Dara*, which caught fire and subsequently sank after a bomb had exploded amidships early on the morning of 8 April 1961. Two hundred and thirty-eight people lost their lives from either burns or drowning. The reason for the bombing was never discovered, but it was thought that it might have been the work of Omani terrorists. Ian Tew gives a laconic account of his escape:

❝ I first went on the *Chindwara*, which was a mistake by the personnel department, because I had been to pre-sea training. She was a training ship but I had already done my training. I was only on her for one trip and then I flew out to Bombay to join the *Dara*. She was on the Bombay to Basra mail run; there were four ships. It was in April 1961 that she was blown up, or that the bomb was put on board and it went off, off Dubai. She was anchored off Dubai when an afternoon storm blew up and she was hit by another ship called the *Zeus*. The lifeboat on the forward port side was damaged and the Master then put to sea. At 0423 the bomb went off when we were about twenty-five miles off Dubai. The bomb had been put on board on B deck. The fireball that was created meant that the boat deck was untenable for twenty minutes. Well it took more than twenty minutes to get the double-banked lifeboats away. I then went with the other cadet to my lifeboat station. We had tried to get the breathing apparatus but fire prevented that so we got to our boat station so he and I lowered our boat, the motor boat it was supposed to be. You can imagine the panic. I then went into the lifeboat and he lowered and unfortunately another lifeboat, an empty one, drifted by beneath, so my lifeboat capsized so I went for a swim and when it got daylight I saw another lifeboat and swam to it and took charge of it because the senior person on board was the assistant purser and he said, 'Oh, thank God, there's a deck cadet,' so I took charge of it. We were picked up by the *Yuyo Maru*, a Japanese tanker, which took us to Bahrain. I then went to Bombay for the initial Board of Trade investigations and then flew home for survivor's leave and then flew back out to Calcutta and joined a steam 'up and downer' called the *Okra*, and then I served the rest of my time out there. ❞

David Sims also served his apprenticeship with British India, and spent some time on a British India troopship. At that time the government had a fleet of troopships on charter from various passenger liner companies. In the late 1940s and 1950s, once the post-war demobilisation was complete, the main route followed by the troopships was to the Far East. Personnel from all three services would be embarked in the UK. The first port of call would usually be Port Said, followed by Aden, Colombo, Singapore and Hong Kong, with contingents of troops being disembarked at each port. The whole process would then be put into reverse on the return voyage, embarking troops who had completed their tours of duty for passage to the UK. It is worth remembering that this was the time of the Malayan Emergency and the Korean War, and more servicemen travelled on the outward voyages than on those returning to the UK. He recalls:

❦ I was put on the *Nevasa*, which was a troopship running between Southampton and Singapore and Hong Kong. That was great fun and I learnt a lot about the army. I was keen on shooting in those days so I used to go down to the range in the morning and shoot a few rounds. The range was on board and the way they did it was they put balloons with some water in, let them go off the stern and, when they got some distance away, the range officer would say Fire. So if you had a competition and you'd got through to the semi-finals, against the Army team, Commodore Reginald Bond OBE was the captain, the troop officer was another member, one of our engineers was another and as a cadet I was the fourth. We had this competition and the idea what was you would hit your balloon, as the balloon was going down. You also got points for the number of rounds you had used, so when Commodore Bond said stop and cadet Sims fired and got the balloon, wow! that was great. I got to know that ship very, very well because you spent half your day doing rounds keeping an eye on what was going on. We had thousands of troops on board.[7] You had troop decks, where there were 120 men to a deck, in three-tier bunks. There were fire doors, which had to be repeatedly checked. The third-class

---

7. Memory is fickle! The troop decks on the *Nevasa* would have held just under one thousand men.

accommodation was for other ranks' wives; the second class was for warrant officers and their wives and of course the first class was officers, the gentlemen and their ladies. The worst thing was when the weather was bad having to go and do the rounds, because they weren't used to the sea and it used to smell horrible, particularly in the third class. I remember one night there was a party on board and the officers and the gentlemen chucked all the veranda chairs overboard and the next morning the Lieutenant Colonel in charge of the battalion was standing outside the Captain's cabin at attention, fully dressed, with a blank cheque in his hand. **9**

Many of the recollections in this book date from the three decades following the Second World War, and many older crew members, including many Masters, had spent the war years at sea. One contributor summed it up by saying, 'There were good times and there were bad times, mostly bad times.' It was a time when the treatment of post-traumatic stress syndrome, or shell shock as it was then known, was still in its infancy. This vignette by Simon Culshaw shows that Blue Funnel Line, at least, were sympathetic to the problem. Alfred Holt, or the Blue Funnel Line, was a well established company based in Liverpool and trading to the Far East. All the ships were named after heroes that appeared in the works of Homer. The last ship was sold in 1989.

6 My mate and I on one trip got a report from the Master saying 'tired and useless'. We thought, 'Oh God, we're going to get the sack before we have really started,' so we went to the boss in India Buildings, head office in Liverpool, with our caps in our hands as seventeen-year-olds do. The boss said, 'Don't worry, because this Captain has been giving Midshipmen "tired and useless" or "useless and tired" since 1943. He is one of the unrecognised war wounded and, gentlemen, you will come across this because we have a lot of Masters who served in the Second World War and you will find that they have idiosyncrasies. You are going to just have to let them be.' This fellow had swum out of six ships in five years and it wasn't until later in life that I realised that I had had the honour of being commanded by gutsy men who were still working and were putting things behind them. **9**

This theme is continued in the recollections of Peter Davidson, who served with Moss Hutchinson Lines. This company was formed in 1934 from the merger of Moss Lines and Hutchinson Ltd, two companies that traced their history back to early in the nineteenth century. It traded to France and the Iberian peninsula, the Mediterranean and the Black Sea. The original Hutchinson Line ships were given the privilege of an exemption from the requirement to fly a courtesy flag when in French ports in recognition of their carrying medical supplies without charge during the Franco-Prussian war. He recalls:

6 Most of the Masters I sailed with, while I was serving my time, had been in the war. Some had sailed throughout but quite a few had been on ships which had been sunk, either torpedoed or shelled, consequently ending up in prisoner-of-war camps.

On reflection I am sure the war had influenced their subsequent behaviour quite a lot. There was one Master who had spent quite a lot of time during the war in the Mediterranean fully loaded with drums of kerosene. This Master had been berthed in Algiers one night when the dock area was bombed and he said his hair turned white overnight. He certainly had a nervous disposition, and no wonder.

There were others who possibly drank too much on occasions, but they were all good seaman and characters in their own right, particularly the one I first sailed with, who had a Master's Square Rigged certificate.

All the bosuns I sailed with initially were company men, and on one ship there was one, Harry Briscoe, who was on a ship that was shelled and sunk by the *Scharnhorst*, a pocket battleship of some renown. Harry had given the possibility of being sunk some thought and had constructed a raft with some provisions and water attached. When the ship was sinking and everybody else took to the lifeboats Harry slipped the raft over the stern and floated away.

Two weeks or so later Harry was surprised when a U-boat surfaced alongside him and the Commander asked him in perfect English, 'Where are you bound?' Harry completed the submarine's tour of duty before being landed in Bordeaux and on to a prisoner-of-war camp. He did however keep in contact with the Commander of this U-boat, with whom he had become friendly, and after the war they met up again.

I was very impressed, and it helped to formulate the belief that all those who have to deal with the elements of wind and sea are genuine types. **9**

Although almost all cargoes were stowed in the ships' holds, it was not unusual to carry some items on deck as well. This might be something such as a railway engine that was too large to go down the hatch into the hold or, not infrequently, livestock. When the latter were carried an extra hand was often signed on the Ship's Articles to take care of the animal or animals. This was not always the case in the Brocklebank Line, as John Gray found out on his first voyage to sea. Brocklebank Line was founded as long ago as 1801 and had a long history of trading to India. The company was sold to Cunard in 1911, but continued to trade as a separate company.

John Gray's recollection touches on the traditional rivalry, and occasional animosity, between the deck and the engine-room departments.

6 As an apprentice you did what you were told in those days for one thing, and the apprentices' job on Brocklebank ships was to look after livestock. We looked after a horse on the first voyage. This involved cleaning the horse out. We were given bales of fresh straw and had to feed the horse morning and evening and wash it down in the hot weather with a hose. It was nearly a full-time job on the way out to Calcutta. The horse, I recall, was called Puffin, and it was a racehorse going out for the Calcutta races, and it needed fresh water and to be cleaned. I had never had anything to do with horses before but you learnt by experience and used your initiative.

Some voyages later we looked after twenty-four cages of monkeys coming back from Colombo for scientific purposes. I always remember that when we got to Tilbury this fellow came along to collect these monkeys, which were in individual cages, and he said, 'How many monkeys have you got?' and we said, 'Twenty-four,' and he said, 'Didn't some die?' We were rather proud of the fact that we had kept these monkeys alive. They used to put their fingers through into the next cage and get the ends bitten off and things like that – they were quite vicious – but we learnt not to put our fingers anywhere near them. We had to feed them and to scrape out the bottoms of their cages every now and again and put fresh straw in. I always remember that we went to Port Sudan on the way home and there was a ship ahead of us loading bags of peanuts and the Mate thought it would be a very good idea to go and pinch a bag of peanuts, so the Mate, myself and the other apprentice went and got a bag of peanuts from the other ship's cargo to feed the monkeys. We found that within two days the monkeys got horrible diarrhoea, so we gave the peanuts to the engineers. 9

Jeremy Procter was an apprentice with BP Tankers, the shipping company of British Petroleum, and recalls an episode from his second voyage:

6 This happened in the early sixties when a great friend of mine and I were sailing on the same ship together. As far as I can recall it was my friend's first trip and I was second trip, as apprentices. My friend had an old pair of jeans that were wearing out and he hit upon the idea of using these jeans as a template to make a new set from duck canvas. Now duck canvas was a very valuable commodity. It was hard to get, but we had an Indian crew and by one way or another we managed to get hold of sufficient duck canvas to do this. So what happened was that my friend cut up his pair of jeans following the seams to make a template. He then used the sections and

This cartoon of the young guitar-playing Jeremy Procter was drawn on the back of the Christmas Day menu by the Radio Officer on the BP tanker *British Patrol*. He misspelled Jeremy Procter's name.

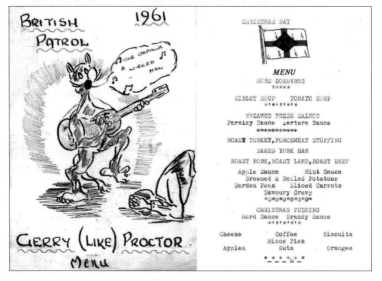

drew out the patterns on the duck canvas, cut out the duck canvas, and then with the aid of one of the Indian quartermasters sewed up the duck canvas into a very presentable pair of jeans and used the uniform buttons for securing the fly and for the top button. All went well and it was quite a work-up over several weeks. It certainly improved my friend's sewing capacity with palm and needle and the 'old' beeswax. Anyway, the time came to try on the said pair of jeans and they fitted very, very well, and so my friend put them on and went out on deck. If I recall properly we were actually doing cargo operations at the time, but unfortunately the weather was not very good and it was pouring with rain. Well, an hour went past, and then I got a call for help. What had happened, because the duck canvas hadn't been shrunk beforehand, the rain caused it to shrink quite alarmingly on my friend. So much so that he couldn't even walk and was in extreme pain from the lower parts, so we had to carry him back into our cabin and literally cut off the garment, much to his relief, but unfortunately leaving all his hard work in ruins. **9**

Not all passenger ships carried apprentices, or rather cadets as they were invariably known in the liner companies, but aboard those that did life was very, very different from that aboard a tramp ship. P&O – the very name conjures up images of the British Empire in the East in the early days of the last century. The Peninsular and Oriental Steam Navigation Company, to give it its full name, had a fleet of cargo ships and passenger liners and is one of the relatively few British shipping companies to have weathered the turmoil of the 1970s and 1980s. Even if you have not been on one of their cruises, you may well have crossed the English Channel on one of their ferries. In this little vignette, Ian Gibb recalls showing a small group of passengers around the bridge of one of P&O's passenger ships when he was a cadet:

❢ My first experience of passenger liners was in May of 1954, when I was appointed to the brand new liner *Arcadia*, and this was a tremendous experience because I learnt to love passenger ships. I loved the passengers, I loved the food, I loved everything about them. It was my metier, I felt. I was always very enthusiastic as a cadet, and one of our roles was to ferry the passengers backwards and forwards when the ships were anchored off the port, and one gained a lot of experience at boat handling, of course, in this manner.

The indenture that bound Ian Gibb as an apprentice to the Peninsular and Oriental Steam Navigation Company in 1954.

Another of the cadets' roles on board was to take passengers around the bridge. In those days there wasn't the security you have today, and if the passengers showed any interest whatsoever in seeing the navigation bridge, the Purser's desk would have a little list and when they had ten or twelve people on the list they would call up to the Chief Officer, and the Chief Officer would organise them to come up at an acceptable time, and Cadet Gibb was frequently called up to the bridge to show them around. And I recall this particular incident when most of the passengers had gone but there were a couple left and one particular gentleman was showing particular interest in the radar. So I walked over to him and said, 'Could I be of assistance and would you like me to tell you all about the radar?' and he said, 'Yes, that would be very nice.' So I explained to him in probably three-and-a-half to four minutes all that I, as a seventeen-and-a-half-year-old cadet, knew about radar. And I could see a small smile playing about the corner of his mouth, and as I finished he said, 'Och, very good laddie, of course you know, I invented it.' It was Sir Robert Watson-Watt. So I can tell you that I told Sir Robert Watson-Watt all about radar. 9

The last recollection of this chapter comes from Michael Keat, and is one that every contributor to this book will share. The thirty-one rules of the International Regulations for the Prevention of Collisions at Sea came in a booklet that certainly was not drafted with learning the text by heart in mind. Definitions, the shapes to be shown by day and the lights to be shown at night under all eventualities, the sound signals to be made in fog, which one of two ships approaching each other 'where risk of collision exists' should give way – it was all there and it all had to be word perfect by the time you came face to face with the examiner at the oral examination for the Second Mate's certificate.

6 An unpleasant memory for me, of another type, was the requirement to learn, word-for-word, the Rules for the Prevention of Collisions at Sea. 'Trippers' had to learn rules one to nine, and each voyage you had to learn more, so that senior apprentices had to have learnt all thirty-one rules by their last voyage. We

had to pass a test from 'Schoolie' on the outward voyage, before we were allowed to go ashore on the Aus/NZ coast. For some this came easily, but for others, not so. I remember one poor lad who just could not learn them. He could answer questions on them, but could not learn the exact wording. Years later, in Mate's and Master's oral exams, the need for this learning was realised. Whatever the examiner asked you, if you quoted the relevant rule, you could not be wrong. **9**

And so, after some four years at sea, indentures completed, the young men would take their Second Mate's certificate, or ticket, as it was more generally called. Almost everyone attended the twelve-week preparation course that was held in all the nautical schools that were situated in the major ports.

The examination was in three parts: written papers, signals and the *oral.* The written papers – chart work, celestial navigation and cargo work – were relatively straightforward, at least to those who had done some pre-sea training that had been followed up by on-board instruction. Signals was a little more problematic. One had to be able to send and receive by both semaphore and Morse code. Semaphore was a thing of the past and never used at sea, so there was really very little incentive for learning it. Morse code was still used, and one just had to have practised sufficiently to have built up the required speed. It was the oral exam that had us quaking at our knees. The examiner did not ask questions, he barked them at you. 'You are heading north-east and you see the green sidelight of a sailing vessel two points on your starboard bow. The wind is from the west. Between what points of the compass could she be sailing?' Or, placing a model buoy on the table, 'You are heading down Channel in reduced visibility when you see this buoy dead ahead. What helm order do you give?'

With this hurdle behind you, it was time to visit the naval outfitter to have one stripe of gold braid sewn onto the sleeves of your uniform jacket, and then to embark on the next stage of your career.

4 • Operation Pedestal

Right from the beginning of their collaboration the authors decided that this was not going to be a war book. However, we are making an exception and including this contribution from a Master Mariner who, as a seventeen-year-old apprentice, sailed on the *Rochester Castle*, one of the five merchant ships that reached Malta out of the fourteen that set out from the Clyde on 2 August 1942. The subsequent battle in the western Mediterranean was both one of the most hard fought and one of the most pivotal of the Second World War. We felt his contribution warranted a chapter to itself.

Jim Whadcoat left school one Friday in 1941 and, apprenticed to the Union Castle Line, joined his first ship the following Monday. It was the second year of the war and it was not going well for Britain. At home the air-raids on London continued, while from early in the year the Luftwaffe had also turned its attention to the ports. In the Mediterranean the Fleet had lost its dominance, and on land our forces were facing defeat in North Africa. However, on 7 December of that year the Japanese launched their attack on Pearl Harbor, which led to the United States of America declaring war on both Japan and the Axis powers. As a result the balance of power gradually shifted in favour of the Allies during 1942.

The Germans and the Italians realised that the conquest of Malta was the key to their success in the North Africa campaign, as whoever held this island, strategically placed between Italy and Libya, controlled the supply lines to Rommel's Afrikakorps. In April 1942 the Luftwaffe commenced a concentrated air attack on Malta, dropping nearly seven thousand tons of bombs over a six-week period. The gallantry of its people under this bombardment so impressed King George VI that he awarded the George Cross to the island. In the light of this, Winston Churchill determined that Malta should not, and could not, be allowed to fall.

Nevertheless, the continuing Axis blockade was having its effect, and supplies on the island were running out since relief convoys were not getting through. By June there was food rationing, and supplies of food, ammunition and aviation fuel were only enough to last until early September. Once the supplies had run out, the surrender of the island would have been inevitable.

In the light of this, a powerful relief force was assembled to break the blockade imposed by the Axis forces in the Mediterranean. This consisted of fourteen merchant ships, twelve of them British and two of them American, with a strong naval escort, which included two battleships, three aircraft carriers, seven cruisers and 32 destroyers. It was given the name Operation Pedestal and became one of the most famous convoy operations of the entire war. The convoy passed through the Straits of Gibraltar on the night of the 9/10 August, and from then on the convoy was under near-continuous attack from German aircraft and Italian submarines and torpedo boats (the MAS or Motoscafo Armato Silurante). Only four cargo ships and the one tanker, the *Ohio*, arrived at Malta. The success of this operation ensured the survival of Malta as a British base, although the price was heavy: as well as the nine merchant ships, an aircraft carrier, two cruisers and a destroyer were lost, together with a total of over four hundred lives. Churchill commented afterwards that 'the loss ... was grievous. The reward justified, the price exacted. Revictualled and replenished with ammunition and vital stores, the strength of Malta revived.'

Many maritime historians have recorded this epic engagement, and a detailed account is given by one of the contributors to this book, Richard Woodman, in his book *Malta Convoys 1940–1943*.

Jim Whadcoat was an apprentice on the *Rochester Castle*, one of those fourteen merchant ships. These are his memories of the events of this momentous engagement, which took place nearly seventy years ago. He takes up the story as they were loading in Glasgow:

❻ There were four cadets, three from the *Worcester* and myself. Of course I was the odd man out because they had had pre-sea training and I hadn't but at the time I had an advantage because I had been at sea longest on that ship, so I did have that advantage. I struck eight bells at New Year, two years running on that ship.

When we were in Glasgow the War Department came round and asked each individual cadet who was under age, and all of us were, whether we were prepared to go, and we all individually said yes. We were on our own, you know, we were just asked so nobody would have said anything if we had said no. I put that in because a lot of people might think that we were just bundled off but we weren't. I can give you the names of the cadets, to the letter: R F Leeds; C G Rattray, who came from Johannesburg – he used to go home on holiday from the *Worcester* each summer on the mail boat; D C B Lockhead, who was born in Burma – his father was in Burmah Oil and when I first knew him he was sixteen. I had just completed one voyage on the *Rochester* when he came and joined. He was my cabin mate. We got on very well together. When we met each other we said, 'That's my half of the desk and that's yours,' and nobody touched anything. (That was what I liked at sea; you could put your money down and go out of the cabin, wander about, do whatever you had to do, and come back and nothing would have been touched. We did get one member of the crew who was a little bit light-fingered but he begged the skipper to pay off in South Africa.)

We were in King George Dock and we were loading there, but we didn't realise at the time because everything was in wooden cases, everything we carried at that time was in wooden cases, but it had the destination on. You wouldn't believe it, but some idiot had told somebody to put something on, but not Malta, so do you know what they had put? If you sat in your taxi and you looked through the mirror 'ATLAM'. That's an absolute fact, that is. That was the sort of thinking. But I think they gave it to an underling, you know, and they had no idea.

We were loading there, and for me there was a certain amount of sabotage because in one of the top chambers we had sugar and there were also, only a couple I think, of carboys of nitric acid for the Malta hospital – and somebody slipped those through the door into the sugar before it was shut and the fumes gradually worked on the sugar; this I think was during the Saturday. On Sunday morning when people were still on deck doing various things I went and reported to the skipper that on his deck, which was the next deck up from ours, there was a ventilator and there were wisps of fumes coming out. So, and you wouldn't believe this, it was caused by the nitric acid working on sugar. The skipper immediately called the fire brigade and the chief man of the fire brigade came down with gold braid up his arms and all sorts of things with all his gear and the fire engines and he opened this door and as he opened it there was a whoosh with a sheet of flame but he managed to close it again. Actually we had got CO_2 in there. So I suppose the flame didn't get back, it only stopped at the door, and anyway he managed to close it down again – and this was the boss himself!

I can't remember how they did it, but they managed to get the carboys out. I think what they must have done was to put in a massive amount of CO_2 with the result that it didn't get a chance to ignite at all. The dockers were there, and when they heard about all this they all jumped over the side, they didn't bother with the gangway, but of course we were well down and it wasn't so much of a jump. As well as the sugar, in the square of the hatch we had bombs for the RAF. That was in number three hatch, which was just between the bridge and the engineers' accommodation, and our cabins were on the starboard side – sort of the first two you come to from the deck, right by number three hatch, and number three hatch was the one that got torpedoed. And we had a hole in us 20 by 25 feet. I went down the engine room on the top grating and a couple of our cadets were down there helping the engineers shore up the bulkhead. By that time we were under way, because they'd stopped the engine, which was a Burmeister and Wain two-stroke double-acting diesel engine, when it first happened, to work out what had happened. We did thirteen knots with a hole in us and the reason that we survived I think was because all the bombs in the square of number three hatch were surrounded by sacks of flour or grain. (The grain was just grain that nothing had been done to and the stink of it, after a couple of weeks, after we got there...)

Going back again to just having left Glasgow, the pilot that took us out had been a pilot from the south, from Gravesend (and I have been trying to remember his name). By this time we knew it was jolly well going to be tough. As he went over the rail, I was sent down to stand by the ladder when he went ashore in the pilot cutter. I passed his bag down on the heaving line and as he went over the side he said, 'Cheer up son, all the ships I have piloted came back.'

So from the Clyde we went out west and gradually the ships appeared and then we were joined up with a load of naval ships including the *Nelson* and *Rodney*. When we were out west, I can't remember what latitude it was, but roughly off the Straits of Gibraltar, then we came in straight and when we came through the Straits it was not only dark but there was a bit of mist and unfortunately an awful lot of Spanish fishermen, but that was how we got into the Mediterranean. Then Lord Lewin who was the gunnery officer on the *Ashanti* at that time told us (at one of the GCIA[8] gatherings) that the morning we went through the Straits, a Vichy French plane went across from North Africa to Marseille and on the open radio said there was a large naval force heading east, which was very nice of them. The funny thing is really, we weren't really bothered too much until the aircraft started to come from Sicily. They came over about every four hours, about fifty of them at a time miles up and the ack-ack was really fantastic. As far as our own guns, on the *Rochester Castle* we had a Bofors by the foremast, on the housing there, another Bofors aft, on the stern, on a platform and the 4.7 was on the next deck down. The 4.7 was very interesting and dated from 1916, it had a brass plate on it and apparently, in about 1916 there was a load of Germans coming down from East Africa and these guns were dragged, or manhandled anyway, up to Mazairu and that's where they were found; one of them was put into a museum, and that is the one that we had. Now another interesting part (away from the actual doings we're talking about the fact that it was from Mazairu) was that we didn't have any armaments at home and at one stage, about 1940, it was deemed that all merchant ships should have a gun aft. The chippy was telling me, Ted Curly by name, that he was ordered to make a wooden gun aft, to make it look like one. That was before I had joined the ship and that was how it went out to South Africa and that was where they got the gun from. Because the Germans always say

---

8. George Cross Island Association.

that we were prepared, which was a load of ...

So going back to Sicily, we were having these air raids during daylight, every four hours roughly. Some of the dive bombers, Ju-87Bs or Stukas I think they were called, with the wings that come out like that. They had a wine in Malta, at twopence a glass, and they called that Stuka juice – you can guess why.

At one stage there were Marmaschettis, I think they were called, about four, five or six of them going round on the horizon, and all of a sudden a flag signal went up, 'ignore surface craft,' and *Nelson* fired a broadside. You've never seen anything like it. Actually you couldn't see the shells but you could see a spout of water behind it and they got roughly to where these characters were and the shells exploded with a puff of smoke and there was nothing there. It was absolutely fantastic, that was. But it was all in one doings and that got rid of the trouble. I discovered then that the enemy, to my mind their heart wasn't in it. It may have been Italians it may have been the Germans, although they all had a cross on. There were fighters on the outside of the group as they came across and mostly stayed as far away as they possibly could. They were only fourteen targets, and fifty aircraft but they didn't come down and try very hard; one lot could have polished us all off. If they'd been British it might have been different, that's what I mean.

When the orders came to disperse from the flagship and make best course and speed that was when the *Nelson* and *Rodney* left us and they cleared off. Our Skipper, Wren, he was a very rough sort of chap in a way; if the firemen gave any trouble on the ships he was on, if they got drunk he'd have them out and he'd knock them out but to my mind he was absolutely marvellous. On that trip, when we got the orders to disperse, he and the naval lieutenant who he had with us, discussed our route (whose name I can't remember but he became a pilot from Dover for the Continent and I met him twenty-two years later when he was piloting). Captain Wren thought that the quickest way from there was straight north of Pantelleria but the naval lieutenant said yes, but it is mined. Wren said 'and so is the south,' which it was, although they had done quite a bit of sweeping there.

Anyway, we chanced it and went north of Pantelleria and we were doing 18 knots. Mattocks, who was the Chief Engineer, came up on the bridge pouring sweat and Wren said to him, 'Is there any more?' and he said, 'If I do the piston tops will come out through the roof' – and we did 18 knots until we were hit. When we were hit, we stopped, of course, as I said, to assess the damage. When the torpedo hit I was coming up from aft, having taken a message. We had an old seaman there, named Jack Darby, who was well over 65, about 67, I think. He stuttered a bit and he said 'Wh- wh-what the bbbbloody hhhell wwwwas tthat?' Actually there were two thumps, one and then two, quite close together and I imagine what it was, was that the E-boat let off two torpedoes. It wasn't actually simultaneous but very close and the thing was that when that E-boat was out on the starboard side, as soon as we were struck he started to come in and he came in right alongside – and if only we had had a hand grenade we could have chucked it over the side onto him, but we had nothing, absolutely nothing, and so he came alongside. All those boats were supposed to be Italian manned, but this one wasn't, so 'Achtung, Achtung,' all in German, so clearly he was a German person. The other thing was that he came alongside, dropped aft because of course we were still making a bit of way and then he fired a cannon at us, across the deck and I'm afraid I dropped down! [laughter] Our guns couldn't fire back at him because we couldn't see him, it was pitch black. The whole thing was engineered by our government to go in, in darkness, no moon, no nothing. Anyway this guy fires across the deck and then suddenly quite out of the blue a circle of lights went in the water and the E- boat disappeared in a cloud of steam and smoke.

In this case the merchant ship had seen the downfall of its aggressor, which was very rare. The E-boat had been hit by *Kenya*, the cruiser, well we guess it was because she was with us in the morning, that's the only reason we think that – the Pink Lady is what they called her. Bletchley Park comes into this because they came to visit us at the George Cross Island Association, at one of our gatherings (we have an annual one in Eastbourne), so someone said 'I think this chap has got a message for you.' This chap said 'What ship were you on?' and I said the *Rochester Castle*. He told me that the E-boat, in the time that it had torpedoed us and run alongside, had got the name of the ship, because of course although the name was greyed out, at the bow it was embossed so it stood out, and had sent it through to Berlin and Bletchley Park picked it up. They got it all through to Berlin before the damn thing blew up – amazing, in a very short space of time.

After we were hit, the thrust of the screw caused the water to come through the bulkhead so we managed to shore it up, and with the bilge pumps running we managed to cope, just. When we arrived, we arrived with the *Melbourne Star* and the *Port Chalmers*. The other two, the *Ohio* and the *Brisbane Star*, didn't arrive until the Saturday, which was the 15th, and we arrived on the 13th. Looking back, it was the first effort that the government had managed to make that was in any way successful, because all the other ones had ended in disaster.

We left Malta on the seventh of December and I remember that very clearly because that was the anniversary of Pearl Harbor which had been on the seventh of December, the year before. So we were in Malta from August until December. When we arrived they had a destroyer there that they were very proud of. They had fabricated a bow and put it on the destroyer and it was lying at one of the buoys and Jerry came over that night or sometime and blew the bow off again so we had the plates from that to go over our own hole. Actually they couldn't do anything with the hull itself because it was all over the blooming place so they just, as best they could, made it more or less flat and built a bit, sticking out a bit on the starboard side, so we had a sort of patch. That was quite a feat because what they did was to put a cofferdam, made of baulks of timber and watertight as much as possible, and put that into place and pump the water out completely, or more or less completely. At the bottom, the cofferdam was sacks of sawdust and when it got wet it got quite watertight and they pumped it out, the cofferdam pushed against the side and made it even tighter. It's a sort of thing that normally nobody ever hears about. And they could go down between the cofferdam and the ship's side and work on it.

So on the seventh of December we sailed to Alexandria, and when we were in Alexandria part of the captured French fleet was there and they used to be allowed ashore of an evening or something and they used to have a boat that came back and, as kids, we used to pull their leg by pointing one of our guns at the boat. It was just monkey business you know, but kids must play sometime, even if it was wartime. From there we went to Port Said of course, through the canal, down to South Africa, empty ship of course and then, in Cape Town we loaded skins and took these skins over to New York and ended up at Todd's Erie Basin as it was called. It was over in Brooklyn and we had a spell in dry dock there and we were repaired there. When the dry dock was flooded the Americans had done a good job with the rivets but they hadn't caulked them and so it was like a watering can. So up she had to come again and they spent a few weeks caulking all the rivets. 9

5 • Third Officer

After obtaining his Second Mate's certificate, the next stage of the deck officer's career was usually a period as Third Officer. There were a few exceptions: many of the larger passenger liners had two officers for each watch, with the most junior being the Fourth Officer, while in the case of the Orient Line all the watch-keeping officers had Master's certificates. The Fourth Officer was relatively uncommon, and reminiscences from time spent in this rank are included in this chapter.

When at sea, the Third Officer kept the eight-to-twelve watch. Out of sight of land, if the sun was visible, his first duty after taking over the morning watch would be to make an observation of the sun in order to obtain a position line. Towards the end of the watch the Master would come on the bridge for the ritual of ascertaining the latitude of the ship by the angular height of the sun above the horizon. The morning position line would then be transferred, making allowance for the speed and course of the ship, to obtain the noon position. When in sight of land, the officer of the watch would plot the position of the ship using bearings of lighthouses and other prominent landmarks at regular intervals. When the ship was in port, ensuring the safe loading and discharging of cargo was the responsibility of the deck officers.

Other duties, performed off watch, included the task of ensuring that the equipment, water and provisions of the ship's lifeboats were maintained. Should one of the Marine Society's libraries be carried on board it was often the Third Officer who acted as librarian.

The experience of taking full responsibility as a watch-keeping officer at sea for the first time remains a vivid memory to many of the contributors to this book, including the two authors.

For a number of years after the end of the Second World War there was a shortage of junior deck officers, and ships were allowed to sail with uncertificated Third Officers.

Anthony Davis was an apprentice with the British Tanker Company, the shipping company of British Petroleum. It was founded in 1915, and in 1956 was renamed BP Tanker Company. At that time and, indeed, throughout the 1950s it had a fleet of some 150 ships, all of which bore the prefix 'British'. He has never forgotten his first few days as a watch-keeping officer:

❦ I had, I suppose, a fairly normal apprenticeship, if that is the right word. The first big thing I remember was, about two years into my apprenticeship, I got sent for by the Master when we were in Llandarcy, which was a BP terminal just outside Swansea. The Marine Superintendent wanted to see me. Aboard ship the Master was God and the Marine Superintendent was somewhere north of him. So I hurriedly tried to work out which of my misdemeanours had caught up with me at that stage. Anyway, I changed out of my working gear and went up to see the Old Man, and rather to my surprise it wasn't what I had done wrong, but they needed an uncertificated Third Mate on a ship. Would I accept? Well, my wages went from tuppence ha'penny a week to real money so the answer was of course, 'Yes'. So twelve hours later I was packed with a train ticket in my pocket heading towards Fawley on Southampton Water.

The ship I joined was the *British Bugler*, which was a small product tanker, seven or eight thousand tons. In tanker terms the average size was twelve, a big ship was sixteen in those days, it was at the bottom end of the range. And the first trip was from Fawley to Antwerp. A relatively short sea trade. But it remains very vividly in my mind because as we exited Spithead I was on watch. Now I had been on the bridge hundreds of times, almost. I knew in theory what to do perfectly, but you suddenly find yourself on the bridge, and all the Master did, a very wise old bird, he just gave me the course and speed and walked off the bridge.

And there was I, heading out of Spithead after we'd dropped the pilot. I suddenly realised just how many ships were around us in the English Channel. There were, I thought, thousands – that was no doubt an exaggeration, there were ships going every which way there was, and suddenly there was me on the bridge, there was a seaman on the wheel, who I'm sure was old enough to be my father, grandfather or even great-grand-father, looking to me to tell him what to do. I had a look-out, the Master wasn't anywhere to be seen. I didn't discover until several weeks later that he was watching me like a hawk from the deck below and had the First Mate on standby. At the time I didn't know this. I thought I was totally on my own.

I had the worst four hours of my life trying to take the ship up through the English Channel. Fortunately I managed to avoid hitting anything, I'm not sure how, but suddenly you real-ise the enormous gap between understudying the officer of the watch as you were as a cadet and having to take the decisions not just in the open sea but in what was then and probably still is the most crowded waterway in the world. Anyway I had a ter-rible four hours, but I managed to survive, and in one sense I probably grew up more in those four hours than in the previous four, five or even ten years. But anyway, I found my confidence – being left alone. As I said, I didn't realise until later that I was very much under surveillance, both by the Master and by the First Mate.

We went on to the Scheldt, and when we entered the Scheldt we had a pilot, and the Master adopted the same tactics that he'd adopted leaving Fawley, and he and the pilot went out into the bridge wing and let me get on with it. So I was the officer of the watch and I took the ship up the Scheldt. Occasionally the pilot might say something, but anyway, you know the Scheldt is a very meandering river and the standard procedure is to head towards the deep water on the far bank, then you do a right-

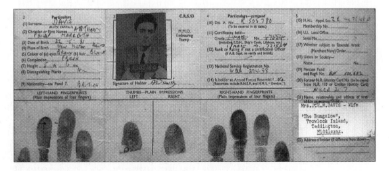

Anthony Davis's Merchant Navy identity card. No one thought to question identity cards in those days.

hand turn and go for the next bend. I took the first bend beauti-
fully, I thought. By the second bend it was getting easier, and
then we came to the third bend and we were heading towards
the bend, and right on the top – the river there had high banks
– was a farmhouse. There were banks because basically it
was floodwater country. The farmhouses were built on top of
the embankments so as to avoid flooding. Anyway, we headed
directly for the farmhouse that was exactly on the bend. We
set it as a marker. I gave the order 'Hard to starboard' and
nothing happened at all. I screamed 'Hard to starboard' and I
don't know how, somehow or other my several years of training kicked in at that stage. I didn't even look to the Master and
pilot, I threw the engines to 'Full Speed Astern', screamed
down the telephone to the Chief Engineer, and sent the cadet
down aft to find out what was happening. She hit the bank but
it was soft mud and then she slid slowly off. I even managed
to stop the engines and bring the ship to a halt in the river. By
this time the Old Man and the Pilot took over. I managed to
manoeuvre more by instinct than by rational thinking.

But meanwhile as we hit the bank there was a problem with
the farmhouse. I think we caused a mini earthquake under
it. The back wall of this farmhouse dropped like a bunch of
Lego bricks, and I always remember the farmer, I think he
was Flemish, I couldn't understand a word he said, but you
didn't need to understand. He was having lunch with his family
or farmhands or whatever it was. I think he was screaming
abuse at us. In fact I'm sure he was. There was the back wall
of his farmhouse had disintegrated and there was the family,
having their lunch and this farmer who was leaping in the air,
I remember him leaping, I am sure he stayed stationary about
three feet above the ground for at least a period of time. He
can't have done, it's physically impossible, but my memory
is that this guy was having apoplexy. Meanwhile the Chief
Engineer had managed to fix whatever the problem was and we
moved gingerly up the rest of the river and arrived in Antwerp.
We were there for, I think, four or five days in total. We had to
discharge cargo and there was an inquiry. So I had gone from
being probably the fastest-promoted apprentice in BP on day

one, to day three having to appear before a marine inquiry in Antwerp and about, I thought, about to make the fastest ever exit from Third Mate at the end of day three.

I always remember this inquiry. It was in Flemish and French. Despite having a French mother, my French is of the *la plume de ma tante* variety. I couldn't understand a word that was said. I had to say a few words and the Master and the pilot did too. Anyway, after what seemed an interminable time, it couldn't have been more than a day in total, eventually it was put down to an Act of God, to whom I was ever after eternally grateful. **9**

Many a naive first-tripper went to sea believing that as soon as his ship was safely tied up in a foreign port he would be allowed ashore. The reality was very different. The turn-around in port was always kept as short as possible, since merchant ships only made a profit for their owners when they were at sea. This fast turn-around was particularly pronounced for oil tankers. As soon as one arrived in port, and tanker terminals were almost invariably well away from centres of population, loading or discharge would commence right away. John Johnson-Allen, who also served in the BP Tanker Company, as it had become by then, recalls just what was involved for the Third Officer:

6 Cargo work in tankers when I was at sea was really rather hard work. Towards the end of the sixties and into the seventies it all changed because then came the era of central control rooms and remote-control valves and all the tanks were filled, the gap at the top between the surface of the oil and the top of the tanks, with an inert gas to make it safer. But before that when we loaded or discharged cargo you had an opening in the deck which had an upstand of about a foot, it was called the ullage plug which was where you also measured the depth, how much was left in the tank, so the fumes could and would come out of the tank and you had to put spark guards over the top of them – you were supposed to but we seldom if ever did.

As Third Mate I shared the cargo work in port with the

Second Officer, doing six hours on and six hours off. So as soon as we arrived in port from doing four hours on and eight hours off doing your watch at sea and then going to stand-by with everybody either on the bridge or on the fo'c'sle or out on the poop coming into port, we then immediately went into cargo work. The Chief Officer was on all the time – he supervised the whole thing, told us which tanks we were going to do next. He did the cargo plan, but the Second and Third Mate actually did the cargo work, and it wasn't a case of standing back and letting the crew do it. There would be one Mate, the pump man and, if we carried apprentices, then one of the apprentices. There'd only be three people, and so it was up to those three to open and close the cargo valves as appropriate for each lot of different grade of cargo, on a product carrier that was discharging, and to close them when a tank was finished, make sure the pumps didn't run dry, as that could burn them out if they were turbine pumps.

The valve wheels were about eighteen inches to two foot wide, diameter, and they took about thirty odd turns to open and close. Some were easy, some were incredibly hard work, and I remember, I think I was an apprentice, being in a club, in South Shields, and we were talking to some girls as one does in clubs, and they said, 'What do you do?' and we said, 'Guess.' And they turned our hands over and said, 'Oh, you're on tankers,' as we all had calluses on our hands from turning valve wheels.

That kept us quite busy, and if, having got to the end of a particular batch, we had to reset the pipelines for the next batch of cargo, then we could find ourselves spending an hour turning anything up to twenty or thirty valve wheels. One after the other to set the valves to make sure the cargo went down the appropriate pipeline from the tank all the way up onto deck then out and over the side. So it was hard work, and then we had to monitor the cargo tank to make quite sure it was going down if we were discharging, and equally important of course, when we were loading to make quite sure that as the oil came in, be it crude oil or a product, that as it got close to the tank being full we warned the appropriate people that that was the end of the grade, that that was all that we were going to need – and they would be standing by to shut off ashore as we shut off the tank when it was full. If it was the end of a grade then they would have to shut off the tank at the right moment when we told them, and if we were loading to a full tank it would be no more than about, in some cases, a few inches below the level of the deck. They had to be fairly active to get it shut off otherwise we would have a spill. I never saw one because they knew what it was all about. But if we were loading and then going on to another tank, then we would have to shut off one tank and open up another tank so that the one tank was full and the next tank was open, so we carried on to the next tank. That could get quite exciting. When we were loading crude oil and it was coming in at two thousand tons an hour and it got near the top it was coming up the tank quite quickly and we really had to watch it very, very closely. When it got to within about six foot of the top we would measure it with an ullage stick, which was a long stick, six foot long with a little bar across the top so we would lower it into the tank and we would keep on watching it and watching the level come up and then we'd wait about an inch and then we'd have to stop it and then move on to the next tank.

What I hoped for in a cargo watch of six hours was a nice slow discharge down a narrow pipeline going to a tank that was some way away, because that would take a long time and with a bit of luck I might have a nice quiet watch so the poor swine who came on after me would have to do all the valve swinging. It didn't always work out like that because they were of the same opinions and so they would sometimes manage to make it work so you did all the hard work and they managed to get away without doing anything.

Tankers, of course, also had other operations where you got involved. Tank cleaning, as of course the tanks had to be cleaned, the sludge had to be taken out of the bottom of the tanks if you were carrying crude oil, and I can remember in the sixties going down the Portuguese coast and we were digging the sludge out of the bottom of the tank and seeing these buckets of filthy crude oil sludge being tipped straight over the side into the sea and there was a brown smear behind us. I mean, what were we doing in those days, it was appalling, this filth going out. And then after the tanks were cleaned, particularly if we were going into dry dock we'd have to gas-free the tanks. They had to be gas-freed so that they could be worked inside, so we had these huge air-powered fans which we would site on opened-up particular plates on the deck. These fans would go on for hour upon hour, and if you were trying to sleep after doing a watch on the bridge there was this eldritch howling going on. Hour after hour to get all the gas out. Then the Mate would go down with his gasometer, or whatever it was called, I forget now, the gas meter perhaps, to check that the gas was out and it was safe to work in the tanks, because if it wasn't and then there was a spark then there would have been an explosion. So there were other aspects of cargo apart from loading and unloading. It was making the tanks fit for cleanliness for dry dock. **9**

The recent upsurge in piracy, especially in the seas off the Horn of Africa, is a cause of concern to all maritime nations, but even forty to fifty years ago violence was endemic in certain parts of the world. Robin Knox-Johnston served his apprenticeship with British India, and once he had obtained his Second Mate's certificate he rejoined them as Third Officer. He recalls:

6 So back I went as Third Mate. I chose to go out East on Eastern service as we called it. There were a number of reasons for that, the pay was better, about twenty per cent more and you paid no tax, you did a two-and-a-half-year contract. After twelve and before eighteen months of that contract you could take a month's flying leave which you could combine with study leave for First Mate's, because by then you had the sea time in; so I went out and joined the *Dwarka* in Karachi. Now, she was one of four ships that we had which were deck passenger ships, basically, with a certain amount of first- and second-class accommodation. They ran the mail run from

Bombay up to Basra. It was a three-week round voyage. Leave Bombay, then Karachi, Muscat, Dubai, Qatar (Umm Said as it was), Bahrain, Bushire, Khorramshar and Basra. It was an interesting run, because in those days Kuwait had just got its first jetties, Bahrain didn't, and Dubai didn't. At Muscat we anchored. Bombay and Karachi of course had ports and we would be alongside. Khorramshar sometimes we would be alongside and sometimes we would anchor.

It was interesting, because we carried 1,200 deck passengers on a 4,900-ton ship with four holds. At many of the ports there were no alongside facilities and people were brought out on dhows. They would just come alongside the gangway and we would load and discharge cargo using the derricks. We put up safety nets to keep the passengers away, and just got on with it.

That year we were, I think, between Karachi and Muscat when we heard about the *Dara* where, basically, a truckload of Egyptian-manufactured, Russian anti-tank mines was exploded on top of the settling tanks in the tween deck and it blew up the deck and set fire to the settling tanks; the ship was pretty soon ablaze and there were about 400 killed. We passed her very shortly afterwards and you could just see the davits sticking up out of the water – that was just before Dubai. Later, of course, we got the full report from the Admiralty as to exactly what had happened, and how it had all occurred. Then we had a series of bombs – we had one on the *Dwarka*, which went off just by number one hatch. Fortunately, because it wasn't enclosed, the damage was quite slight and we only had one passenger who was only slightly hurt. We were very, very lucky.

Thereafter I led a charmed life. I joined a ship that had just had a bomb and I left a ship just before it got one and I'm surprised more people didn't follow me around. But all sorts of things used to happen. If the passengers got hold of alcohol that could cause a lot of trouble, causing difficulties when you asked them to move to get out of the way when you were loading stores – then they weren't going to move. I remember once, one tried to punch me and that was a mistake. I was quite a

good boxer and I just hit him and I remember his nose explod-
ing and his mates ran away, but we had to be careful because
we had had a situation a few years before where some Somalis
had got loose, killed one of the officers, paralysed another,
and it was quite serious. They overpowered them and one of
them was standing there with a knife challenging the Chief
Engineer, who picked up a soda-acid fire extinguisher and set
it off, firing it into the chap's eyes, and while he was doing that
hit him over the head with it so that was the end of that little
battle – a complete knockout to the Chief Engineer.

But we had to be a little bit careful. There was another time
when we had to put the fire hoses onto them as they were riot-
ing. I suddenly found I had no fire pressure, and one of the little
bastards had got behind me and cut the hose. He was a bloody
fool because I still had the nozzle in my hand and his knife did
not compete with the fire nozzle and he came off second best!
There was no particular protection to stop people getting into
the accommodation or up onto the bridge – if someone was
determined they could have done it. We weren't armed. There
was a pistol in the safe but nobody could ever remember the
combination. We did have some bullet-proof jackets but they
were bulky and I don't think anyone ever brought them out to
wear. On the whole it was fairly simple. After that Arab tried to
throw a punch at me everyone got out of my way in the tween
decks – word got round. Although I was only the Third Mate
people got out of my way more willingly than they did for the
Mate. Some passengers that you never had any trouble with
were the Bedouin, never any trouble with them whatsoever,
they were absolute gentlemen, and they were very courteous
always. It was the town Arabs that were the problem. **9**

After they had spent a number of years at sea, many young men, deck
officers included, decided that they would rather be working ashore.
A few of these used their off-watch time furthering their education.
The Seafarers Education Service and the associated College of the Sea
provided libraries for ships and arranged correspondence courses for

seafarers. Volunteer tutors made up courses to suit the individual, and sent out appropriate learning material, and then corrected the work that had been set as well as giving the often all too necessary encouragement. It was a protracted process as it could be up to two months or more between writing an essay aboard ship, sending it back to the UK for correction from one foreign port and then receiving the comments when the ship arrived at another port. Richard Goss recalls studying with the College of the Sea after he had passed his First Mate's certificate:

❦ I took and passed the certificate first time then I did a voyage with Buries Markes as Second Mate on a ship called *La Cumbre*. That company is a subsidiary of Louis Dreyfus of Paris. They are primarily grain brokers but they had some ships of their own. *La Cumbre* had been built as the *Clan McAlpine*, a merchant aircraft carrier during World War Two. She was a very wet ship. She was the only ship that I have sailed on where I had two inches of water in my cabin in bad weather – not nice. I decided that I didn't like being a Second Mate because of the twelve-to-four watch but also because by that time I had got interested in studying economics and was doing so under Ronald Hope at the College of the Sea.[9] There is a distinction between them and the Seafarers Education Service but it is not important; they had the same management in the same building. I got interested in economics and I wanted to study, you see. The twelve-to-four watch is no watch to keep if you are studying; on the other hand the eight-to-twelve watch is an ideal watch because you had every afternoon off and you can have a little bit of a kip after lunch and then get down to reading books and writing essays, which is what I proceeded to do. I went back to being a Third Mate with Ellermans; they put me on a ship called the *City of Brisbane* in Tilbury to see whether I was half decent, and evidently I was, because then they put me on a ship called the *City of Khartoum*, another five-hatch job but a five-cylinder Doxford engine and a pretty good

---

9. It is a pleasure to be able to mention that Dr Ronald Hope received an Honorary Degree from the Open University in recognition of his pioneering efforts on behalf of education for merchant seamen.

ship it was. A very fine ship, going out to India, from there to New York, and back to India. When I say India, I mean Ceylon, Bangladesh and so forth. We had railway locomotives on deck and all sorts of things.

By that time I had taken and passed GCEs. I was the first student to take GCEs on a merchant ship. It is now fairly standard and several dozen people do it every year, but at that time it hadn't been done before and I had to go to Senate House, the office block of London University. London University had a long history of being extremely generous in creating examination centres elsewhere, and I went and saw one of their officials. It would have been so easy for him to say there is no precedent, we have never had it on a ship, no, no, no. Instead of that he said we have never created a ship as an overseas examination centre yet, but I don't see why we shouldn't start. Marvellous! And I have always thought of Senate House as being an extremely beautiful building ever since.

So this was done on the *La Cumbre*, with the Captain invigilating. The Captain was barely literate and certainly did not know what invigilation meant. When the examination papers arrived on board he opened the envelope and handed it to me so I had to explain that you're going to put me in a room at a certain time and so forth. The university insisted that the examination should take place at the times for starting and finishing stated on the examination sheet. However, the university did not know about apparent time, Greenwich Mean Time, local time, ship's time or anything like that – and trying to clarify this I gave up. They said, well at that time! So we used ship's time, which I am quite sure they thought was very reasonable. If, however, nasty-minded people had wanted to telegraph the papers around the world because they were in some different time zone this would have enabled them to do so.

Then I did advanced levels. I did advanced-level GCE economics, I did economic history, I did British constitution and English language as well. Most of this was a little like falling off a log because in the first place it was very easy. I was using Samuelson as a textbook, which I thought was marvellous, and Cairncross's book, but I can't remember what textbooks

I had for economic history. All the time that I was doing this I was Third Mate. I used to study very hard at sea, literally, when voyaging, because there was peace and quiet and I could write two or three essays in an afternoon – oh, it was marvellous. ⁹

The Sovereign's Review of the Fleet dates back to 1415 when Henry V inspected the ships that were to take his army to France before the Battle of Agincourt. In more recent years a naval review has traditionally been held to commemorate the coronation of a new monarch and any subsequent jubilees. Following Queen Elizabeth II's Silver Jubilee review it was decided that there should be no more of these commemorative reviews. However, a further review was held in 2005 to mark the bicentenary of the Battle of Trafalgar.

John Redman was fortunate to be serving on one of the ships chosen to represent the merchant navy at the Silver Jubilee Naval Review held at Spithead on 28 June 1977.

❻ In 1977 I was Third Officer sailing aboard the SS *Opalia*. I had been promoted to Third Officer in 1975 following my cadetship with Shell Tankers (UK) Ltd. The *Opalia* was Shell's cadet ship of the fleet. She was manned almost entirely by cadets – there were twenty-eight of them aboard plus a full complement of officers and petty officers. When I joined, *Opalia* was trading around the Caribbean, the east coast of the States and the Mexican Gulf.

Prior to joining I had been told that the ship would be attending the Queen's Jubilee Review at Spithead in June 1977. We loaded our last cargo of oil in the Caribbean for discharge at Rouen and as we sailed up the River Seine and approached the berth, standing on the quayside ready to join was the Commodore of the Shell Fleet, Captain Simon Darroch RD, RNR. He boarded together with other superintendents from Shell and representatives of Tilbury Graving Dock, as it was then. The men from Tilbury came aboard to measure up for modifications, which were to be done in preparation for our attendance at Spithead.

We were aware that guests were being invited on board for the review, and in order to accommodate their needs cabins on the first accommodation deck were converted into gents and ladies washrooms. Whilst that work was going on the ship was painted overall. She was also fitted out with signal flags to be dressed overall between sunrise and sunset. There was a lot of preparation work, and of course as Third Mate I was responsible for signal flags. Boxes and boxes of these flags were put on board and rigged up on a wire running from the foremast to the mainmast and then from the mainmast down to the poop deck. Several practice runs were necessary hoisting the flags, and of course the final job was to actually look at the letters to make sure that there were no inappropriate messages spelt out. Between sunset and sunrise the ship was to be lit overall so a second wire was rigged which carried light bulbs. I can't remember how long the work took, but it was only a matter of three or four days and at the end the ship looked really smart with new paint and dressed overall.

We sailed from Tilbury and arrived at the Nab Tower in the Solent on Saturday 25 June to pick up the pilot. Once the pilot boarded we were escorted by a naval tug to our designated anchorage position just to the north-west of the West Ryde Middle Buoy. All the naval ships had already arrived and were at their anchorage positions. As we steamed up the line many of them were using *Opalia* to practice for the review day, when they would cheer ship when *Britannia* reviewed the fleet. It was quite marvellous to be the centre of everyone's attention, especially for the wives aboard our ship. Of course naval etiquette demanded that the ensign be dipped as we passed each naval vessel, keeping our flag party very busy. We eventually anchored around midday and spent the rest of the day ship watching and preparing for our guests the following day.

During the next three days, Sunday, Monday and Tuesday, we had various visitors on board. Sunday was 'Family Day'. Shell had arranged for the families of all those on board to assemble at Clarence Pier, Southsea, and be ferried out to *Opalia*. My then wife was sailing with me and our parents travelled up for the day from our home in the West Country. After a tour of the ship we joined the reception on the boat deck and spent the afternoon enjoying the occasion. Of all the days at Spithead this was the most enjoyable, being able to share it with family whom we had not seen for some time.

On the Monday the guests on board were shoreside staff from Shell Centre. Safety was a concern and access to certain parts of the ship was restricted. We had to make sure, as far as possible, that spaces were locked so that inquisitive guests couldn't gain unauthorised entry, although this didn't deter some of them. We tried to make the bridge a restricted area and had fashioned varnished mahogany notice boards spliced with decorative rope and tied to the bottom of access ladders, saying NO ADMITTANCE. Adventurous guests ignored the signs, untied the rope and came up to the bridge anyway. Then we had the usual questions from people who don't have any practical experience of ships such as, 'How many gallons do you carry?' An unusual question, we thought, from people employed by one of the largest merchant tanker fleets in the world. Although I don't remember the answer, one was provided that seemed to satisfy their curiosity. Then, after they looked into the radar visor we would be asked, 'Which one is our ship?' Rather than explain the principles of a relative motion radar display we took the easier route of switching on the reflection plotter and drawing a chinagraph ring around the nearest ship to us, with an arrow saying 'SS *Opalia*'. This worked a treat.

The cadets had been told that they absolutely had to be on their best behaviour, and I have to say they were a credit to the company. You can imagine that, with twenty-eight young men on board aged between seventeen and twenty, adventurous, high-spirited and so on, keeping control of them was sometimes difficult. When the guests from Shell came to leave they assembled on the main deck before walking down the accommodation ladder to the waiting launch. Suddenly a lady at the top of the ladder said, 'Two people are missing. The couple I came with aren't here.' We searched the ship but couldn't find them. We did a head count on the launch and sure enough there were two people missing. We then did a more thorough search of the ship and in one of the fo'c'sle spaces they were found. We had run out of padlocks so weren't able to lock the watertight access door. Instead, all eight dogs had been hammered hard, but somehow they had managed to gain access. Having been surprised in the fo'c'sle, the young couple emerged and walked along the main deck to the top of the accommodation ladder. The young man had dirt patches on his elbows and knees, and as we saw the young lady disappear down the accommodation ladder we noticed that the seat of her jeans was filthy. At that moment it was rather difficult to maintain discipline, and there were quite a few ribald comments from our cadets as the couple disembarked.

Tuesday 28 June 1977 was review day, and our guests that day were senior personnel from the office and clients of Shell. On a personal note this day was also my wife's twenty-first birthday. I discovered later that on the launch on the way out to the ship a huge birthday card had been passed round and signed by all the dignitaries from Shell and their customers. This was presented to my wife by Frank Whitely, the Managing Director of Shell Tankers (UK) Ltd. She was also presented with a key mounted on a mahogany board which had been made by the ship's engineers. The key had the ship's name and my wife's name cut into it and, as I discovered later, had been sent ashore in Tilbury to be chrome-plated. A wonderful surprise, and more was to come. It's not everyone who has the Queen turn up for their twenty-first birthday.

I don't remember too much about the day but the format pretty much followed previous days, except of course this was *the* review day. As *Britannia* reviewed the fleet and sailed past *Opalia* the ship's company lined the main deck in full uniform. We cheered ship with caps off and held in the right hand, which was extended upwards at forty-five degrees. On the cheer hip, hip, hip, hurray, the right hand described a clockwise circle with the wrist not falling below shoulder level. We had spent days practising. We were specifically told that the cheer, at the Queen's request, would be HURRAY, not HURRAH.

Anchored to the west of us, at the head of our line, was the 270,000 dwt BP tanker *British Respect*, the largest ship at the review. I don't know what her complement was but she was a normal merchant ship, not a training ship. We could see her crew all lined around the poop deck leaning over the rail. They hadn't particularly dressed for the occasion and they didn't cheer ship as we had done. Our radio officer told us that he had received three telegrams following *Britannia*'s review. The first telegram was from C-in-C Fleet to *Opalia*, and it read 'Very smart.' The second, we were told, had also been sent by C-in-C Fleet to the *British Respect*, reading 'Kindly show more British respect.' Nice to get one over on BP again. The third telegram was from the Queen herself to the entire fleet – 'Splice the mainbrace' – and the celebrations began.

That evening my wife and I were invited on board HMS *Fearless*. By happy coincidence her uncle, a serving Chief Petty Officer on board *Fearless*, had sent a message to *Opalia* inviting us to the Chiefs' mess for a party. He was paying off the following day and had put a barrel on to celebrate. I spoke to our Commodore and got his permission to use the launch to take us to the *Fearless*. *Opalia* was anchored at the western end of our line and *Fearless* was almost at the extreme eastern end of the line. The launch took us down the line past all the naval ships, which were lit overall. A truly fantastic experience. Needless to say we had a wonderful evening in the Chiefs' mess and later on went up on deck to watch the fireworks display which marked the end of the review.

It was a great privilege to be present at the Spithead Review in 1977, and experience four wonderful days in my seagoing career which were completely different from the day-to-day business of operating a Shell tanker. 9

Finally, to end this chapter, two little vignettes. Jeremy Procter remembers a railway journey with a difference:

6 As a young Third Mate around 1965 I was asked to escort an Indian crew from a ship in dry dock on the Tyne to one about to sail from dry dock in Falmouth. The crew and myself travelled

by British Rail, the latter attaching two flatbed trucks to the train for crew's luggage. The crew and luggage were successfully embarked on the train and I was ensconced in a second-class compartment. After a few hours from our departure you can imagine my surprise when there was a knocking on the compartment door and there was one of the Indian stewards complete in his uniform with a tray of food for me. Quite how they had prepared this I never did discover, but it was gratefully received. The other passengers in the compartment were amazed, and it made me feel like royalty! **9**

And Adrian White recalls one Master under whom he served:

6 When I was Third Mate in the *City of Poona* the Master enjoyed more than a glass or two of gin. On that ship the staircase to the chart room rose from the Captain's deck. One evening about eleven o'clock I was on watch when I heard a scrabbling coming from the direction of the staircase. I went to investigate and saw two hands holding on to the top step. They belonged to the captain, who was stretched out to his full length on the staircase. He looked blearily up at me and said, 'Third mate, does Jesus want you for a sunbeam?' I replied, 'I don't think he would have me, sir.' 'That's just what I've told the Purser,' he replied, and at that point his fingers slipped and he slid gracefully back down the staircase. **9**

6 · Second Officer

The Second Officer normally kept the twelve-to-four watch at sea and, on cargo ships, was night duty officer when the ship was in port. As well as his watch-keeping duties, he was the navigating officer, with responsibility for plotting the ship's course, keeping the chart portfolio up to date and looking after the gyro compass if one was fitted. Another important duty was taking responsibility for the daily winding of the ship's chronometers, of which there were usually two. These were mounted in the chart room and had to be wound at a fixed time each day. Making a fair copy of the logbook for transmission to head office at the end of the voyage was an unwelcome chore that was usually done by the Second Officer, and in many companies looking after the dispensary was also one of his responsibilities. The woefully inadequate qualification for this latter task was a St John's Ambulance first-aid certificate, normally obtained whilst ashore studying for the Second Mate's certificate.

David Smith records some memories of this last aspect:

❦ There was a dispensary on every foreign-going vessel, and in the Royal Mail Line responsibility for looking after it on those ships that did not carry a doctor was given to the Second Officer. This meant that for over two years, when we were at sea, I opened the dispensary every morning at eleven o'clock and waited for custom. What follows is thematic in nature. All the incidents happened, but I can't be sure in which ship or in what order they occurred.

The dispensary itself was a small cabin with a bench and sink, a couch, cupboards and drawers, and on a shelf, a copy of that exemplar of do-it-yourself manuals, *The Ship Captain's Medical Guide*. A hot-water steriliser stood on the bench, the cupboards contained large bottles of medicines such as cough linctus and prickly-heat lotion, while the drawers contained bandages, plasters, needles and thread for sutures, scalpels, splints and dental forceps, a large syringe for ears and small syringes for penicillin, and everything else that was on the Board of Trade list. Each time we returned to the UK a pharmacist would come aboard and replenish the stock. Basically, the crew were a healthy lot. It was mainly made up of young men living in an atmosphere that was unsympathetic to hypochondria or self-pity, but nevertheless on most mornings there were usually one or two patients. Generally this meant filling a small medicine bottle from one of the large ones, handing it to the patient, and making an appropriate annotation in the dispensary log. It was only a matter of days before I was able to treat routine cases without reference to *The Ship Captain's Medical Guide*. Once we reached port, arrangements were always made for anyone who was ill to go ashore and see

SERIAL No. 6197

Sperry Gyroscope Company Ltd

CERTIFICATE OF GRADUATION

This is to certify that

N. J. D. Smith

has completed a course of 5 days instruction in the fundamental principles and operation of

Sperry Gyro-Compass Equipment

and has given satisfactory evidence of his ability to operate this equipment.

Given under our hand this Seventeenth day of December one thousand nine hundred and fifty six

Sperry Gyroscope Company Ltd

Instructor

Managing Director

During the period covered by this book, gyroscopic compasses were being introduced, and responsibility for their care while at sea was usually given to the Second Officer. The gyroscope was housed in a small room deep in the bowels of the ship in order to minimise disturbance from the pitching and rolling movements of a ship in a seaway. If one lived within daily travel of the Sperry factory at Brentford in West London, the week's course was a pleasant addition to the normal leave at the end of a voyage. Given the length of the course there is, perhaps, something just a little pretentious about the certificate itself.

a doctor, so it was only on the long ocean passages that one was at risk of being put on one's mettle. And inevitably emergencies, both big and small, did happen.

One of the more dramatic incidents involved a seaman who had sprained his hand. He had been sent ashore in one of the Brazilian ports, where a doctor had wrapped his hand in cotton wool and then strapped it up with sticking plaster, giving instructions that twice a day the bandages were to be taken off so that the hand could be given an ether rub. This doctor had then given the seaman a large bottle of ether together with a supply of spare cotton wool and strapping. The seaman soon decided that removing the bandages was a complete waste of time when the relief resulting from the cooling effect could just as easily be obtained by pouring the ether liberally over the bandaged hand. So early one evening he did just that, but then made the mistake of deciding to have a cigarette. The moment he struck a match the ether-soaked cotton wool, strapped to his hand, caught fire. Some of his shipmates managed to catch the by now crazed human firebrand, smother the flames, and bring him to me. Once I had given an injection of Omnopon I set about cutting off the charred bandage. As soon as I removed the bandage the skin of his hand came away like a very old glove. The next hour or so was spent carefully covering the exposed surfaces with tulle gras before bandaging the hand. Fortunately we were not all that far from port and we were able to put him in hospital the next day.

Not emergencies, but rather the all-too-frequent sequel to shore leave in South America, were the cases of gonorrhoea. A few days out to sea and one of the clients at the morning dispensary would come in and shut the door before announcing, perhaps slightly shame-faced, more often defiantly, 'I've caught a dose.' The Ship Captain's Medical Guide laid down the procedure to be followed, complete with illustrations. First a glass microscope slide was produced from an ample supply in one of the drawers and given to the patient, who had meanwhile dropped his trousers, with instructions to provide a specimen. This was then covered with another slide, taped together, and put aside to be sent ashore when the patient was referred to hospital at the next port of call (where, I expect, it was promptly binned). Next, an injection of penicillin in the buttock. Syringe and needle were placed in the steriliser and boiled for a few minutes while an ampoule of sterile water was broken open. Then the water was drawn up into the syringe, injected into the little bottle containing the powdered penicillin, the bottle shaken, the solution drawn into the syringe and then injected into the buttock at the site so clearly delineated in the photograph. (I don't recall this particular duty of a Ship's Officer appearing in the pages of the sea stories by Percy F Westerman that I read so avidly as a boy.)

On one long ocean passage a seaman had toothache and, not surprisingly, the recommended pledget of cotton wool soaked in oil of cloves proved ineffective. As the days passed his pleas for me to extract his tooth became ever more urgent – something that I was reluctant to do, since although dental forceps were to be found in the dispensary, local anaesthetic was not. Eventually his badgering wore me down and I gave in. By careful comparison with the illustrations in the book I was able to select the correct forceps – lower jaw – and give them the requisite ten minutes in the steriliser. Three of the apprentices were recruited as assistants, one to read out the instructions as I proceeded with the operation, one to hold the man down should this be necessary and one to steady the head. 'Place the forceps on the tooth with one beak on each side,' read the apprentice. 'Exert downward pressure so that the beaks of the forceps are forced between the tooth and the gum.' After each sentence there was a pause while I executed the manoeuvre. 'Gently rock the tooth to and fro to loosen it in its socket. Push firmly down on the handles of the forceps to break the tooth out from the jaw bone.' Incredibly, while this protracted procedure was going on, the seaman sat there quite still making no sound. Sure enough, as I pushed firmly down on the forceps so the tooth came out. After a few minutes spent biting on a piece of rolled-up gauze, the man stood up, thanked me and went back to work. 9

Navigating close to a coastline has always been hazardous, and over the centuries an elaborate network of buoys, light vessels and lighthouses has been developed to assist the mariner when sailing close to land. The Corporation of Trinity House is the body invested with the responsibility for the lighthouses and buoyage around the coasts of England, Wales, the Channel Islands and Gibraltar. It traces its origins back to a religious foundation, based at Deptford on the Thames just downstream from London, founded to say masses for the souls of 'shipmen' lost at sea. More prosaically, its written history dates from 1514 when King Henry VIII gave a charter to 'the Guild or Fraternity of the Most Glorious and Undivided Trinity of St Clement'. Over the intervening years its responsibilities increased, and it became increasingly concerned with the ensuring the safety of sailors living in this world rather than the next. Today Trinity House owns a small fleet of survey ships and tenders that are used in the day-to-day maintenance of the buoys and offshore lighthouses.

The body responsible for lighthouses and buoyage in Scotland and the Isle of Man is the Northern Lighthouse Board, while in Ireland it is the Commissioners of Irish Lights. Both these bodies are relative newcomers, having been founded by Act of Parliament in 1786. Despite their more prosaic foundation, both these bodies have their eccentricities. Based in Dun Laoghaire in the Republic, the Commissioners of Irish Lights is a cross-border body and its lighthouse tender flies the Irish flag when in Irish waters and a defaced Blue Ensign when in UK waters. The tenders of the Northern Lighthouse Board fly, when a Commissioner is aboard, a White Ensign with the pre-1801 union flag in the upper left-hand quarter, the only time this early version of the union flag without the red saltire of St Patrick is used.

Richard Woodman recalls his time as Junior Second Mate aboard one of the Trinity House vessels in the late 1960s:

❥ The ships, in those days, had a Commander, a First Officer and two Second Mates, a senior and a junior, who shared a lot of the practical work on the ship. You weren't a Third Mate but you were very definitely a Junior Second Mate and did all the boat work and a lot of the buoy work. It was a very physically demanding job, just what you wanted at twenty-two. So I took to that like a duck to water and they sent me down to Swansea for three weeks and I ended up staying for three years and becoming permanently appointed to THV *Alert*.

We were working in the Bristol Channel and the Irish Sea looking after a wide spectrum of aids to navigation which had a nice mixture of all of them – we had buoys, five light vessels and three or four major offshore lighthouses to look after, which kept us very busy and gave me a tremendous experience in a variety of work. That particular area that we looked after was particularly good from my perspective because the span of seamanship was as good as it got in Trinity House and I loved it.

The crews were pretty steady, almost all permanent men, all accomplished seamen who knew their jobs. The ships were basically run on quasi-naval lines so you were much more an officer in charge of men rather than a bloke who kept a watch on a merchant ship who either had to go and see the Mate if you wanted anything done or go and negotiate with the Bosun. I was much more an officer of a ship's company, which I liked, and it suited me and I suited it. You had, as a greenhorn officer coming in to that job, to earn your spurs, particularly with regard to the crew. Once you had done that they were brilliant, they were very good and they were extremely loyal and supportive, but you had to go through this sort of slight period where you had to decide how you were going to behave, were you going to throw your weight about and come along as a brass bounder full of piss and importance or whether you were going to take a slightly observational seat, because one of the jobs we used to do as Boat Officer was be in charge of the motorboats wherever they went. Now if you went into a rock landing in a heavy sea or swell you knew that the coxswain of the boat, who'd been doing it for some years, was better at it than you were. I thought myself something of an expert in small boats, which I wasn't actually. So you had this difficult relationship. You were responsible for anything that went wrong, but he did the job and it was a question of marrying those two responsibilities together. If you hit it off right the boats crew were brilliant. I was fortunate to work with some very good boat's crews.

We also, of course, in those days had acetylene-lit buoys, which did go out occasionally and had to be relit. If they did you would get a call-out for a job. I am not exaggerating to tell you – I am really not exaggerating – that we boarded buoys from ships' motorboats in extreme conditions. I boarded the St Anne's buoy off Milford Haven on a lee shore in a south-westerly force nine and that wasn't that unusual. There was superb seamanship, from lowering the boats to picking them up again, on the part of the Mate, the Master, the hoisting crew, brilliant seamanship on the part of the sailors, the boat's crew, and the coxswain. As the Boat Officer I jumped the buoys and relit them with one sailor, the middleman in the boat . He and I jumped the buoys, did what was necessary, got off and went back to the ship. It was very physically demanding but it was easy to earn your spurs in that way because once you showed you could do it and you were up for it and game for it the boat's crew were then on side.

There were all sorts of compensations – we went to some beautiful spots. We would spend the day recharging a lighthouse with oil and water and again, as Boat Officer, you were in charge of the shore party supervising the oiling, which in those days was done one barrel at a time, so that it was almost nineteenth-century in its adventurous, demanding way. I was always knackered because we worked very, very hard for long hours. There were no regular watches. We did work extremely long hours, but it was very interesting. 9

Although radar had played such an important role in the Second World War, its introduction aboard merchant ships in the immediate post-war period was slow, and it was quite a few years before it became a standard feature aboard ship. Certainly, a number of older Masters were wary of it – a caution that was not completely unfounded. Reliability was problematical and the training of deck officers in its use was by no means universal, and it was not long before the expression 'radar-assisted collision' entered the seaman's language.

Bill Allen was serving with the British Tanker Company, and he was lucky to be sent on a radar observer's course soon after he had obtained his Second Mate's certificate. He recalls:

❦ After I got my Second Mate's ticket I got another urgent telegram instructing me to join the ship as Second Mate. I got a very nice letter, which contrasts with what some ship owners were like. I went on the radar course at Leicester, which was a typical course for those days and lasted for five days. I hadn't seen a radar set in my life before and after five days I was qualified to take charge of a new set. I got a letter after I had been on the course saying that they only paid for bed and breakfast and meals and I had to pay back £1 and some pence, which was not included. They had to send that out to me on the ship at Colombo, which had to be signed by the Master and by me in order to recover that money. What the money had been used for was to buy a cup of tea and some newspapers.

The radar set was a very good one for its day, but the Old Man didn't like it at all. We were coming back from Australia and we had had the radar serviced while we were in Australia. I switched it on as we came up to Ras al Hadd. That was so we could pick up the headland. The story of that light was that the light was only lit when the sheikh was in the harem. As he was an old man, nine times out of ten you couldn't see the light. So I had the radar on to pick up the headland. It was two o'clock in the morning and the Old Man was down below. I was up on the monkey island trying to see if I could see the light. Suddenly there was an almighty bang. The radar stopped going round. I shot down into the wheelhouse. The man at the wheel was crouched behind it. He said a great big green flash came up out of that. I opened the front cover and there were thirty-two valves inside. I can always remember, there was a big valve sitting on top of a transformer. It had a cap on the top of it. And there was a bit of wire clipped on to the cap. When I opened the front, the whole thing was an absolute mess. I picked out this bit of blue wire with the cap on it. I knew where that bit went. I then walked into the chart room, just behind the wheelhouse. The Old Man came pounding up the inside staircase because he had heard the bang. He said, 'What's up, Second Mate?' I said, 'The radar has blown up, sir.' He looked at the little blue wire in my hand and said, 'Is that all you've got left?' 9

Some goods were carried on deck rather than in the holds. These were always more at risk of damage in bad weather. In this short vignette, Bill Allen, who had left the British Tanker Company and joined Clan Line, recalls a deck cargo shifting in bad weather. Clan Line was founded in Liverpool in 1877, but moved its headquarters to Glasgow in 1881. It traded mainly to India and the Persian Gulf, Southern and East Africa and Australia. The company went into administration in 1988.

6 When I was on the *Clan Urquhart* we were carrying railway carriages on deck. The terms of carriage were that the shipper insured the risk. We were in the Irish Sea in a bad gale, and early in the morning the Old Man called me up to the bridge. The railway carriages had broken adrift and although I was the Second Mate, the Mate, whose job it was to secure them, was drunk and incapable. The apprentices, the junior engineers and I had to secure them, because the Indian crew were too scared. By rigging the insurance wires, fore and aft, we managed to secure them. When we unloaded them in Mombasa, the engineer from the East African railway company who inspected them said they only had superficial damage. They were lifted onto the jetty and towed away. When we got back to the UK I left the ship but before I left I went to see the Old Man, who gave me an envelope, which had some compensation from the railway company for our efforts in saving the railway carriages. However, the biggest envelope had gone to the Mate, although he was at the time drunk in his cabin. 9

Ian Gibb recalls another deck cargo from the time he was Second Officer aboard the *Salmara*:

6 One of the strangest cargoes that we ever carried, or that I ever carried, on the P&O cargo ships was on *Salmara*. The *Salmara* was a cargo ship of about eight or nine thousand tons

and we were employed on the Far East trade from European ports to Hong Kong and the Philippine Islands, and on our arrival in Bangkok we were advised that we were going to have a cargo of water buffalo and pigs. Our Chief Officer and I decided that the best place for the pigs was on the afterdeck and the herd of water buffalo would be on the foredeck. There were 100 water buffalo and 250 pigs. The cadets were given the task of mucking out the pigs, and interestingly enough, one of the cadets of that time became Commodore of the P&O passenger fleet and I have some lovely cine-footage of him mucking out pigs. The water buffalo – which we carried between Bangkok and Hong Kong over a period of about four days, I think it was – were quite a problem in the sense that they lowed and they mooed at all hours of the day and night. On one occasion, I think after we had been at sea for a couple of days, the Chief Engineer rang the bridge in a state of high excitement to say that one of the water buffalo had somehow managed to lodge its head into his porthole and couldn't extricate itself. He didn't know what to do. Fortunately the Chief Officer, who was an Extra Master Mariner with a great deal of logical thought, came down and by half past five in the morning we had managed to extricate the water buffalo and the Chief Engineer was able to get back to sleep again. I had never seen a cargo of livestock being moved before, but we didn't lose either one pig or one water buffalo on the trip round and they were all discharged safely in Hong Kong four days later. 9

The next account mentions the Dreadnought Seamen's Hospital. This was originally built as an infirmary for the Royal Naval Hospital, Greenwich, between 1764 and 1786. It closed as Royal Naval hospital in 1869 and the building was then leased to the Seamen's Hospital Society for use as a hospital for merchant seamen. Prior to this, the society had maintained hospital ships moored on the Thames at Greenwich, one of which had been HMS *Dreadnought*, and this name was retained for the land-based hospital. Responsibility for running the hospital was transferred to the new National Health Service in 1948, but the dramatic decline in the number of ships using the London docks resulted in a drop in patient numbers, and the hospital was closed in 1986. A dedicated service for sick and injured merchant seamen is still available at St Thomas' Hospital in Lambeth.

John Johnson-Allen was promoted to Second Officer in BP Tankers. He recalls:

6 My first ship as Second Mate was the *British Chancellor*. I was just twenty-two when I joined her in February 1967, only about two weeks after actually getting my Mate's ticket. I remember when I signed on, the Shipping Master, who seemed to be a somewhat soured man, perhaps by years of signing on ships' companies, looked at my new shiny Mate's ticket and said, 'Another bloody boy wonder.' We were all new on that ship because it was my first ship as Second Mate, it was the Third Mate's also, his first trip, we had a radio officer who had never done the job before, it was his first trip on his own, and the Chief Officer likewise. And I think the engineers, all apart from the Chief Engineer, all were new to the job and were finding their feet. I think the Old Man was fairly laid back about it actually.

We went eventually to load in Mina-al-Ahmadi in Kuwait, and we loaded a cargo of benzene for Australia. In those days we loaded with open ports on the deck and this benzene had a specific gravity of about 0.6, so it was much, much lighter than even aviation spirit. It was the height of summer up the Gulf so it was about a hundred and something in the shade, and this stuff, the surface of it was boiling as we loaded it. We had to shut the boilers down, the galley, everything, there wasn't a single light allowed aboard anywhere, so we had to load this stuff and because it was so light you could see the fumes were coming out of the ullage plug and running down the side and across the deck and we were loading to ninety-eight per cent capacity, so we had literally to wait until we could see the boiling surface of the liquid coming up into the ullage plug and then shut it off as quickly as we could and slam the cap on to keep it in. So after we had loaded that, which took about two days – it came from tanks presumably some way away down a small pipeline – we took this off to Australia. We discharged it in one or two ports from, I think it was Newcastle in New South

Wales, went round to Kwinana in Western Australia to load, I think to head back, probably, towards the Suez Canal, starting to come home.

The Chief Officer was a very nice chap, and he and I managed to get an afternoon ashore so we went into Kwinana. His hobby was knitting and on a long trip he would knit a sweater, and he had an idea that he wanted to knit a Fair Isle sweater on the trip home. So we went into Fremantle and we managed to find a wool shop and in we went. Well, in Australia in the sixties, two men looking to buy wool in a wool shop was clearly unnatural to the shop assistants. We got some very, very strange looks, but it didn't matter because he got the wool he wanted and we went back and I believe he did knit a sweater on the way home.

My next ship as Second Mate was the *British Poplar*. I joined her in November 1967. She was a permanent coaster although she was 19,000 tons. She spent all her time round the UK and northern Europe and the Baltic, so everybody on board had some particular reason why they couldn't go deep sea at that time. Mine was because my mother was very, very ill and BP had been very kind and said we will keep you within close range, the other Second Mate was unfit and the Master, Captain George Appleby, was a wonderful character, he was a Geordie and great fun but he suffered from psoriasis, so he wore white gloves all the time because the skin was flaking off his hands. But going into port he would always put on his best uniform and his white cap and be there on the bridge with his uniform on and his white cotton gloves to protect his hands, but his psoriasis grew worse. We left the Isle of Grain to go to Malmö and on the way across he became very ill – and fortunately we had two wives on board who had both been nurses, so they were able to dress him because the psoriasis had taken him from head to foot and we had enough zinc and castor oil, basically, to coat him from head to foot and then bandage him, so he was in his cabin.

I was by that stage doing the Chief Officer's job and the Chief Officer had taken over the Master's job, and we went into Malmö and I was on the fo'c'sle getting ready to pick up the tug, except we didn't have a tug up forward, I remember, there was only one tug aft, and we were heading towards our berth and I was watching because we were heading straight for a berth on which there was a small coastal tanker and I rang up the bridge and I said, 'We've only got about, sort of, two hundred feet to go, we should be stopping, can you please start us going astern as we are getting very close.' And I rang up shortly after that and I said, 'We are now down to a hundred feet and it is getting dangerous. We must be going astern now.' And then I rang up and said, 'We are now clearing the fo'c'sle, because we are about to hit this coastal tanker.'

So we all cleared the fo'c'sle except for the Bosun, who stayed up as he thought, well, 'If we hit it we are all going to hell, probably, so I might as well watch what is going on.' So he stayed there, and he was looking over the bow and there was a man painting the side of this coastal tanker and, as most people know, ships are incredibly quiet. They don't make a lot of noise when they are going slowly. But all of a sudden, whether there was a shadow, but this man looked over his shoulder, apparently, and saw fifty foot of steel bow coming towards him very, very close. He jumped from a sitting position onto the deck of his little tanker and ran like fury for the gangway and got ashore just as we hit it, and we opened it up, and there was a complete silence, there was no bang at all, and there was no pollution because it had a cargo of white spirit aboard so nothing happened. No pollution at all. There was an inquiry afterwards, but of course George Appleby, the Old Man, was in his cabin so he wasn't involved in that.

We went from there straight back to the Isle of Grain, and he was still in his cabin all the way so I was still working as Chief Officer, and we got into Grain and we made fast to buoys. To do that we had to 'hang the anchor off', which is a seamanship exercise which is fascinating – we had to disconnect the anchor chain near the anchor whilst the anchor was secured, so we could then use the chain to connect to the buoy.

So we did that, and then George Appleby had to go to hospital, so he was prepared by the wives of the engineers and the Third Mate, I think, who bandaged him up. We had used all the zinc and castor oil for a six-month deployment on his psoriasis over about a three- or four-day period, and he was bandaged and he was put on a stretcher. Because he was on a stretcher, and he was quite a large chap, we couldn't have taken him down the accommodation ladder, so he was taken up and one of the lifeboats was brought down to deck level and held in tight so that he could be manoeuvred in his stretcher into the lifeboat and then lowered down to such level so that he could be transferred into another boat and taken ashore to go to hospital. He went to the Dreadnought Seamen's Hospital, which was then in Greenwich, and I remember going to see him when he was in hospital and he was unbelievably angry because of the food he was getting. He had been used to BP food – a five-course lunch, a five-course evening meal and probably a four-course breakfast – and I arrived just before lunchtime and he said, 'Look at that.' There was this little green dollop of spinach with green slime running out of it and a poached egg. He said, 'Just look at that. You call that food? How can I eat that?' And I think he never went back to sea. He retired after that. 9

Roy Jenkins was a Second Mate with Walter Runciman & Co, a tramping company all of whose ships names ended in *–moor*. It was very involved in the Welsh coal trade and, because of that had many Welsh officers, of whom he was one. He recalls having to abandon ship:

6 The *Fernmoor* was my first ship as Second Mate, and I joined her on the London River, at Purfleet. She had been built in the 1930s, she was an economy Doxford, nine thousand tons, nine knots, and nine tons of fuel a day, an open shelter decker. She had been in Port Said during the war for years as a naval depot or maintenance ship, with workshops fitted in for supporting other ships. After the war the Superintendent insisted that she be put back as was. Everything that the Navy had put in as extras was to be taken out. The only thing that was left was the screening on the monkey island. Everything else was stripped back to be exactly as it was when they took her on.

She wasn't in very good nick at the time. The engines weren't at their best, they were Doxford diesels and she was showing her age with everything. In fact when we sailed one of the engineer superintendents came with us on the first part of the voyage just to see that things were running, just to get from one port to the other. She was a terrible sea ship. The forepeak was dry, so that any wind you sailed in you made a tremendous amount of leeway. Going into Port Said and going up the channel the starboard-hand buoys were about six points on the bow, we were crabbing up the channel and there is a place where you get to where the wind seems to stop so if you didn't watch it you would be out of the channel. This was in ballast. We were going out to load phosphates for Japan. She was struggling now engine-wise and could only do six or seven knots.

We went to Miri in Borneo to take bunkers, going up through the Palawan Passage, checking the Ocean Passages and the Pilot Book. It said for that season there would be a very, very strong easterly set. So we compensated for this with an allowance to the west – but as it turned out the drift was the other way so we had compounded the error. The Mate that we had, well, one of his boasts was that he hadn't taken a sight since before the war. When we grounded it was about half past seven in the morning and I went up to the bridge and you could see mountaintops and when you looked at the chart, from the fixes that he had got we would have been doing about fifteen knots, so he hadn't been very careful. We didn't get a proper fix until I took a sight, so then I was able to correct the position and we were about forty miles away from where he had got us. And we were hard aground on a pinnacle. What you could see was a small piece of rock no bigger than this room, toward the side, which had just cut her open all the way down until it had got to number four hatch and then stopped. The engine room was flooding with water in the first quarter of an hour. There is no way that anything was going to be saved. The distress call went out. Everybody packed their bags. There was no panic. When you think of it, a large proportion of them had been at sea during the war so some of the senior people and some of the senior ratings were very calm and said just get the boats ready, just a routine thing. Get your bags packed and we will put that stuff in the jolly boat and we'll take it all with us. It was dead flat calm; we were lucky in that. You could see these mountaintops thirty miles away. It's a fairly remote part of the world but our distress call had been received. During the day an American plane came over and spotted us and relayed our position and the *Liberal*, a Panamanian-flagged ship with a Chinese crew and a Norwegian Master came to us in the early evening. By that time she was settling right down, in fact you could step from the main deck into the boat when we left her.

We didn't abandon ship until the ship turned up to save us. We were there overnight. They waited before setting off again until she went down. They waited through the night to get a proper fix again before they set off, then one of the Shell ships, one of their T2 tankers, the *Tomogerus*, came along and we were transferred onto her and she took us down to Singapore where we landed.

We were offered a flight home by KLM for the whole crew but oh no, no, no, we're not having that, we will look after it – and they sent out a Dakota. It was out doing a delivery job in Pakistan. She came down but she couldn't take everybody, there were about forty of us, and there were about ten or twelve that she couldn't take, so how they selected them I don't know but some stayed back in Singapore. They cut down our flying allowance to five kilograms, to arrive back in the UK in February. The Old Man just wouldn't have this at all so a balance of twenty-five kilograms was put on a British Airways – BOAC in those days – flight and that was to meet us when we got home. The rest of the stuff was packed up and left in Singapore until another company ship eventually brought it home in the fullness of time.

As it happened our kit was waiting for us when we got home. It took us five days to fly home. There were only two pilots and an engineer and a steward on this plane. We had to wait first to have a replacement engine before we set off; it was BKS – the pilot jokingly said it was 'British Kangaroo Service'. They operated out of Southend and that's where we were bound for. So we worked our way up the coast, to Malacca. The first night we stayed in Calcutta. Next morning we set off to Delhi and then to Sharjah. It was an RAF place that, just sand and a few huts that was one of the refuelling stops, then it was Baghdad overnight. I can't remember after that where we refuelled but then we went to North Africa for an overnight stop at a place called Benina. It was an old Italian Air Force base. It still had the symbols in the plasterwork. We stayed in the huts there and the next day we flew to Cannes and then Southend. Five days flying home. After that we went home on leave, and I think I was home for a fair while. **9**

'Man overboard' – a shout that is dreaded since it is only very rarely that anyone who has fallen, or in some cases jumped, overboard is picked up alive. Malcolm Borland had more than his fair share of 'man overboard' experiences during his time at sea. He recalls:

6 After my Second Mate's ticket I made six voyages on the *Strathaird*, another big P&O passenger ship running between London and Australia. We used to carry the £10 Poms and also called in at Italy and Greece to pick up emigrants. I cannot remember the exact figure but we used to carry a lot of passengers. On my six voyages we lost somebody overboard on five of them. Of these five, three were not discovered until the following day, the ship was searched and because nobody had seen the person missing for some twenty-four hours before we never turned back. However, the other two cases are worth recalling.

For the first case, I was on the twelve-to-four watch at about half past one in the morning – two officers of the watch – I was the junior with the Second Mate. I was in the wheel-house, he was in the wing of the bridge. There was a noise from the chart room then some tapping. The quartermaster said, 'There's somebody in the chart room.' So I went into the chart room and there was a young girl of about nineteen or twenty. I said, 'What do you want? What are you doing here?' She said, 'I don't want to cause any trouble,' so I replied, 'Look, you are not causing any trouble, what's the problem?' She said, 'This is the bridge, isn't it?' 'Yes,' I replied. She said again, 'I don't want to cause any trouble' – and this went on and by now the Second Mate had come into the chart room and said, 'What's the problem?' and still this girl would not spit out the problem. Anyway, after about four or five minutes she said, 'I think someone has fallen overboard.' So immediately the helm was put over and the lifebuoys let go. We went back but never found anyone. But if only this silly little girl had spat out rather more quickly her problem, who knows?

The other Man Overboard happened at about five to midnight. The Junior Second Officer was on watch, I was with the Second Mate on the twelve-to-four. Some of the bell-boys were messing about on the fo'c'sle head and the Junior Second Officer who was watching them sent a quartermaster forward to clear them away. Before he got there one of them sat on the rail and the officer of the watch saw him fall off back into the water. He immediately put the helm over, and let the lifebuoy with a light on go and sounded the accident boat signal. I took the boat away. We were about halfway between Colombo and Perth. On the face of it, quite a nice night with not a lot of wind. When we let go the lifeboat falls, the ship was still doing about three knots. We sheared off and the ship went on to turn around. She was a 25,000-ton passenger ship, but within a few minutes the swell was such that when, in the accident boat, we were in the trough, we couldn't see the *Strathaird*, she had disappeared. When we came up on the crest we could see her. Because the Junior Second Officer had let go the lifebuoy quickly we managed to pick up the light. As we got closer we heard the boy shouting. Luckily, though he said he couldn't swim when he fell in, he was close enough to the buoy to get to it and to hold on until we managed to pick him up and successfully got him back on board. But he was very, very fortunate indeed that he was seen to go overboard by the OOW. ⑨

There is a duty to answer any distress calls. Near to land, at least in the busier seaways, the response to a 'Mayday' call is likely to be coordinated by the appropriate coastguard and lifeboat services, but on ocean passages far from land this responsibility devolves onto any ship or ships that may be in the vicinity. Malcolm Borland was serving aboard a ship that went to the rescue of the crew of an ore carrier that was sinking. He recalls:

❦ The next little story is when I was Second Officer on the *Carthage*. I did about six trips on the trot, London to Hong Kong and back. On one occasion we were coming from Bombay to Aden. There was a very heavy south-western monsoon which had been running for a long time with very heavy seas. Halfway between Bombay and Aden we picked up a distress message from a ship called the *Allegra*, under the Panamanian flag, sailing from Goa to Bremen loaded with ore of some sort. She was about eighty miles astern of us and making water forward, well down by the head and sinking. We turned round as we were the nearest ship and got back to her about half past eleven at night. By then the foredeck was awash, the Italian Master was extremely agitated and said his lifeboats were leaking and he couldn't use them. The seas were very bad and the Captain of the *Carthage* said that no way was he going to put down one of his boats in those conditions. They would have to manage with their lifeboat. I was rather relieved at that because I would probably have had to take our lifeboat away. Anyway they lowered their boat and we put over scrambling nets and pilot ladders. We also streamed ropes from aft and we manoeuvred the ship quite close to the lifeboat. They picked up one of the ropes we had streamed and we pulled them alongside. There was a crew of fourteen, and the first member made a grave mistake because he jumped for the scrambling net when the lifeboat was in the trough. He was halfway up the net when the lifeboat came up on the next crest and crushed him between the lifeboat and the ship. He fell away and was gone. All the rest then quickly realised that they must go for the net only when they were on the crest. We got them all aboard except the Italian Master, who was about twenty stone. He shouted up that there was no way he could climb up. Too fat and too big. So we threw over a few heaving lines which he made fast around himself and we pulled him up. All the time he was shouting, but the weather and the noise was so bad that we couldn't really understand what he was saying. After we got him aboard we discovered that what he was screaming for was another heaving line because he had an attaché case in the boat with two thousand pounds or something like that. Of course it all went. Two thousand pounds in those days was quite a lot of money.

Eventually, a couple of trips later, the owners of the *Allegra* sent a certain amount of money to the P&O for the crew of the *Carthage*. The company decided the way they would distribute this was to give everybody one day's pay. So even the stewards who were asleep during the whole exercise all ended up with one day's pay. We who actually got heavily involved got just one day's pay also. Life is not always fair. 9

Malcolm Borland also has memories of one particular passenger:

6 My last little story is about the most famous passenger I've ever carried. Field Marshal the Viscount Montgomery, Monty. He joined the *Carthage* in Bombay and we took him to Southampton. When we arrived in Bombay the Captain was told that Monty was joining, so he called the three officers of the watch up to his cabin and informed us Monty was coming as a passenger. He said, 'I propose to invite him onto the bridge any time he likes, so when he comes up look after him and give him anything he wants. Be courteous to him, etc. etc.' We all said 'Yes, of course.'

I was on the twelve-to-four watch and Monty got into the habit of coming up after lunch for half an hour or so. He used to relate to me how he won the Second World War single-handed. He was quite pleasant but rather arrogant. When we first met him he said, 'Don't call me Viscount, just call me Field Marshal.' And he used to call me by my surname, not my Christian name, my surname, Borland. When we were in the Mediterranean, we used to go through the Straits of Messina and then through the Straits of Bonifacio, between Sardinia and Corsica, and of course he was in his element recounting how he had fought his way up Italy – again single-handed.

One amusing little story concerning Monty. We were coming through the Straits of Gibraltar. I was on the twelve-to-four watch. We used to produce a newspaper on board the ship – the news used to come through in Morse at 3 am GMT. When I came off watch at four o'clock, I used to go into the radio room to read the football or cricket scores or any news. On this occasion the radio officer said to me, 'Malcolm, look at this.' It was a message from Monty to his son, although I discovered later it was his stepson. Of course it was confidential and he shouldn't have shown it to me, but this is Monty cabling his son: 'Arriving Southampton ten o'clock on 21st. Meet me. Signed: Montgomery of Alamein.' To his son. No 'Dad'. Quite amazing. 9

One final story for this chapter. Jeremy Procter recalls:

6 I was second mate on the BP tanker, *British Trader*, which called in at Singapore, and I visited a cousin of mine who lived there at the time. My cousin had a sulphur-crested cockatoo and offered the bird to me because it was rather noisy. I took advantage of this and took the bird back to the ship. I was fortunate that the Master of the ship was quite a keen ornithologist so welcomed the bird. I made a perch out of an old vent cover and a couple of broom handles and the bird settled in very well. He used to come up on watch with me on the bridge, and he enjoyed an afternoon cup of tea and took great delight in having a biscuit and dunking it in the tea. His main dislikes were engineers, I don't know why, whether it was the white boiler suit, and he also did not like members of the Indian crew. We had a ship's cat on this particular vessel and the bird certainly wasn't troubled by the cat at all. In fact, quite the reverse. One day the cat came into my cabin and saw the bird on my bunk and thought, 'Mmm, nice dinner,' and jumped up on the bunk, and was approaching the bird, when the bird turned round and let out the most ear-piercing screech, causing the cat to freeze, almost as though it had been given an electric shock. The cat disappeared out of my cabin in a flash and was never seen in the cabin again.

The bird had a limited vocabulary but enjoyed flying. After I came off watch he was let go and allowed to fly in the accommodation, and he used to fly to the Master's cabin, where he received a little treat in the shape of some cake, and he would perch on the Master's desk and he would sort of say 'Hello'. This was a fairly regular occurrence around quarter past four, but on one occasion when we had arrived in Kuwait all the usual officials – immigration, health, customs – were ensconced in the Master's cabin, and they were very surprised when the bird suddenly flew in, perched on the Master's lamp, looked around and said 'Hello' to all of them. They were really open-mouthed in amazement. **9**

7 · Chief Officer

The Chief Officer kept the four-to-eight watch at sea. Morning and evening twilight usually fell during his watch, and out of sight of land, if the sky was not obscured by cloud, he would make sextant observations of three or more stars in order to ascertain the ship's position.

In most companies the Chief Officer was responsible for the stability of the ship and for the stowage and discharge of the cargo. On a cargo liner this could be an exacting task. A ship would normally be discharging cargo at a number of ports on the outward voyage, and similarly loading cargoes at various ports on the homeward voyage. He had to ensure that the ship was not overloaded at any stage. The passing of the Merchant Shipping Act of 1890 made it compulsory for all British ships, and all foreign ships entering British ports, to be surveyed and to have a load line (the Plimsoll Line) painted on the hull amidships that had at all times to remain above the water line. As well as this the ship had to be loaded so that she remained on an even keel and did not list to one side or the other, and at all times the ship had to remain stable. Fuel and fresh water were stored in tanks in the ship's double bottom, and during the course of a voyage these would get used up, causing the centre of gravity of the ship to rise. The Chief Officer's most important duty was to ensure that the centre of gravity remained below the centre of buoyancy, as otherwise the ship would turn turtle. Every morning the carpenter, a petty officer, would sound all the tanks and report to the Chief Officer. If necessary sea water could be pumped into some of the tanks to maintain stability.

His other main responsibility outside watch-keeping was for the maintenance of the deck equipment and above the water-line paintwork. The Bosun, another petty officer, reported to him every morning to discuss the day's work for the deck hands.

Before the Second World War Robert Atkinson served both as apprentice and as Third Officer with the Temple Steamship Company, a wholly owned subsidiary of Lambert Brothers Ltd. His time aboard their tramp ships took him around the world, but, like many a young man at that time, he was keen to obtain a full-rigged ship's qualification. At that time nearly all the remaining ocean-going square-riggers belonged to Gustaf Erikson and were based in his native Finland.

An application to join an expedition to the Antarctic was unsuccessful. Had he been accepted, he would never have had experience under sail, as the expedition was cancelled in the run-up to the outbreak of war. However he did manage to obtain a berth as Mate on the *Penola*, a small topsail schooner of around 300 tons which was trading around the Scottish coast. (The *Penola*, rigged as a three-masted schooner, had been the ship on the 1934–37 expedition to Graham's Land in the Antarctic.) He recalls:

❝ To get to Finland and join up was difficult and I hadn't the funds. But I knew of a ship that was a topsail schooner, taking cargo around the coast. In fact I had applied to the government to join the RRS *Research* to the Antarctic. They interviewed me and they turned me down and said, 'We were seeking more than seamanship qualifications. Each of our members has an additional qualification. The doctor might also be a dentist, the professor of XYZ would have to be something else – and you only have the qualifications of being a First Mate'. But they mentioned the *Penola* that had been on the Greenland expedition. She was now taking cargoes around the coast of Britain. Would I like to join? And I said I certainly would, and I did, I think, six months in that ship with a crew of about nine or ten which included the Bosun and some Able Seamen. The Captain and I were the only officers.

She had a small auxiliary engine. She was only capable of about four or five knots, so it was quite a small engine. It was used occasionally, because that ship, when I joined her, was used for carrying bricks from Amble on the north-east coast round and through the Pentland Firth down the west coast of Scotland, calling at Mallaig and the islands. She was a very stiff ship. I suspected that the Captain had a financial interest in the ship, but I didn't know. Carrying those bricks was quite a difficult operation. He was so mean he would not use the engine except as a last resort. I can remember one special circumstance, if not two, where in the Pentland Firth we could not go through on the square rig, we had to use the engine as well and he also used it occasionally for coming in and out of harbour. The owners were very mean and they wouldn't fit a larger engine, which might have done about ten knots.

Each person had to take his turn in the galley, except the Captain. I had to take my turn and of course I hated the idea. The galley was about five feet square and there were fiddles to stop the food from rolling about. We also had to take our turn with trimming the sails of the square rig, as required. I didn't mind that at all. To this day I enjoy going aloft. I was on the roof of this house painting when we first moved in, to the astonishment of the neighbours.[10] There was one chap who was dead scared, and I realised this from the beginning. He hesitated going up the ratlines or anything like that. So I said to him one day, 'You don't like going aloft and doing the sails, things like that, do you?' 'No,' he said, 'I do not.' So I said, 'I will take your turn going aloft if you will take my turn cooking.' This had to be put to the Captain because you just can't do that sort of thing in a small crew like that. So we put it to him and he said, 'In a little ship like this, this will have to be put to the crew.' So the crew was consulted and they readily agreed. They had only had about two experiences of my cooking but it was clear that they didn't like it.

The rations were provided, but, by today's standards, you wouldn't get away with anything like that. There was no fresh food, it was all from a tin. It was very poor and of course, as it was a small ship, the freight rate for the bricks would be low, so they had to keep the expenses down. There was no coffee in the morning, it was tea if you were lucky. There was no bread baked on board, it was all bought and enough for two or three days at a time, so it was pretty stale by the time you got to the last loaf. You didn't expect very much but it was below the tramp-ship level. The food was cooked by chaps who weren't cooks.

---

10. At that time, Sir Robert Atkinson was nearly ninety.

Sometimes we would have to call in at Peterhead, for example, and then it might be two to three days until you got to Lochinver on the north-west tip. To my astonishment, a thing I learnt, which I didn't expect, was that we would not go through with the tide. Not a bit – you would lose control, because the tide would take you, so you had to adjust your course and speed to get to the Pentland Firth just on slack water, so you would stem the tide as you went through. Otherwise you had no control over your ship. With a ten- or twelve-knot tide and your sail and a small engine you would lose steerage way. Twice we had to call in and wait at a port for the right time to go through, and I remember going to a terribly small port on the west side but we didn't go into the harbour, we waited in the estuary so that we wouldn't have to pay harbour dues. You had to think about those things, you see.

The accommodation was very basic. There was no such thing as a private cabin, except for the Captain. The rest shared cabins for about three or four people. She was in port for a lot of the time and only doing very short journeys. I shared a cabin with a couple of the ABs. There was one bathroom and heads for the crew. It was better than one ship I sailed on when I was an apprentice, on a tramp ship, where the four apprentices had one cabin on the boat deck and their facilities, as you might call them, were right near the stern and you had to walk all the way along the open deck if you wanted to have a bath or anything like that. In those days apprentices were units of labour. So really, the accommodation was about the level of that of a tramp ship.

I was lucky to have employment, because it was very hard to get a job at sea at all. Although this was a special ship, not everybody wanted to go on such a ship. The Captain was a qualified Master Mariner and he had been in the ship long enough that it was his life. I think he had a financial interest in the ship. There was some relationship with the brick manufacturer as well. To get their bricks to Mallaig, it was cheaper to take them round the coast than it was by road. I only went to that ship for the reason that I needed six months' seatime. I had my Second Mate's certificate and I would have been away for quite a long time, up to two years, and would have fallen behind my personal schedule. So this was six months to make up the time for my First Mate's ticket. **9**

It is normal practice, and often mandatory, to take a pilot when entering port, but pilotage services are also available for the English Channel, the North Sea and the Baltic. Company policy varies, but generally these deep-sea pilots are only used by Masters who are unfamiliar with North European waters. Peter Adams had been working as a North Sea pilot, but when these pilots lost the right to pilot ships in the Baltic their income dropped markedly. With a young family to support he felt he had to find another job. He recalls:

6 I knew I had to go back to sea into paid employment but it wasn't easy to find. Very, very fortunately I was in Ghent and I looked at the *Lloyd's List* in the agents' offices and the Thames sludge boats were advertising for officers and I knew that these were a good job because I knew somebody that worked on them. It sounds appalling but the ships themselves were very good. They were nice ships, they were owned by the Thames Water Authority. The Master and both Mates all had Master's certificates. All the engineers had Chief Engineer's certificates.

We did one week on and one week off, with six weeks annual holiday, which gave us a working year of eighteen weeks. The salary was not bad – they paid the pension payments. Promotion was a bit slow. Because there were no reserve Masters it meant that when the Master was on leave, the navigating officers would fit in as a relief Master. This gave you plenty of docking and undocking experience. We had plenty of that in any case because the Masters were quite happy for you to do it.

It was all work in the river. They were all around three thousand tons and carried three thousand tons of sludge at a time. It was loaded at one of the two drainage works on the Thames. All the London sewage drains down from the north bank and the south bank to one of these two sewage-processing works. One was at Becton, near the Royal Docks, and the other one was a little further downstream opposite Dagenham, which was the Crossness works. The biological degrading tanks were the huge concrete tanks that reduced the sewage to a viscous black liquid. This was loaded tanker-fashion and you took it out to the Barrow Deep off Clacton and you'd dump it, by pressing four buttons on the bridge, opening four valves in the bottom of the ship allowing the sludge to fall out, with the aid of gravity, in about ten minutes. You then ballasted the ship with sea water on your way back up again and you did two round trips per twenty-four hours, using the tides, sailing from the berths an hour after high water, so you went with the tide down the river, a fuel-saving operation.

The fact that dumping at slack water out on the Barrow Deep means that the stuff comes up on the next flood tide didn't seem to bother anybody very much, and on your next trip you would meet the same stuff off Southend-on-Sea. However, it was a very nice job and I was more or less settled there. I thought I can go on until the age of fifty-seven when my pension will kick in at retirement age and, in addition, it gave you a whole other life. I am a marine artist and I had a friend in Nottinghamshire who was interested in setting up an art gallery. She was a painter as well so we had an art gallery going so I had a whole other life. Unfortunately it only lasted for four years because Margaret Thatcher privatised the water authorities. They went from being local-authority-owned to a private company and the last thing they were going to do was to pay Foreign-going Masters to run up and down the Thames – so we were all made redundant and the job was put out to Crescent Shipping in Rochester, who were a not very well thought-of coastal company, who put their own personnel on board. The water company were extremely generous with their redundancy pay and I got far more than I would have done from the shipping industry, so I left without too many hard feelings.[11] ❥

---

11. Dumping sewage into coastal waters has since been banned by the European Union, and the sludge is now incinerated.

Penola – one of the last of the small sailing coasters that had been such a large part of our maritime heritage for so many centuries. Robert Atkinson was Mate for some six months when she was trading around the coast of northern Britain just before the war. In this photograph *Penola* is rigged as a barquentine.

◄ Coaling at Port Said. Peter Richards-Jones experiencing the reality of an apprenticeship in a tramp company.

▲ In 1948, when David Smith was at Warsash, there was a collective obsession with the value of military drill as a tool for character building. It might not be obvious from this photograph, but we were civilians being trained for a civilian service.

John Gray, on the right, with 'Puffin' in 1953. He little anticipated that one of his main duties on his first voyage to sea would be looking after a horse. ▶

The end of the Great Singapore Canoe Race, organised by the British India ship *Canara* in 1960. All canoes were built on board. In the middle are Robin Knox-Johnston (left) and David Sims, then Third Officer (right).
▼

Sketch of the *Glenbeg*, drawn by Ken Owen in 1953. She was one of the American 'Liberty Ships'. Ken was a keen artist in his youth, and many of his sketches and paintings now hang in his home.

Sketch by Christopher Daniel of P&O's *Patonga* in 1960. ▼

THE FIRST LAP HOMEWARD : THE P & O. S.N. COY'S "PATONGA" CROSSING PORT PHILIP BAY
ARRIVAL MELBOURNE, 24th. MARCH, 1960.

The Grand Priory in the British Realm of
The Venerable Order of the Hospital of St. John of Jerusalem
AMBULANCE DEPARTMENT.

The St. John Ambulance Association.

Name of Candidate Anthony Philip Meredith DAVIS

Rank in the Merchant Service Cadet R.N.R.,

Home Address of Candidate (if any) 98,Kenilworth Avenue,
LONDON, S.W.19

CERTIFICATE OF ATTENDANCE AT LECTURES.

No. of LECTURES AS PER PAPER 58	PLACE OF ATTENDANCE AT LECTURE.	DATE OF LECTURE.	SIGNATURE OF SURGEON-INSTRUCTOR.
1			
2	H.M.S. "CONWAY"	May	
3		to	
4	12 LECTURES	July,	
5		1948.	
6			

CERTIFICATE OF EXAMINATION.

This is to Certify that A.P.M.Davis

has been examined by me at H.M.S. "Conway", Menai Straits.

on the 23rd day of July 1948 and has qualified to render
First Aid to the Injured.

Signed Leslie W. Jones
                        Surgeon-Examiner.

Countersigned J.W.Goddard

Chief Secretary or Local Representative.

ST. JOHN AMBULANCE ASSOCIATION.
The Surgeon-Instructor and the Surgeon-Examiner are requested to read the instructions on the back hereof.

◄ On ships that did not carry a doctor, the Master or, more usually, a delegated officer, was responsible for looking after the ship's dispensary and, while the ship was at sea, treating any illnesses or injuries that might occur. Although life-threatening illness was uncommon, serious accidents were by no means unknown. The standard of training required to undertake these duties was a first aid certificate like this one of Anthony Davis's.

MV *Otaio*, cadet ship of the New Zealand Shipping Company Ltd.

Cadets on the *Otaio*. Malcolm Parrott is at the centre of the second row, as Cadet Captain.

The navigating officers of MV *Northumberland*, of the Federal Steam Navigation Company Ltd, taking midday sights. Malcolm Parrott, aged 22, is second from left.

▲ SS *Everglory*, the tramp steamer on which Peter and Eunice Elphick spent their honeymoon.

▲
Anthony Braithwaite was Chief Officer of the *Port Nicholson* when he took this photo of her moored to a buoy in Sydney harbour.

▶
David Sims on watch on the bridge wing of the British India ship *Barpeta* in 1963.

Malcolm Parrott in command of MV *Orient Express*, run by Sea Containers as a 'cruise ferry' in the eastern Mediterranean in the late 1980s.
▼

On a cargo liner, carrying a mixed cargo to several destinations, the cargo plan was an important working document both for the ship's officers supervising the unloading and for the master stevedore at the port of discharge. For days before loading started, a warehouse in the company's home port would be filling up with wooden cases, cardboard cartons, bales, pieces of machinery, cars and lorries, and all the myriad products of a major exporting nation. Loading would be supervised by the company's cargo superintendent, who had to ensure that the cargo was evenly distributed between the different cargo holds (usually five), so it could be discharged quickly. The weight of each parcel of cargo had to be calculated to ensure that the ship remained stable and on an even keel after each port of call, and after the fuel and fresh water stored in the ship's double-bottom tanks became used up. A further requirement was that cargo for early ports of call must not be blocked in by cargo for later ports of call.

▼

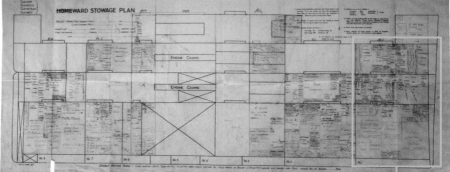

This detail of the cargo plan above, based on a very schematic printed representation of the ship's cargo spaces, is for one of Glen Line's general cargo vessels in the late 1940s. It shows how cargoes for various ports in Malaya were stowed in the No.1 hold, nearest the bow. The colours crayoned in made it easier, at a glance, to identify elements of cargo with a common destination.

The 16,000-ton tanker *British Fame* in icy conditions in the Gulf of Bothnia in the spring of 1965, when John Johnson-Allen was her Third Officer.

Taking seas on deck in the South Atlantic on the 28,000-ton tanker *British Skill*, on which John Johnson-Allen was Third Officer in November 1965.

Christopher Daniel using the cross-staff aboard the replica of Sir Francis Drake's galleon *Golden Hinde*, en route from Devon to San Francisco by way of Panama in 1973. The insurance wouldn't cover Cape Horn.

John Redman standing on the deck of *Opalia*, Aldis lamp in hand, during the 1977 Silver Jubilee Naval Review at Spithead.

Ian Tew in 1983, surveying the grounded VLCC *Wind Enterprise* in the Persian Gulf. She had a full cargo of 350,000 tons of crude oil, and was successfully salved by him.

The *Sea-Land Lightning*, of which Ken Owen was in command when he was 66, past the age of retirement but still in demand.

MacAndrews & Co Ltd was a shipping company that ran a regular service to Spain, Portugal and Gibraltar. When the service was started in 1857 the name of the Company was the McAndrew Line, but this was changed to MacAndrew in 1870, reputedly to make the name more easily pronounceable by the Spanish and Portuguese. The ships were small, around 1,500 tons, and had tanks for the bulk carriage of wine.

Herbert Jones recalls his time as Chief Officer aboard one such ship:

❛ When we got back to the UK the red wine tended to be short in measure but the white was full. The reason was that we'd loaded the white wine from chilled bodegas and as the temperature increased slightly that kept the tank full, but with the red wine, because there was a fall in temperature, there was a reduction in volume. This caused a problem with the Customs. Eventually I left and went to the passenger ships and this young cargo officer took over. I warned him about this problem, having trouble with the Customs. I had made out proper tables which would explain the situation because the Customs expected the tanks to be full all the time but they did not understand that there had to be an ullage in the tank. I still remember it because he said 'I don't want all this paperwork.' We had a place under our bunk where we dumped everything and this chap put the tables there. The cargo superintendent said to me that the young man had never been on a tanker in his life but he was doing better with the wine than me, which made me a bit peeved so I went to see him about it when I was in London and said, 'How do you manage with the red wine?' He said, 'Very simple, I just add some water to it.'

We carried some remarkable cargoes. We took all the gear out to Spain for the film of *Lawrence of Arabia*, to Almeria. We took the Rolls Royce car from the Imperial War Museum. It was insured for more than the ship was worth. We used to load grapes in Almeria in little barrels, on pallets, probably 100,000 of them at a time. The barrels must have been worth more than the grapes. We also carried sherry in barrels. The big ones were called pipes. We would load about two thousand of those, and each one was just over half a ton, so nearly a thousand tons. They were all loaded bung up and a bilge free. You start it off with the first tier, the stevedores did all the work of course, so that the whole weight of the barrel was on a metal hoop, on the bilge and the bung was up. The pipes went in first, and the smaller barrels went on top, and they always gave one small one for the ship. That was to prevent people broaching the other cargo. I don't know whether it was on the manifest. We used to try and get cork bark to fill in the spaces. When they were stored they never moved.

Some of those ships had two holds and some had three. The *Valdez* and the *Velasquez* were lovely ships – they were treated like yachts. They carried twelve passengers. They had a special chef. They were on a regular run. They left from London on Friday night and arrived in Gibraltar on Tuesday morning. They had three days in Gibraltar, they carried all the stuff for the shops in Gibraltar and stuff for the Navy and diplomatic mail. The next port was Barcelona, two days there, and then three ports on the Costa Brava. One of them was Tarragona, the main wine port, for table wines, and then Valencia, which was the main loading port for oranges. After being on tankers, it was a change to be on a ship with a hold full of goodies like that, sacks of almonds, anything you could wish, fruit. There wasn't much pilferage. The odd sack would go. In Gibraltar it wasn't the dockers. It was only years later that I spoke to a seaman who had been on the ship who said that they used to get into the hold from the engine room. Another time we had some cars for an exhibition in Barcelona. I locked each car up in the hold but the stevedores broke the doors off the cars to get at the radios, using cargo hooks to get in. 9

All mariners have a duty to offer assistance to those in distress at sea. This is a duty that is becoming increasingly onerous as a result of economic migration and the search for political asylum. More and more people are taking passage in overcrowded and unseaworthy craft in search of a better life. Until relatively recently anybody rescued at sea would be landed at the next port and then repatriated, but an increasing number of countries are becoming reluctant to accept these migrants. An early example of this new tension is illustrated by Anthony Braithwaite's experience picking up some Cuban refugees in the Florida Straits. He recalls:

❢ The Chief Officer didn't keep a watch in Port Line, but it was the custom for him to go on the bridge at seven o'clock in the morning, relieve the Second Officer so the Second Officer could go down and shower and change into his uniform. So during that time the carpenter and the Bosun would come up and discuss the day's work ahead. On one occasion, coming up through the Florida Straits we saw ahead of us two small boats with people in them and we warned the engine room that we were about to reduce speed and put the boats directly ahead. I didn't need to call the Master because it was two or three minutes to eight and he was the most punctual man that I have ever met. I knew that as the quartermaster rang eight bells, the door would open and there he would be, and so it was. And I said, 'Sir, there are these two boats ahead and we are reducing speed.' 'Fine.'

So a very short time later the two boats are alongside. There are thirteen people in them including several children. We had a gangway already rigged that the quartermasters were going to varnish that day so it was very easy for me to go down with one of the passengers who spoke Spanish to speak to them. Unfortunately the lady who spoke Spanish wasn't able to communicate, but it was quite clear that it was thumbs up for America and thumbs down for Castro. Hurried back to the bridge and the Captain said 'Bring 'em aboard and put an axe through the boats.' There were a lot of crew around the gangway and they went down the gangway and picked up a child each and brought them up. We had a doctor aboard and they were all taken down into the surgery. The crew gave up their mess room and by half past eight I was able to go up and report to the Captain that they were all safely aboard. Where was the Old Man? He had gone down to his breakfast. It was half past eight. He really was a very punctual man.

When we got to Charleston the Red Cross asked us if we would keep the thirteen Cubans on board for an extra day as they had arrived at the weekend, which we were very happy to do. As they went down the gangway I gave them all a photograph of the ship, with the ship's stamp and the date, signed by the Captain. I wanted those children to know that they had been rescued by a British ship. Later in the day, when we were about to sail, I went down to sign the cargo papers in the office on the quay and the head clerk rolled his cigar to one side, shook my hand and said 'Goodbye, Mr Mate, and next time you come to Charleston, don't you bring any more of those Cuban bastards for Uncle Sam to look after.' **9**

When a new ship was being built, it was the custom for the senior officers to join while the vessel was still on the stocks. Ian Gibb was standing by during the building of the *Spirit of London*, and he explains just why this was necessary:

6 Having been Chief Officer on some of the P&O cargo ships for a number of years, I was selected to become Chief Officer of the first of the purpose-built cruise liners for the P&O, which was to be called the *Spirit of London*. The *Spirit of London* was being built in Riva Trigoso in Italy and then was transferred to La Spezia to be completed, and my job as Chief Officer, while 'standing by', was to ensure that all the safety practices were in line, and indeed, all the lifeboats and the lifeboat equipment were up to the standards of the Department of Transport, because the Italians had slightly different standards. So the Chief Officer and the Staff Captain sat down and did the Emergency Plan. We knew how many of the ship's company there would be, we knew what their roles were, and we had to decide, indeed, the master plan for the evacuation of passengers and ship's company, and we did this in conjunction with the Department of Transport inspector who was also standing by at the shipyard. The regulations are particularly stringent for passenger ships flying the British flag and, basically, the Chief Officer was there to ensure that the ship's company knew exactly what they had to do in an emergency situation, whether it be a fire, whether it be a stranding, or to evacuate passengers first and then the ship's company. The mustering of everybody in the various public rooms had to be dovetailed, and the majority of the time that I spent over there, which was several months, was making sure that this happened perfectly. We did a lot of testing of all the emergency equipment with the Department of Transport inspector, and he then put us through our paces before the ship was allowed to sail for Southampton.

I think, if I recall correctly, there were something in the region of 250 members of the ship's company, and of course many of them were not required until ten days or a fortnight before the ship sailed from La Spezia. Trials were held and the ship did her training during the trials with a full complement of officers and crew, and we then had to test that all the paperwork, the administration work that we had done during the months before, worked to the satisfaction of the inspector. Basically that is what the Chief Officer had to do while standing by. The technical side was all looked after by the engineering department and we had very little to do with that. The administration and safety was our prime consideration. 9

In 1950 a 10,000-ton tanker would have a crew of around fifty: Master and three deck officers, four apprentices, Chief Engineer and three engineer officers, a radio officer, Chief Steward, four stewards and two cooks, Carpenter, Bosun and twelve deck hands, lamp-trimmer and twelve engine-room hands. Today a 200,000-ton supertanker will have a crew of around twenty: Master and three deck officers, Chief Engineer and three engineer officers, two apprentices, a petty officer and six general-purpose hands, Chief Steward and three catering personnel.

Roger Woodcock was serving with British Petroleum in the 1970s during the transition from ships having separate deck ratings and engine-room ratings to one of General Purpose manning for ratings. He recalls:

❻ We did have problems when we had guys coming in from the Grey Funnel Line. When the Navy were having a clearout we did get quite a few ex-naval ratings, either ABs or stokers. They came from a very different ethos so there was a bit of a problem. The discipline set-up was much slacker in the merchant navy than it would be under Queen's Regs, so that did cause a few problems. Some were very good and very capable seamen but some of the others were very good at knowing where not to be at the right moment. It was sometimes a case of years of undetected crime in the Royal Navy. Sometimes, if detected, they got a bit vocal about it, but that was about it.

We had some funny incidents with them as well. I remember on one particular occasion when I was Chief Officer on one of the VLCCs, I think it was the *British Inventor*, coming up the west coast of Africa from the Cape when the Old Man had been making noises about painting the funnel – so we got that organised. The Chief Petty Officer got the stages rigged and about mid-morning he came up to me and said we had a problem with one of these guys, who I knew was ex-RN and was a GP One,[12] which meant he was supposed to know what he was about. He said that this guy refused to go up on a stage on the funnel. I said, 'Well, I'll have a word with him when I go on watch this afternoon.' So at four o'clock, when I was on watch, I sent for him and the Chief Petty Officer. I said to him, 'the Chief Petty Officer tells me you don't want go on the stage. What's the problem?' He said, 'Well I'm not used to going on stages.' I asked him what branch he had been in, in the Navy. He said, 'I was a stoker.' So I said, 'Well, even down in the engine room you must have done maintenance on the boilers and up round the skylights and been used to going on stages doing that.' He turned round and said, 'Yes, well, that's right, Chief, but I was a stoker in submarines!' There was no answer to that, so we kept him on deck after that. ❾

---

12. General Purpose, grade one.

Many a retired seafarer will look back on his time at sea and have especially fond memories of one particular ship. Terence Jewell is no exception:

❢ My favourite ship was probably the oldest ship in the company, on which I was senior apprentice and then had my first trip as Chief Officer, an old ship called the *Trewellen*. She was not the world's best but I learnt a lot as an apprentice, I enjoyed it, I grew up and became a man on that ship – and then it was my first ship as Mate and we had all sorts of problems. She had been in dry dock and came out. We had a Somali crew. She had been in a dry dock for about four or five months and as we came out, because the ropes were not in good condition I had warned the Master that not too much strain was to be put on them – however, it was blowing old boots coming out of Cardiff dry dock so the head line parted, the stern went across onto the harbour wall with the propeller still going so we took the tips off the blades, so we had to go back into dry dock. They took off the prop and welded on new tips.

After six or eight weeks off we went again and we got as far as Las Palmas and we were getting a vibration. We got down to Freetown then as far as Lagos and the Chief said to me 'I think we've got a problem here. Do you think you could tilt the ship, bow down, to bring her propeller out of the water so I can have a look at it?' The tips that had been welded on were just like Aero chocolate, they were completely perforated. So we had to take that one off and put the spare on. That was an interesting exercise in seamanship. ❣

Roy Jenkins has vivid memories of one voyage:

❢ The *Brockleymoor* had an Indian crew, the only one in the company. They were good – you could get the occasional bad one amongst them, but not very often. Yes I have remembered, it was on the *Brockleymoor* that one of them ran amok and killed the serang[13] and nearly killed one of the ABs. He used

---

13. Indian equivalent to bosun.

a chipping hammer. It was a right mess. It happened in the middle of the night. We had sailed from Manchester and we were coming down off Land's End. I was Mate on that ship. At two o'clock in the morning the Old Man woke me. I put the light on and he said 'I think you better get up, the serang has been killed.' I thought that I'd better get up and see what this was all about. Apparently tobacco had been found by the Customs when we were up in Manchester and this particular bloke had taken the blame for it and there was some argument about his compensation from the others. Anyway this was the story that came out afterwards and he decided that the serang had caused the problem, so he would deal with him. He just went into his cabin and put a chipping hammer through his skull and then went after the other one, who got away, badly injured.

We had to apprehend him and locked him up in one of the cabins. He wasn't cooperative at all, so we put him into a Stevenson stretcher and tied him in it, because you can get out of one of those, quite easily. It was just the Old Man and I who had to restrain him, there was nobody else to help. The engineers said, 'Nothing to do with us, that's the deck department.' The Second Mate was on watch on the bridge, and I can't remember if we even called the Third Mate. He wasn't a big chap and he didn't have the chipping hammer on him and was quite relaxed and said, 'Oh no, nothing to do with me.'

We rendezvoused with a corvette off Plymouth who took the injured bloke ashore. We went into Plymouth and the police came aboard and held an inquiry.

It was a shock seeing the serang with his head stove in. The naval surgeon was quite a young man – I don't think he'd been in the trade a long time. By this time the serang had died and this surgeon was a bit offhand and he really got up my nose so I said, 'Will you come down and view the body?' 'Oh no, no, no need for that.' The attitude was rather it's all right now, the Navy's here. So I got him to go down. What I really wanted to know was what we could have done to save him, and he couldn't really get out of that. We went down, and of course there was the serang in his bunk and a smear of blood and brain matter right up the bulkhead and onto the deckhead. He did go quiet at that, which gave me some satisfaction because his attitude had not been too good. They took a couple of the seamen off as well as witnesses. They put these two Indian seamen into the Mission there. They couldn't get Indian food, there were no facilities for them at all, so when the time came for the trial they were excellent witnesses for the prosecution, yes, yes, yes, and when the defence was asking them questions, yes, yes, yes. So the case just collapsed and the chap who had done it was flown back to Calcutta. 9

The second half of the 1960s was a time of considerable social unrest in Western Europe, especially in Germany and France. In 1967 the German police killed an activist during a rally held to protest against a State visit by the Shah of Iran. This prompted a left-wing sympathiser called Andreas Baader to plant bombs in two department shops in Frankfurt. Baader was caught, tried and imprisoned, but subsequently escaped with the help of Ulrike Meinhof, a young journalist. Together they formed a group of urban guerrillas called the Red Army Faction to fight what they perceived as an authoritarian tendency of the German government. The Red Army Faction or Baader–Meinhof gang, as it was popularly known, then conducted a campaign of terror, assassinating several prominent public figures. The two most notorious of their terrorist attacks involved the seizure of the German embassy in Sweden, when two diplomats were murdered, and the hijacking of Lufthansa flight 181 taking tourists from Frankfurt to Majorca. Both Baader and Meinhof were caught and imprisoned, Meinhof committing suicide in 1976 and Baader doing the same in 1977. The group continued in existence, operating at a lower level, until it voluntarily disbanded in 1998. John Williams recalls:

6 When I was Chief Officer – it was the time of the first real terrorist threats with the Baader–Meinhof gang, and we had a circular from the British Council of Shipping, or whatever they were called in those days, warning Masters of a potential piracy situation, with this terrible terrorist organisation, the Baader–Meinhof gang, and it was one of those circulars which

came, we read it and we discarded it.

Some weeks later we were going up to Rotterdam – this was on a very large bulk carrier – and we were going to pick the pilot up and it was foggy – it was very thick fog and we were steaming up to the entrance buoy – the Maas buoy at the entrance to the Rotterdam Channel. I was on the bridge with the Master when out of the gloom ahead of us appeared a helicopter, hovering over the ship. In the light it looked black, and as it lowered towards the deck, this was about six hundred feet away, a ladder came down and a man in black clothing came down the ladder. The Captain in total panic looked at me and said 'My God, it's the Baader–Meinhof gang. Get up there, Chief, and stop them.' He went onto the radio to say the ship was being attacked by the Baader–Meinhof gang and I ran along the flying bridge without even thinking, and as I got there this chap, with a peaked cap on, carrying a briefcase, came down the flying bridge and introduced himself. He said, 'Hello, I am the pilot.' When I got back on the bridge, by which time there had been a general muster, everybody was on the bridge including my wife who was in total panic by this time fully expecting these terrorists – and I came onto the bridge and reported that this was the pilot and the Captain said, 'Oh well, these things happen.' 9

Here is an account of what must be the most unusual voyage to appear in this book. After he had obtained his Master's certificate, Christopher Daniel left the sea and joined the National Maritime Museum at Greenwich. He recounts how he was enticed back to sea, albeit only temporarily:

6 It must have been about the summer of 1972, when I was on holiday with my family down in Devon, quite close to Appledore, when we went round the yard of Hinks, the shipbuilding yard, and I saw this vessel under construction and she really looked beautiful. She was the *Golden Hinde*, a galleon being constructed in wood, and I thought that I would love to sail in her. And on

returning to the National Maritime Museum, where I was on the staff, I commented about this to a colleague of mine and he said, 'Oh, I know the right person for you to see,' and he put me in touch with Captain Adrian Small, who was the Master, and I had an invitation to go and see him in Brixham.

I would have been happy with any role aboard ship but he said he wanted a Mate. He wanted a Chief Officer, and would I be prepared to accept that? So I said yes I would, and in due course the following year I joined the *Golden Hinde*. First of all, I saw her launched, but I joined her when she was being rigged down in Appledore, and I had several months' experience in helping to rig this ship under the direction of two ancient riggers who were well into their nineties, I think, and that was my first experience with her.

We set sail, if I remember rightly, initially in August 1973, and it was an occasion when, despite being August, it was overcast. We set out into the Bristol Channel, and we were going to go to Milford Haven. We couldn't really get back, even if we wanted to, because our draught was rather too deep. And at one time when we were in the middle of the Bristol Channel, round about midnight, it was scudding clouds and a waning gibbous moon, a cross-channel vessel closed with us, tried to shine a searchlight on us, then veered off suddenly, probably being surprised at seeing a sixteenth-century warship in the Bristol Channel in the middle of the night.

In October 1973, having spent time in London and Plymouth and that sort of thing, we finally set sail south towards Lisbon. We had a following sea, we had with us a crew of eighteen, including a gentleman from the SAS, and various people who had applied to join. They were all hand-picked, people knew people and that was how it was done. We were supposed to have a radio that worked, but in fact it seldom worked. We were even allowed, having put into Lisbon for a bit, to set sail without the radio working. Since the vessel had been paid for by the Americans, and it was principally an American venture, with an American designer, etc, it was the Americans we were supposed to please. I don't know that they were very pleased because our Captain was much more concerned about the ship sailing in an old-fashioned way. Indeed, I had problems with him when, in hot weather, he wanted to use a system of putting a beaker up high on the yardarm, if you wanted a glass of water you had to climb up, get the beaker, bring it down, have your water and then take it up and put it back again, so the benefit of having your drink of water was lost in going up and down the rigging.

The National Maritime Museum had given me initially a year's sabbatical leave, and finally two years' sabbatical leave, and one of their conditions was that I should do some navigation using period instruments. They provided me with a cross-staff, copied from Thomas Tuttle, which was a very nice instrument, and I managed to supply myself a mariner's astrolabe and one or two other bits and pieces. So I made use of these instruments to see how accurate our navigation was. We did carry a chronometer which again, surprise, surprise, I actually supplied. I had been responsible for getting the charts together, and I had organised a lot of the supplies – including the Captain's tobacco supply, which kept him happy.

Well, we had a following gale down to Lisbon, and then we picked up good fair-weather winds down to Barbados, and in Barbados we discovered we were alongside the berth with the QE2. The QE2 very kindly invited us over to visit their ship, and the first thing they wanted to know was, would we like a bath or a shower? I'm not quite sure why, they seemed to think we might have smelt a bit! And then they offered us breakfast, which was very good, and I don't think I have ever seen anything quite like it. We helped ourselves to everything from bacon and egg to cornflakes, and it didn't matter what order it was in. And that was very welcome. The people of Barbados were very kind to us and looked after us very well.

We subsequently learnt that the QE2 did ask us when we were aboard how we navigated, and they showed us their navigation system. They could use GPS to within a third of a ship's length, and we pointed out that we navigated using a long piece of wood, a graduated piece of wood with a sliding cross-bar, and using this instrument, that's how we determined our position. Evidently, a fortnight later the QE2 went on a reef! I'm not sure what that tells you.

We then sailed on to Cartagena, which was a place that Drake used to sack with monotonous regularity, and finally we ended up anchoring in the bay of Nombre de Dios, which again was one of Drake's watering holes. He used to put men ashore, march them across the peninsula and waylay the Spanish gold trains, that sort of thing. And then he went on to Portobelo, where subsequently, in 1596 if I remember rightly, he died of a fever. We anchored in Portobelo and it was absolutely stunning. It was completely out of history – you could feel yourself with the jungle around you, up on a hillside looking down on the bay, and there was nothing to indicate that it was the modern era, and there was the *Golden Hinde* at anchor. This was a really exciting part of the voyage.

Then we sailed on to Panama. We didn't go round the Horn, our insurance wouldn't cover this. We sailed through, or we were dragged through, the Panama Canal alongside an enormous tug which was probably bigger than we were, but it gave us a little bit of time to relax. We were very well looked after by the Americans in Panama, who took us to an island in the vicinity of the Canal, Isla Colorada I think it was, where we experienced water skiing and looking at furry creatures in the middle of the night and crocodiles under the weed, and things like that. It was really quite interesting. And then we left Panama and sailed up towards Acapulco, during which time we had Christmas. And we were very lucky, we had provided ourselves with a turkey, or a goose I think it was, but the question was, who would kill the goose? We felt a bit squeamish about killing the goose, but the SAS sergeant was quite happy to do that. He said, 'Leave it to me.' Thwack, and that was it, and we managed to cook the goose. We did have a very fine Christmas, and we even managed to chill some wine down. We had some packs, a strange pack which when you managed to mix two chemicals together by banging the pack, it would freeze. This was in case we had some kind of problem where we needed this to put on somebody's hand as a poultice or something, but we thought it was better used chilling the wine down!

And we then sailed on up to Acapulco, and at this time

the Americans were getting somewhat annoyed because our radio was not functioning well and they sent a radio operator down specifically to check the radio and to work it himself. He, actually, was much more on our side. He managed to have two pieces of equipment, one of which the Old Man kept and thought he was the only one using it, and meanwhile down in the lower hold the radio operator had the other one. The Old Man used to communicate with the owners, while down below in the hold we could communicate with our friends and families, which was rather nice. We had maybe a fortnight in Acapulco, and then sailed out of there and went briefly to another port called Manzanillo, and then we had to haul out into the Pacific with fair winds so that when we reached the latitude of San Francisco we could sail in on a parallel of latitude. We needed, we desperately needed, to get well to the west to pick this up, and having arrived at the right parallel of latitude we turned in on an easterly course towards the land.

At about this time we ran into a very severe storm, at least it seemed so to us, I would have put it about Force 10, perhaps more, I don't know. The ship was rolling heavily, we were under bare poles, and during the course of the night the Bosun fell out of his bunk and cracked a rib. We actually had a doctor aboard. I had managed to pick him up in Eltham[14] when he was taking his car in to be serviced. He had a tie with a yachting device on it, so I was cheeky enough to ask if he was a doctor. And he said yes, so I asked if he sailed, and he said yes, and I said, 'How would you like to sail aboard the *Golden Hinde*?' His partner managed to take on his duties for him, so he sailed with us, and he managed to strap the Bosun up.

We were very worried because we saw lights, which looked like the lights of a power-driven vessel coming towards us, closing on us, and we managed to shine an Aldis light on ourselves, but still this didn't seem to do the trick, and then, all of a sudden, the sky cleared and to our astonishment these lights turned out to be the stars of Orion – so we were not on a collision course! The weather improved and we were able

---

14. In south London.

to set some sail, and finally we made landfall in the morning, arriving to a hero's welcome in San Francisco. They had something like 250,000 cars on the road all trying to have a look at us. They had a huge display of yachts, and vessels of all kinds came out to greet us, and quite illegally they gave us a twenty-one-gun salute, which should have been reserved for royalty. And in San Francisco, again, we had a fabulous time, treated like astronauts, and we were entertained by the Mayor of San Francisco, who had invited the Lord Mayor of Plymouth out, and the Lord Mayor of Plymouth had his gold chain of office with him and the Mayor of San Francisco in welcoming us said, 'Here is the Lord Mayor of Plymouth wearing his magnificent gold chain of office, and what I would like to know is why the people of San Francisco don't give me a gold chain of office?' And a voice at the back said, 'Cos I guess you'd keep it!' 9

It is no exaggeration to state that without the British merchant navy, the Falkland Islands would now be under Argentinian control. In order for the land forces to arrive at the Falklands in the spring of 1982, the officers and men of the merchant navy – serving aboard both the ships of the Royal Fleet Auxiliary and chartered merchant ships, which were not all from British owners – provided the essential means of transport for men and material.

No naval operation can succeed without supplies of fuel, ammunition and other stores. Supplying this is the role of the Royal Fleet Auxiliary, which was formed in 1905 for that purpose. The early RFA ships were constructed to merchant-ship standards and, indeed, in the post-war period, they were still using tankers that had been acquired from commercial operators. More recently, the ships have become highly specialised purpose-built vessels which can operate helicopters and launch landing craft as well as replenishing warships at sea. The merchant-navy crews of the ships are all employed by the Ministry of Defence, although now they are all naval reservists as well, reflecting their more active role within the Royal Navy's operations.

In 1982 the RFA was active in the Falklands War, supplying the ships of the Royal Navy. At this time Jeremy Carew was a Chief Officer, and in this short extract he describes the operation of transferring fuel from the BP tankers that had been 'taken into service' to provide fuel for the war, to the RFA ships that delivered it to the warships in the Falklands waters.

❦ I was down there as Chief Officer on a ship called the *Olmeda*, which was a replenishment tanker with a helicopter deck and two helicopters. We did 185 replenishments, taking fuel from the *British Wye*, the *British Esk*, and all the BP River class. We used to pull out, go well out of the threat area. We sent our refuelling rigs across to them, and had some Chief Officers sent to them so they would know what was expected. The trouble was we had to be careful that people weren't washed off, because the seas would break over the deck. Under ten knots it was difficult to steer, and over twelve knots there was too much water coming on. So if you wanted 10,000 tons of fuel we're talking about ten hours alongside, which is a bloody long time just to keep station on a ship. ❦

Replenishment at Sea (RAS) was a very important part of the RFA's role, and unlike in the previous extract, where they were receiving fuel, normally they were refuelling other ships. The following description, also from Jeremy Carew, explains some of the techniques involved in connecting to ships that were steaming side-by-side in the open ocean to allow the transfer of supplies, in a highly skilled and dangerous operation.

❦ Another way of replenishment was to start further out. With two big ships, if you haven't got enough manoeuvrability, you start about a quarter of a mile away and you steer in by ten degrees. You have to be prepared to take helm off and only steer in by five degrees because otherwise when you turn or try to, it won't work. So you come in at an angle of ten degrees, getting closer and closer and you've got to judge the distance, and this is where I got twitchy, until you have got the gun line across. The first runner that goes is the distance line, with flags at about five-metre intervals, then telephone lines, then before the hose line there would be a messenger line, and onto the messenger was the hose line and onto the hose line came the hose or, if you're doing a jackstay, the jackstay wire. If you had enough manoeuvrability and enough speed to do it you'd come through like that [demonstrates with two pens], and you'd have a bloke standing on the fo'c'sle as your bow went past his stern. If you rang on the revs for the speed that you wanted, you'd think, the first time, you're never going to slow down fast enough, but by the time you got up there, you had decelerated very fast. You couldn't do it on a bog-standard steamship, to get the revs off quickly enough, but on the Fort boats, the *Fort Victoria* and the *Fort George*, which had six propellers and twin engines, you can slow them right down so you'd come up and sit there quite happily. **9**

8 • Master

The Captain, or Master, carried the ultimate responsibility for the safety of the ship and for the discipline of the crew. It was in many ways a lonely life, with periods of relative inactivity alternating with busy periods in bad weather and when navigating in congested waters. The Master would be on the bridge entering and leaving port, and at times of reduced visibility, especially in coastal waters. Out of sight of land, with officers in whom he had confidence, his main appearances on the bridge in good weather would be for the time-honoured ritual of the morning sights. The Master, the three watch-keeping officers, and possibly the senior cadet would, so long as the sky was not overcast, take a morning sight of the sun soon after eight in the morning. This was then repeated at noon, when it was possible to calculate the latitude from the angular height of the sun above the horizon. Advancing the morning position line by the course and distance steamed then gave the noon position.

Oliver Signorini reminisces about his time in command. His views on maintaining crew morale would have seemed a little idiosyncratic to many serving Masters at the time. However, he makes a most important point when he talks about how some older Masters became out of date. At a time when technology was moving very fast, there was little in the way of continuing training for deck officers and Masters once they had obtained their Master's certificate. This is not the case today.

❦ Regarding my career as Master, it's a very exciting day when you are told you are getting your first command. Of course, it is a long haul to get there. I was serving in Trident Tankers (owned by P&O shipping company) at the time when I was appointed to my first command, the MV *Maloja*. It was so important to me that my house has been named after it for the last forty years. I joined it in Copenhagen, and at that time you were assigned to the vessel for an extended period of time, with a relief Master taking over when you had some leave. It was company policy that the relief Master endeavoured to manage the ship without radical change until your return. At the end of each voyage you had to answer for the vessel's performance by attending a voyage seminar with the fleet manager in London at the head office of P&O.

One issue that I always remember was that during my sea career, sometimes we didn't enjoy very good food. There was not exactly rationing, but a day rate set by most shipping companies in order to exercise control over cost. Some Shipmasters stood by it whilst others cut it, but I elected to completely ignore it. When I joined the MV *Maloja*, one of the very first things that I did was to call the Butler up to my office – they called the Chief Steward the Butler on those ships – and I said to him, 'You can dispense with all that paperwork with regard to feeding rates, because there will be none of that while I'm on this vessel.' I considered that this aspect of financial control by the owners was indirectly detrimental to the vessel's performance, through loss of crew morale. It was very difficult for the Butler to get his head round this because they are very fastidious with record keeping and he found it difficult to grasp, but he did. To my mind, good food was paramount to building good rapport with the officers and crew. Occasionally, we had candle-lit dinners and lots of other subtle changes to the menus that improved the general atmosphere on board. Where possible, an effort was always made to make things more enjoyable on board, e.g. at Christmas, we'd have a Christmas tree regardless of location, or rounding the Cape we would telex ahead for something special, including requests from the wives on board. My wife Valerie had the privilege of joining me on my first trip as Master.

In so doing, everything fell into place and I never had any problems with crew morale. When I attended the voyage seminars I never had any difficulty answering questions, as the ship performed very well. To this day the question of feeding day rates was never raised.

Regarding the duties of the Master aboard, the Standing Orders were, of course, the dominant thing on the bridge because that was how you wanted to run the ship, especially when it came to navigation and safety on board, both of which were critical.

Port performance of the vessel when loading or discharging had to be closely monitored, as this was analysed at head office and you could be sure to be questioned on the subject at the voyage seminar. Once alongside and the clearance inward documentation out of the way, the agent would send a car down to pick you up and the driver would take you either to the agent's office or more likely to his home for an informal meal. Of course, it was a common sight to see the Master going down the gangway with his briefcase. Some would say, 'You went away with the agent, and what did you do?' Well, from my experience, the agent did everything required from liaising with the British Consul for repatriation of crew to ordering the pilot for departure and everything in between. Signing documents was about all that was asked of you.

Yes, there are a couple of things I would like to say about Trident, later called P&O Bulk Shipping Division. P&O was operating liners and cargo ships worldwide and purchasing very large quantities of fuel from the oil industry. They woke up to this fact and approached the oil companies, more or less saying, 'Look, we're buying all your fuel, so we think we should be allowed to ship some of it.' It was at a time when sub-chartering was big business, and it resulted in the formation of Trident Tankers.

They built a lovely fleet of ships and offered good conditions. The trouble was that it happened very quickly, and when it came to manning the ships experienced personnel in the tanker trade were hard to find. It resulted in many P&O Group officers manning these vessels, and I sailed with many. In fact I was often the only officer in the deck department who was not RNR, and usually they were all ex-*Worcester* and *Conway*. Quite frankly, in the early days they operated the vessels like the liner trade, especially in port. The vessel would load at Mena-al-Ahmadi and start loading crude oil, then shut down for gin and tonics followed by a very long lunch and a leisurely restart to load after that. In the industry it was well known, but it was not that they were doing anything particularly different to what they were used to. Anyway, all that had to change and they started to take in experienced tanker people. I had a lot of experience because of Caltex and Overseas Freighters for a good number of years, and so I got rapid promotion – and thus Trident was good to me.

Regarding experience serving under Masters in general, I think firstly about my cadetship and then all the way through the ranks. In cargo ships it was a long road to get your own command, but in tankers the opportunity came much earlier. The old brigade of Masters over the period of their time in command sometimes distanced themselves from what the Chief Officer was actually doing in the ship to the point where, as technology moved on, they weren't really fit for purpose to take over as Chief Officer if something happened to him. The advent of the younger Master changed all that, as they were more attuned to the new technology demanded by the industry in the sixties and seventies, as the younger Masters were coming in, particularly in oil and gas ships. They had to keep a close eye on what was going on because technology was moving so fast that they just had to take a part in all of it, and the owners were very insistent on this. 9

Peter King recalls the time that he became Master of a vessel trading in the South Pacific:

6 As far as I was concerned changes started before 1970 because within the New Zealand Shipping Company it was obvious that containerisation was coming over the horizon and the whole of the ethos of the old shipping lines was going. Something new called containerisation was arriving. I was not impressed by this, and in those days the Thursday edition of the *Daily Telegraph* had all sorts of bloody good jobs in various parts of the colonies working for the Crown Commissioners

and I remember seeing these, going back many years when I was at school. As a treat the geography master at school used to read from a book called *A Pattern of Islands* by Sir Arthur Grimble. That lodged in my brain, and over the years, trading through the Pacific islands in the New Zealand Line fleet, one would see these chunky little islands ships in Suva and places like that.

In early 1968 a job for a marine officer, ship's Master in the Gilbert and Ellice Islands colony[15] was advertised in the *Telegraph*. I saw this job and dreamed into the office, got all the information I could and went home and told my wife we were going to the Gilbert and Ellice Islands. She said you haven't even applied! To cut a long story short I ended up in the Gilbert and Ellice Islands as Master of their principal cargo and passenger ship. It was the most extraordinary job then and would probably be so now. You did everything yourself. I was a government officer who, in practice, was seconded to command the Cooperative Society's ship. I took command of this splendid little ship, which basically traded around the islands and every three months went down to Australia via the New Hebrides and then back up to the islands by way of the Marshall Islands then, in between, down to Fiji. We did everything which in any normal shipping company would have been done by the Marine Superintendents and the Catering Superintendent. We did everything ourselves, our own docking, our own compass adjustment, surveying and everything else that was necessary. You ran the ship as a division of the wholesale society, reporting to the board – and at the age of twenty-eight it was an extraordinary experience. It left a deep impression, never to be forgotten. I was there for two and a half years, after which they had to prise me off the ship.

When I went out to the Gilbert Islands I had never sailed with a Gilbert and Ellice Islands crew. The islanders were two different ethnic groups, flung together by the British government. The Gilbertese were Micronesians and the Ellice Islanders were Polynesians, with different languages. I was not without my reservations as to how I would fit into this organisation.

---

15. Now Kiribati and Tuvalu, respectively.

I will never forget my first Sunday at sea in command of my first ship at the age of twenty-eight, with glistening new gold lace dripping from every corner of me. I said to the Chief Officer, 'We'll have inspection on Sunday.' We had extra accommodation provided because we carried a large crew for the size of the ship. We did need a large crew because we worked all our own cargo, we carried 150 passengers and we also had to do all our own stevedoring as well as our own boat work. They were a very hard-worked crew. They had cut off the after accommodation in the number two tween deck to provide extra accommodation for the crew, and the officers had the old after accommodation. We went round the after accommodation with our glistening uniforms finding a bit of dust here and a bit of brass that needed cleaning there and I thought, 'King, you're making a significant impression here.'

They seemed pretty happy with it, so having finished that accommodation I went to step out onto the deck. There was a high step over the sill into the side alleyway. As my body was at the point of no return, going forwards, so an enraged boar pig came down the side alleyway and I had no option but to run for my life with this pig chasing me and leap for cover into the accommodation block. Just by magic the whole crew happened to assemble at that moment in time. The Gilbertese, when they laugh don't just laugh, they roll around, tears come down their faces. You had a very brief moment to decide your future on the ship – do you come the dignified commanding officer or do you laugh? So I laughed, whereupon they all laughed. They were the most brilliant crew. ❯

Watch-keeping in busy waters, especially when coasting, can be very exacting. Keeping track of all the other ships that are visible or can be seen on the radar, taking appropriate action to avoid risk of collision, and in addition ascertaining the position of the ship every twenty minutes or half an hour to ensure that the ship is following the course that has been plotted on the chart, is very different to that when out of sight of land on a long ocean passage. When crossing the Pacific or the Southern Oceans it may be days between the sighting of another vessel. Nevertheless Michael Twomey recalls, against all the odds, rescuing a yachtsman in the middle of the Pacific Ocean:

❦ Now a nautical adventure, on a container ship which is unwieldy, going about our business in the Pacific, southbound from Panama to Auckland. It was a lovely calm Pacific morning, with no perils or adventures anywhere, and I was in the bathroom abluting – and pitter, patter, pitter, patter, urgent feet, never a good sign on board ship, and a telephone ringing. Fortunately there was a telephone in the bathroom. 'The Junior Third officer, yes?' 'There's a yacht, sir.' So? A yacht. Justifiably I was somewhat annoyed having been interrupted in my ablutions but I thought to myself there is a reason for this young man telling me about this yacht. I said, 'What's the matter with it?' He said, 'It doesn't look right, sir.' OK. So hastily gathering myself together I shot up onto the bridge, by which time the yacht was abeam and this young man was quite correct. The sails were up but not drawing properly and the yacht was going in a sort of odd direction, a northerly direction.

I gave it a long look and thought I'd better come a bit closer, so we went round in a circle and there was a single-handed man in a very small boat gazing fixedly ahead and I thought, oh, he's dead. Eventually he looked up so I thought, well he's not dead but he is not well – so it was round in another circle and slow down and try to get alongside him. His sails were still up, and although there wasn't much breeze there was enough to keep him going. I thought to myself, drop your sails lad, but not a bit of it, so we stole his wind and I leant on him which is not easy to do with a bloody great container ship and got him alongside and on board him. My splendid Bosun went down a ladder, took a line and made it fast. At this stage the chap came to and eventually we got him on board.

I went down and said to him, 'Look, we can give you food or whatever you want but I can't do anything about the boat because I don't have anything to lift your boat out of the water,' because we just had a stores crane. When he came on board he came to a bit and we put him in the hospital. He had run out of food but he did have water and some currants and raisins, but that was all. He was nearly dead. Before we put him in the ship's hospital we managed to get some information from him, who he was, what he was doing and so forth. I thought to myself, what can we do about the boat? It was stuffed full of polystyrene for buoyancy and was virtually unsinkable. If we had let it go it would just have been a nuisance to everybody concerned, in the middle of the Pacific. So I said, just slip it when I give the word, so I went half ahead and hard a star-board and ran the stern right over the top of it. It didn't sink, of course, but it broke up. I thought that was the end of that. I got this fellow into the hospital so he could not see what I was doing because he would not have liked it.

So off we went. After carefully stuffing some food and water into him he came good and he told me afterwards that when we had appeared he was hallucinating and thought that we were just a delusion, and 'It wasn't until I came alongside you ...' I said, 'No, we came alongside you. I thought it was pretty good, coming alongside a little yacht.'

He was so archetypal, aged thirty-three, divorced, a lec-turer in art history at Berkeley University, and he was sailing from Sausalito, California, to Easter Island to find himself. I thought to myself, oh God, how archetypal can you get? He nearly lost himself in the process of finding himself. He was a very, very lucky man because he wouldn't have lasted very much longer. **9**

Construction of the 77-kilometre-long canal across the isthmus of Darien in Panama, to join the Atlantic to the Pacific, began in 1904, and it was opened to shipping ten years later. Much of the canal is higher than sea level, so locks are necessary at both ends to raise and lower the ships making the transit. When they first opened in 1914 these locks were big enough to handle ships of up to 295 metres in length, 32.2 metres in beam and with a draught of 13.5 metres, but the advent of container ships and supertankers from the 1960s onwards meant that an increasing number of ships were unable to transit the canal. On a passage from the western seaboard of North America or the eastern seaboard of Asia to the ports on the north-east coast of America transiting the Panama Canal saves up to six thousand miles and, as is especially the case with oil products, until a pipeline was laid, it could be more economical to transfer the cargoes of super-tankers to smaller vessels (Panamax ships) that could pass through the canal, rather than routing the supertankers around Cape Horn. Construction has now begun on new locks, which will operate in par-allel with the existing locks. These new locks will allow ships of up to 426 metres in length, 54.9 metres in beam and with a draught of 18.3 metres to transit the canal.

Roger Woodcock recalls his time as a berthing master aboard the *British Renown*:

❧ On that ship, where we were doing that lightening, I was the berthing master, one of two. We had two berthing masters on each ship, all of whom had had experience on VLCCs as Mate or Master. This was before the completion of the pipeline across the isthmus. The building of the pipeline got out of syn-chronisation with the production of oil from Alaska so we had two mother ships anchored west of the Panama Canal. The VLCCs used to bring the crude down to us and then we used to back-load it into ships to get through the Panama Canal. The berthing master's role was to put the VLCCs on, take them off, put the small ones on and off,[16] so that was quite an interest-ing job, probably the most interesting I had because it involved getting it right every time and it was seamanship and naviga-tion. We had two tugs, three at one stage. Under the Jones Act, non-American ships could not trade between American ports, which meant that our ships, to comply with that, had to be at anchor all the time. It was a case of having to berth ships on what was in effect a swinging jetty. It was sometimes a very interesting experience. We learnt quite a lot, because of the interaction between ships, loaded and light, wind and cur-rent, so you had to balance all this up, and with two relatively low-powered tugs, manoeuvring a VLCC onto a swinging jetty took a certain amount of skill. We had to be fairly robust with the engine movements as well to do all this. We only had one

16. Making fast alongside and letting go.

slight contact, a paint-scraping job – there wasn't any serious damage.

Talking more about those ships in Panama, there were two Masters, two berthing masters, three Chief Officers, three Second Officers, who were on watch on the bridge doing paper-work, one Chief Petty Officer and two petty officers. Because there was a fair bit of accommodation on those ships, having been built for a bigger crew than was actually on them, it was possible to fit everybody in without hot bunking. The galley was running twenty-four hours a day. There was a Chief Steward, Chief Cook, and two second cooks. The crew was pretty much the same but it was a hundred per cent deck operations. There was very little painting and decorating going on unless there was a slack spell in the operations or the weather was too bad to get the ships alongside – it could be blowing a bit and quite nice but too rough for lightening. The cafeteria system worked there, of necessity, but it met a lot of resistance when it was coming in. I think people tolerated it. There was nothing wrong with the food, it was just the concept of everybody in one mess room – it was a significant change. People were served from a hatch. Because the ships had been built with a saloon and a mess room, there was a bit of tension.

I did fall overboard on one occasion, during the lightening operation off Panama. I had brought this small American ship alongside the *British Renown* about nine o'clock in the evening. We were in ballast with very little cargo left, just enough to pump into this small ship, which had come alongside in bal-last. The ships that came up from Panama used to bring our mail, magazines and that sort of thing, so the Old Man gave me a packet for the ship. There were two walkie-talkies in a haversack on my back, newspapers and stuff under my arm. Forgetting the cardinal rule of one hand for yourself and one hand for the ship, I knew if I didn't bring the mail back I would get lynched by the crew, so I went down on the deck to go back and used the accommodation ladder and walked down – I hadn't been drinking, because they were dry ships – stepped onto the bottom platform of the accommodation ladder, which was damp because of the evening air – my foot slipped and I swung around and realised I wasn't going to be able to hold my weight with one arm. So I let go, and as I went down I thought, 'What am I going to hit?' because we had the big fenders between the ships, ten-foot diameter joined with rope pennants and shackles. Fortunately I didn't hit anything – I went through the five-foot gap between the fenders, and between the pennant and the ship's side. I was very lucky. As I went down I heard the crews on both ships shout man overboard. I thought as I came up, 'Some clown's going to throw a lifebuoy down and hit me with that.' On the *Renown* they had the sense to lower the accommodation ladder right down to the water, so I swam to the platform and they lifted me up on it. I got a lot of flak because of the soggy mail, magazines and stuff. I went up to the radio room with these two wet walkie-talkies, handed them to the radio operator and said, 'Hey Sparks, is there anything you can do with these, d'you think?' And he sort of told me to go away, or words to that effect. The next morning we measured it, and I had fallen thirty feet. Added to that, we knew that there were sea snakes around the ship. **9**

Until the 1980s, a succession of colliers made the passage from the coal terminals on the north-east coast down to the power stations on the banks of the Thames, returning in ballast once they were discharged. So long as they lived up north, the crew generally got home about once a week. Many a deep-sea man, once he got married, joined coaster companies such as Stevenson Clarke. Alan Storey was one of these. He recalls:

6 The first ship I was on as Master was called the *Amberley*. The accommodation for the Master was beautiful. The accommodation for all those amidships was beautiful – it was panelled in dark wood, as though it had come from a passenger ship. The Master had a day cabin on the first deck immediately below the navigating bridge. It had two windows in it looking forward and another window on the starboard side. Inboard of that was a sleeping cabin with a double bed so you could take your wife with you – or girlfriend, whatever you wanted! Whatever you were allowed to, I should say! And that was excellent accommodation. For the crew the accommodation was good as well.

They were small ships. You normally spent four to six months on board before you had any leave. On the first ship that I was on we were running from the north-east coast in to the Thames, running to Becton gas works, which has now been demolished, and the up-river stations. It was a flat iron collier where the masts and everything came down. We would have traded between Methil, in Scotland, and Blyth, in Northumberland, the Tyne and all the loading stations, the Wear, Seaham Harbour, which was affectionately known as the 'hole in the wall', because that's what it was, and West Hartlepool. They were our loading ports.

We used to work what was called a North East Coast trading agreement. The crew were divided into half. There were six sailors on the ship, that included the lamp trimmer, instead of the Bosun. I don't know why he was called the lamp trimmer because there were no lamps to trim. They were all Able Seamen, there were no ordinary seaman or deck boys, and then you had a Chief Steward, a cook, a second steward and a cabin boy. There was the Chief Engineer, Second and Third Engineer, Mate and Second Mate and Radio Officer. So on the North East Coast agreement, which the majority of ships were on, because we were trading from the north of England to the south of England they were split in half. Most, if not all, of the crews came from the north of England because it was advantageous to you to do so. So when you went up to load, if it was your loading watch, the Mate would be on duty and would remain aboard the ship, with three of the ABs, one of the engineers and two of the catering staff. Oh, there was also a donkey man, but I think he was on day work. All the others would go home immediately, as did the Master and Chief Engineer, and you were communicated to by telegram or telephone and you waited at home. If you wanted a telegram you paid the Mate, he would take the money from whoever wanted a telegram. Or you'd get a telephone call if you were on the phone. Not everyone was on the telephone in those days.

If you came into a quay like the Commissioners in North Shields, which we used to dread, you could come in on a Saturday morning because they only worked till lunchtime at weekends, and Sundays they didn't work at all. So if you came in early enough on a Saturday morning you could be loaded and out by lunchtime, so you would go up to the waiting buoys – and if you came in on Friday and there was no berth you could be there until Monday or even Tuesday. You were always at home once a week. The watch on-board people didn't work right round the clock, they did two shifts, and once the catering staff had finished the evening meal they would go home. That was all unofficial of course, and if the ship was safe, locked into a nice harbour like Seaham, if the weather was good, at the discretion of the people on board the Mate would also go home if he was on loading watch and come back in the morning. Of the three crew sleeping on board, one would be the night watchman and of the other two, one would be on day work, shifting the ship up and down the quay and opening and closing the hatches so the people on board perhaps still got a chance to slip home in the evening. It wasn't official, but everyone did it and everyone knew it happened, and I don't ever remember any unforeseen circumstances because the crews generally were mostly married guys, most of them had an allegiance to the ship and had a contract with the company. They used to refer to the 'new boy' who might have been there for six years. They were mostly in their forties and some of them in their fifties. The lamp trimmer in one ship had been on board since the ship was built and the ship then was about fourteen years old. He had never been on another ship – he had taken his leave but stayed on the same ship.

The crew's accommodation was aft, below deck. The mess room was on the deck above that, right at the stern. You'd go in there and there was a washbasin on the starboard side, and on the port side was the mess room which was about eight foot square and there was a table, secured to the bulkhead, a form either side, with a bit of a upholstery on it, and at the end of that, on the bulkhead, there were six coat hooks. They all had their own hook. They were great guys. When I was Second Mate I would be saying, 'We'd better start lowering this down,' and the guys would say to me, 'It's all right, Second Mate, we know what we're doing, we've been on here for ten years.' So I found this totally different from deep sea, where the attitude was that you had to tell the sailors what to do. But this was totally different because the ship ran like clockwork. Apart from navigating the ship you could have taken the officers off and the masts would have come down, the hatches would have been opened and closed, safety nets would have been put in place, everything would have been done. I can't say how good they were, the crew. They were totally trustworthy.

You would load numbers two and three hatches first, right up to the top. Trimmers would come on and push the coal right into the corners of the hatch. The hatch was about six feet deep so if there was any movement when the ship rolled it filled up the hold. Then you would put three hundred to five hundred tons into number four hatch. The next thing was to fill number one hatch until you were on your mean draft. You would then finish off in number four hatch until you got to the right trim, about six inches to a foot by the stern. The Mate would stand on the quay and watch the load line until you got to the right draft.

There were lots of guys with no certificates at all. I sailed with one Second Mate who had no certificate but he was a good navigator, and a good seaman. He didn't have the theoretical knowledge, but he knew how to load because he'd been taught to do it that way. The lamp trimmer could load the ship, because he also knew what to do.

There were chutes, with railway lines on high wooden pilings, which came out over the ship so that small trucks could come out and teamers would release the coal from the truck into the chute, which would have been moved to position the coal where it was needed. Some places had conveyor belts, like Jarrow. The Mate stood on the quay and watched the finishing draft and the Plimsoll Line. The loaders were good, you never ended up with a list even if the Mate was on the quay, and the guy in charge knew you had to be upright. But if there was a slight list, the trimmers would correct it. There wasn't much freeboard on the well-deck ships, you might only have a couple of feet. On the main deck there would be six feet.

Sometimes we had to shelter in bad weather. Bridlington Bay was well known, particularly for shelter from a northerly, Spurn Head was another. There weren't many other places south of there. Because the prevailing wind is south-westerly, we used to hug the coast really, really close in, half or quarter of a mile, down through Yarmouth Roads and then through the Barrow Deep, past the Sunk Lightship. Oh – one last thing – we steered by points, not degrees. I had to relearn my quarter points. 9

Eric Beetham was the Master of a refrigerated cargo ship in the 1970s. He recalls the changes in manning levels that occurred around that time:

6 All the changes were evolutionary. They were not the result of any act or report. The crews reduced and the work they did became more operational than maintenance-based. Probably at the same time there was an improvement in the paint. The routine on a reefer ship in the 1950s when you left the UK was that you stripped down all the gear and then you would put it up and then start painting. The bad bits you would chip – as apprentices we used to spend a lot of time chipping the paint-work. And as you went through the different layers of paint you saw the different colours going back to the grey in wartime. Sometimes on the bridge front you would take off the paint and find bullet-holes bunged up, sometimes with chart paper. It was as good as anything. We started using International Paints, on the outside of the hull, and that was much better, because you scored the plate to make a key for the paint. It didn't imme-diately rust everywhere. It was like a rubberised paint.

Machinery was also improving. Unmanned engine rooms had come in. Manned engine rooms had a tremendous effect on social life on board. The three mates still kept watches, but the engineers did not keep watches at night time. The numbers of engineers reduced. In the old days, on a 10,000-ton single-screw reefer ship you would have a Chief Engineer, Second, Third and Fourth Engineers and then three junior engineers, as assistant watch keepers. There would then be two refrigeration engineers with an extra junior engineer for refrigeration machinery. Possibly two or three electricians as well. That came down to one electrician, one reefer engineer, a chief and three watch keepers, usually one junior for training. Junior engineers were time-served apprentices. And then engineer cadets came in. All the engineers would work in the engine room during the day. One would be the duty engineer overnight, and the alarm systems went to his cabin. If that wasn't responded to within a certain time it would then sound off in the Chief Engineer's cabin, and after that on the bridge. The duty engineer would go down to the engine room during the evening for rounds. They would be a time lock on the engine-room door but you couldn't get in without resetting the alarm. This would mean that if he had an accident in there the alarm would go if he wasn't out of the engine room within an hour. Because of this the number of greasers had reduced. It had reduced to a total of three.

At the same time ship's bars had come into being. This was instead of drinking in cabins. Before air conditioning came into use, cabin doors were always left open with only a curtain across. On air-conditioned ships, curtains were often not fitted by the builders, so cabin doors were closed. This helped encourage the introduction of bars, to prevent secret drinking. For a small number of people loneliness was prevented by the bar. Bars were a good thing because, for example, I would speak to the Fourth Engineer most days – otherwise you would not normally speak to one another. Even so the Master, Mate and Chief Engineer would still tend to have some drink in their cabin. 9

Like many another British seafarer in the 1970s, Eric Tinney realised that his promotion prospects would be poor if he stayed with a UK company. He worked for a while for a Ghanaian company before joining ZIM, an Israeli company. Founded in 1945, ZIM's first ships brought immigrants to Israel. In the 1960s they had a fleet of tankers bringing crude oil from Iran to Israel. He recalls one voyage as Master:

❦ A little bit of history now. After the Arab–Israeli conflict of 1948 when Israel became a nation, Egypt banned all Israeli flag ships, and ships carrying strategic cargoes to Israel, from passing through the Suez Canal and the Straits of Tiran. After the 1956 war, when Egypt nationalised the Canal and Britain, France and Israel attacked Egypt to protect their rights over the Suez Canal, Israel only agreed to withdraw from Sinai if they were granted free passage through the Straits of Tiran. Freedom of passage was ratified by the United Nations and the port of Eilat opened for business in 1957.

The *Nora* was a tanker of 70,000 tons with Liberian flag. Apart from myself there were three other northern European officers. The rest of the crew were Israeli. ZIM Line, the Israeli shipping company that I was working for, did not send any vessel flying the Israeli flag to Eilat, to avoid any possible conflict with the Arabs.

We operated to a routine like clockwork. After discharge we sailed from Eilat to Djibouti, where we bunkered for the round trip. We always transited the Straits of Tiran in daylight – the navigable channel is about two kilometres wide and two kilometres from the Egyptian shore and the guns at Sharm el-Sheikh. From Djibouti we then proceeded to Kharg Island in Iran, loaded crude oil and returned to Eilat. A round trip of some twenty-three days.

Interesting aside – although everyone knew that we were bound for Israel no one said a word. Iran is, of course, not an Arab country but it is Muslim. My bill of lading always said that I had loaded a cargo of Iranian crude oil for a company based in Switzerland and I was to proceed to Land's End for orders. A day after clearing the Persian Gulf I received my orders to proceed to Eilat.

Early in May 1967, my wife and two young sons travelled from Scotland to join me on board the ship for the round voyage. The voyage from Eilat to Kharg Island was uneventful, apart from the fact that my wife did not consider her clothing suitable for the tropics and I had to go shopping in Djibouti.

During the return voyage, we were sailing along the south coast of Saudi Arabia towards the Gulf of Aden, when on 22 May we heard on the radio that the President of Egypt, Colonel Gamal Abdel Nasser, had claimed that the Straits of Tiran were within Egypt's national waters and all vessels wishing to transit the Straits had to seek permission from Cairo.

I received a telegram from my owners ordering me to reduce speed, not to continue the voyage to Eilat, to maintain radio silence and await further instructions whilst the Israeli government requested the United Nations to order Egypt to lift the blockade and abide by the UN resolution of 1957, which granted free passage to Israeli ships. I did not know at this time that Israel had told the United Nations that if Egypt did not lift the blockade they might be forced to attack Egypt to protect their interests.

I started to look for a bay where I might be able to anchor and save fuel. All on my starboard side were Arab, and there were none suitable on the Somali coast. One possibility was in the roads off Massawa in Ethiopia, but my chart showed that the distance between sandbanks was not great and the area had not been surveyed for some considerable time. Therefore I moved out of the main shipping route, stopped the engines, hoisted the signals for a vessel not under command and drifted where the current took me in the Arabian Sea.

A couple of days later my orders arrived. I should enter the port of Djibouti and load sufficient bunkers to reach Haifa, which is on the Mediterranean coast of Israel, via the Cape of Good Hope. This was my first problem. The port of Djibouti only had a depth of thirty feet and my draft was forty-two feet. I broke radio silence and sent a short message in code to Haifa saying that because of draft problem I could not enter Djibouti, but was altering course for Haifa and I would bunker en route.

My second problem was where on the coast of East Africa could I obtain fuel. I had already discussed this with the Chief Engineer, and we had calculated the optimum speed to give us maximum range before bunkering. I consulted the various Pilot Books that we had on board, which give details of all ports, rivers etc, and discovered that Mombasa did not have the type of fuel that we required and did not have the depth of water, Beira similar, Zanzibar had no fuel and no depth, Lourenço Marques (now Maputo) had no fuel. Durban had fuel but insufficient depth of water. They did however have a small ship that they used to bunker ships in the harbour, and I hoped that it might be able to come out to the roads and supply my ship.

On 30 May, we heard on BBC World Service that Egypt had claimed to have sunk a tanker at the entrance to the Straits of Tiran. This was the day that we were due to pass through the Straits of Tiran, and when we didn't show the Egyptians claimed a victory. We all had a little smile. The BBC did not mention the name of the vessel, but my wife was concerned that we were unable to tell the family at home that we were safe. The families of the Israeli crew members were all informed by the company in Haifa that all was well. We were still maintaining radio silence.

On 5 June Israel attacked Egypt, and on 10 June the war was over.

I received new orders: return to Eilat. This was my third problem. We had by now passed the point of no return and did not have sufficient fuel to return to Eilat. However, we were no longer required to maintain radio silence. I spoke with the Harbour Master of Durban, who told me that the bunker barge could barely get across the harbour and would never get outside the breakwater. The next suitable port was Cape Town which had an oil berth with forty-two feet of water and could provide fuel oil. The Harbour Master at Cape Town told me that he could not accept my vessel as the pilots required at least two feet clearance underneath the keel in the entrance channel, which was also forty-two feet. Problem number four. We did not have sufficient fuel to proceed beyond Cape Town. I informed the owners in Haifa. This was now a diplomatic problem, and the Israeli government began talking to the South African government.

After a few days of discussions the Harbour Master agreed that we could enter – but only in favourable conditions. It must be at high water, no wind, no swell etc, and the vessel should enter with tugs fore and aft and no use of ship's engines because of the possible effect of 'squat'.

We arrived in Cape Town roads and anchored to await our turn and favourable conditions. The first night there was a storm and the vessel began to drag anchor – we were heading for Sea Point before we got the anchor up. I told the port control that I was dragging and was going round to False Bay and would anchor off Simon's Town. He told me that I would lose my place in the queue. At that moment that was the least of my problems. We remained in False Bay until the Harbour Master told us to come in. All went as arranged, and we berthed alongside the tanker berth in Cape Town.

Problem number six! When we sailed from Kharg Island we had loaded to our Tropical Load Line. Now, here in Cape Town, in June, it was winter and the vessel was overloaded. The Harbour Master did not like me at all. He said, 'I can't allow you to load two thousand tons of bunkers when you are already overloaded by about two thousand tons.'

More diplomatic wrangling. The Israeli government offered to sell all or part of the cargo to South Africa. We could discharge here and return to Iran for another cargo. This solution did not find favour with the United States, who pointed out to Tel Aviv that there was an embargo against South Africa because of apartheid and if Israel was to break the embargo they might have problems with the USA.

During all these discussions the crew had a great time. There was no TV in South Africa at this time, but our situation was in all the newspapers and radio stations. We were heroes of the war. There is a large Jewish community in Cape Town and many came to visit the ship. When they found out that I had a crew of healthy young Israelis, the mothers, particularly those with daughters, were arranging dances, soirees and in some cases visits to the homes. I didn't feature very much because, as well as not being Jewish, I had a wife and two children in tow.

Finally all parties, Israeli government, South African government and US government, were in agreement, and the Harbour Master gave me permission to load sufficient fuel to proceed to Haifa, the agreement being that if I sailed north from Cape Town I would be in the summer zone very soon after leaving Cape Town and within about a week I would be in the tropical zone, whereas if I were to sail east I would be in the winter zone for some considerable time. (This was before the Load Line regulations were altered, and there was no summer passage round South Africa as there is now.)

The Harbour Master came down to see us off, and in the privacy of my cabin said to me, 'Good luck, and for God's sake don't turn round until you are over the horizon and I can't see you.'

After sailing I received a telegram, as expected, ordering me to proceed to Eilat. We arrived in Eilat on 2 July and were royally welcomed. All crew members were sent on leave to be reunited with their families. The officers were also granted leave, and I took the opportunity to tour Israel with my family. I hired a car and drove around, visiting Tiberius on the Sea of Galilee and Jericho on the West Bank. Old Jerusalem was now open to Israelis and other visitors, so we spent a day there before Bethlehem and home. **9**

The 1960s and 1970s saw not just the change to containerisation, but the introduction of two new types of vessel: the hovercraft and the Jetfoil. Both these brought new challenges. Christopher Laycock was one of the first of those who served as a Master of the newly introduced Jetfoils. He recalls his time on these high-speed ferries:

6 Coming home after my second voyage as First Officer on the container ships I spotted an advertisement in what I think was the *Evening Standard* in London advertising for Master Mariners to train and to operate Boeing Jetfoils between a new terminal under construction at St Katharine Dock in London and Ostend. This struck me as being a very interesting development, and I applied forthwith and was accepted as a trainee First Officer with P&O Jet Ferries.

The Jetfoils were only just being delivered – the first one

had just arrived and the second one was still under construction – but to provide a two-vessel service, Boeing Marine Systems was chartering their older Jetfoil to P&O to get the service under way as quickly as possible. Before the service started, everybody who was involved with the service had to undergo an extensive training programme operated by Boeing on the handling of the craft, the systems of the craft and the completely different concept to vessel handling. Most of the training was conducted in Ostend, and it was here that I made a claim to fame and something of name for myself. Arriving on board for some boat handling training one morning, my footing was carelessly misplaced on the gangway edge, resulting in an unplanned fall into the water. Fortunately, this was without injury or any other repercussion, but needless to say I never managed to live that down, and to this day there are some that still call me by the nickname that I was given at the time.

The Jetfoils were powered by two Allison 501 marine gas turbines, connected to water pumps. I can't give you the quantity of the water they would pump out, but I am sure that

Serial Number 017

TYPE RATING CERTIFICATE

I certify that **Christopher W. Laycock** *has successfully completed a course of instruction in the handling (normal, abnormal, and emergency procedures) and systems operation of the Boeing Model 929-115 JETFOIL.*

In my judgment, he is qualified to operate the JETFOIL subject to existing regulations and the weather condition limitations as defined in Section 1 (Limitations) of the JETFOIL Operators Manual.

Exceptions:

Boeing Marine Systems, a Division of The Boeing Company

Authorized Representative _____ Dated *16 May 1980*

The certificate of competency for operating Jetfoils was issued by Boeing. However, this was in addition to a British Master's certificate.

Commodore Barrett will have that information ready to hand. We had the most tremendous, but challenging, training period in Ostend with the Americans. The craft being built by Boeing was obviously equipped with extensive aviation systems. The principle of the Jetfoil flying through the water on retractable foils was very similar in principle to aircraft flight, the only difference being the density of the medium through which the foil or the wing was actually travelling. Apart from learning the American language – completely different to our own – we also had to learn and to understand these new systems that were going to control the attitude, the speed and the means of handling for these craft. It was definitely a case of forget everything about transverse thrust, rudder angle and the rest of it. We were learning a completely different system really, revolving around the action of the water jets.

We trained and we trained, and there was a very, and quite rightly so, stiff examination conducted by Boeing at the end of the training course. To the best of my belief, I think all of us passed, but we had a lot of work to do and it was a very long exam, both practical in demonstrating our ability to handle the vessels and also demonstrating our knowledge of the systems such that we could deal with faults in the right manner should they occur. After a while working as First Officer in the early days, an opportunity for promotion was offered to me as a result of one Master being taken sick, I think – anyway there was a vacancy for another Master, and I was offered the appointment and became Master of these Jetfoils.

Promotion to Master, I think, on any ship, or aircraft come to that, is a very daunting prospect. Suddenly you are the ultimate as far as decision making is concerned because there is nobody else to go and ask. The buck definitely stops there. However, I was thrilled by it, and in the middle of the North Sea suddenly awoke to the realisation that I was there with upwards of 150 passengers sitting behind me, umpteen million pounds worth of Jetfoil all on my own. A very difficult position to be in, but one that I relished, enjoyed and, hopefully, made a reasonable job at.

The challenges of navigating a narrow river or any restricted waterway, even at five or ten knots, can sometimes be demanding. Whilst the Jetfoil was a depth-critical craft in that we always had to maintain enough water beneath us to land in the case of emergency, we would fly foil-borne at forty-two knots on high-tidal conditions all the way up the Thames to the Lower Pool. Whilst that could be exhilarating it could also be extremely scary. We were required to carry pilots, but the river pilots were, of course, not used to the speed. Certainly flying round Greenwich Reach and the various other busy points in the Thames needed you to be very much on the ball. There was no room for error, and flying like that, also through the Thames Barrier, which was close to the end of its construction period, required one hundred and ten per cent concentration.

Rough weather was also a challenge in a different way from on conventional vessels. The Boeing Masters that I sailed with when I was acting First Officer with them on the charter boat taught me some quite interesting manoeuvres in heavy weather – one of them being the ability to increase speed by some three to four knots by flying down the back of waves. It was most incredible and it worked, and it was more comfortable than just trying to keep on a safe course.

We had many happy transits, very busy, very demanding, both mentally and sometimes physically. There was the most tremendous camaraderie, I do remember, among all the staff, whether it be the cabin attendants, the First Officers and technicians, there was a camaraderie amongst that group that probably surpassed many of the other ones that I have come across at sea. 9

In 1980 Richard Woodman was promoted to Commander (at that time the Trinity House Service equivalent to Master) of the Trinity House Vessel *Winston Churchill.* He recalls that while serving on that vessel he had an unusual secondment:

6 Then, during the summer months in 1982, 1983 and part of 1984, I was involved in Operation Channel Cable. This was a

project to link the national grids of France and the UK, a massive civil engineering project which required a safe area one kilometre by half a kilometre, to be driven slowly across the Dover Strait as cable trenching and laying was carried out on the seabed from a large barge, rather like a pipe-layer with all the facilities on board, plus a workforce of some eighty persons and their accommodation. To ensure the area was safe it was buoyed and guard ships were attached, stationed at a tactical distance 'up-threat' to warn off any international shipping and deter it from making a close approach. As the safe area was required to advance as the seabed work progressed, the buoys were leap-frogged from rear to van, so a small buoy-laying vessel was attached which deployed as an additional guard ship when required.

When things got up to speed in 1983 there were two such complexes, one run on behalf of the Central Electricity Generating Board of the UK and the other one, coming from France, run for EDF. Each was to lay two cables and each had a squadron of three guard ships, although we started off with just one complex. Eventually, four trenches were dug, cables were laid and they were covered over.

This was an ambitious project, and the preliminary work in 1982 required the seabed to be cleared of any unexploded wartime ordnance, which, given the history of these waters, could vary from coastal artillery shells and anti-aircraft rounds to mines and even torpedoes. To achieve this two mine hunters were deployed, HMS *Kirkliston* and HMS *Nurton*, and with Trinity House providing the guard ships I was seconded to take the first of these from Harwich down to the Strait to join them. For this first part of the operation we chartered a small cruising cutter, the *Preceder*, from our own pilotage department, and at one point had a Trinity House lighthouse tender deployed, but it was rather odd to be in a red-ensign vessel standing guard on two busy white-ensign ships, especially as the number of bangs they made was disappointing – but we didn't lack excitement and it became rapidly clear that keeping shipping clear of our charges would be difficult and demanding. Our deterrents were International-shape light and flag signals – useless; an Aldis – helpful; and a Shermuly rocket-launching mortar fixed to the bridge – hugely satisfying and very effective until successive recoils destroyed the extempore mounting. We had to resort to hand-held maroons, which were a lot cheaper than the £50 Schermuly rockets, and we developed some rather interesting techniques for rapid-fire, but we did get results.

Once the civil engineering phase began things took on a different hue. We deployed three guard ships initially, then six when the French joined. Each of our two squadrons consisted of two distant-water trawlers – because they were available, could work up to fifteen knots from a standing start and were remarkably manoeuvrable. Although each flew a Trinity House ensign, she had her full crew and was commanded by her skipper. But each also had a small Trinity House team of a Commander and two Second Officers, one of whom was required to speak French. The third guard ship in each group was the buoy tender. To the first group was attached Guard 3 – a former French seaplane tender, much converted and altered in a long life with the splendid name of *Hydragale*.

I transferred from Guard 2 – the *Boston Lincoln* – to the lead ship of the second squadron, Guard 4 – the *Northella*, just back from the Falklands. I had under my wing Guard 5 – the *Arctic Raider* – and our buoy tender, Guard 6 – the *Geotek Beta*, better known as the former RRS *Shackleton*. We worked-up off Harwich before running down to the Strait once the EDF complex began work, enjoying the grandiloquent title of Guard Commodore!

Both squadrons worked in conjunction with HM Coastguard at Dover, who mustered extra staff to feed each Guard Commodore a stream of information regarding the approaching traffic if it looked likely to pose a threat – and much of it did, from large tankers to small yachts, from warships to ferries who should have known better. We learned a lot – you could always tell when a ferry had changed her crew – and the number of ships with poorly manned bridges, even empty wheelhouses, was terrifying. I shall never forget the two small yellow-pig-tailed girls who regarded us as we surged up alongside their father's coaster with megaphones blaring, lamps flashing and our trigger-happy fingers shooting maroons over the Strait. Papa appeared from the after accommodation and asked on the VHF how he could help.

On another occasion a Dutch yacht asked who was firing cannon balls at him, then dismissed our warning – we were icily polite on all occasions, it was the only way to handle the situation – by declaring the complexes that lay right athwart his hawse were not on his chart! We patiently explained that was why we were firing cannon balls at him, and he got the point.

Despite radio nav-warnings and inclusion on the regular traffic information broadcasts from the Coastguard's CINS half-hourly broadcasts, we were kept constantly on the run, particularly when out of the inshore traffic zones and crossing the south-west or north-east lanes. It was all rather depressing and extremely tiring. My team 'opened fire' on the Royal, United States and Soviet Navies, and I think my opposite number scored a hit on a West German U-boat making a transit of the Strait. Looking back it was all rather terrifying, but the cooperation we had from the trawlermen, especially the skippers and mates, was fantastic – I think they rather enjoyed it. Our technique in good visibility was to head off trouble before it got close when a small alteration of course resolved the situation. We would approach close under the port bow, if possible, calling initially on VHF. Once we could read the threat's name we called incessantly, and often this was sufficient, but if this was no good we fired a maroon as close as we dared – which was pretty close – and then swung under the bow of the threat, still firing maroons. That usually worked. If not, we ran alongside until we got a reaction. Most watch keepers were so alarmed that they cooperated immediately, but one British master of a Hong Kong registered vessel threatened to report me to the DoT. I assured him that that was fine, because I should be reporting him for failure to keep a proper watch. Although we had had to work out our modus operandi according to circumstances, we were on station at the Department's insistence and, given the size of the large OBO concerned, we were at the greater hazard.

We had some very, very hairy moments, including one that was near catastrophic but, by the grace of God and some good luck, we avoided any problems. It was a very foggy night and it is etched forever in my memory. All three of my guard ships were 'up-threat' in arrowhead formation when several large echoes approached. We had a tactical plot running and managed to shepherd the first threat just past one corner of the complex, thanks to the *Geotek Beta*, then the second approached doing about fourteen knots in thick weather and heading right for the centre of the complex where the barge was working. We ran directly towards it in *Northella*, then dodged out of the way as she passed us. *Arctic Raider* then moved to stand in the way while we brought *Northella* up astern, firing maroons, calling on the VHF and aware that we were in the screw-race of this monster but quite unable to see a thing. The barge had been fully alerted and Dover CG were equally aware that a disaster was looming; it was a dreadful few moments as *Arctic Raider* then had to let her pass and we told the barge we had done what we could. Mercifully the barge-master had rung the alarms, mustered all hands and let go all his tensioned head mooring wires. At the point at which the rogue vessel passed through the position of the barge, its stern moorings had plucked it clear, and as the rogue tanker swept past within yards of the barge the visibility lifted just sufficiently for the highly efficient barge-master – whose heart must have been, like mine, in his mouth – to read the vessel's name.

Consular or diplomatic protests were made but I'm not aware that anything came out of it except that I recall giving a lecture on the subject to the Command Seminar in 1984. There have been one or two similarly such exciting moments in my career in Trinity House, though few teetered on the edge of dis-aster quite in the way those few moments did. I, like a number of my colleagues, was on secondment for Operation Channel Cable, but we needed extra personnel to provide us with our small teams. Altogether there were twenty-seven officers involved in this task, all on a rotational basis, and of those nine were ex-Blue Funnel. Several of the French-speaking officers were women, and this was my first experience of working with female deck officers. The young lady attached to *Northella* was impressively professional and efficient, and most helpful in the staff-work necessary to answer all the queries that fell about our heads in the wake of the incident I have just described.

The requirement for guard ships arose from events in 1971 when there was a collision between the *Texaco Caribbean* and a Peruvian ship called the *Paracas*. Cut in half, the *Texaco Caribbean* sank just off the Varne Bank. We got a Trinity House vessel on station before dark but her warning signals did not stop the *Brandenburg* striking the new wreck and sinking with terrible loss of life. Even after the deployment of over twenty buoys and two light vessels, a Greek ship called the *Nikki* penetrated the danger-zone and she too sank. This was the catalysing event that bought in the IALA buoyage system, because the wreck-marking signals that we were using under the old 1934 lateral buoyage system were not universally recognised, evidence for which was produced by the surviving OOW of the *Brandenburg*.

I don't think anyone was really to blame except perhaps the original people who caused the collision, but the aftermath was pretty ghastly. This, of course, was in the minds of the people setting up the Channel Cable project. **9**

That the Niger Delta might be a source of oil has been known since the early years of the last century, but it was not until 1956 that Shell–BP struck oil at Oloibiri, leading to further exploration and development of the new oil fields. This in turn led to considerable resentment by the indigenous inhabitants of the region, who were concerned at the likelihood of environmental degradation and also expressed fears that the new oil wealth would not be equitably returned to the region. In 1967 Mobil discovered huge oil reserves offshore, while at the same time the Nigerian province containing the oil riches seceded from the rest of the country and set up the Republic of Biafra. It took three years of vicious civil war before Nigeria was able to defeat the forces of the newly declared republic. These three years saw a dramatic drop in oil production and a sharp increase in lawlessness. The latter, a combination of criminality and environmental protest, continues to this day.

In 1967 John Gray was Master of the MV *Martinetta*, engaged in surveying off the coast of Nigeria when the Biafran war broke out. He received instructions to take his ship to Papua New Guinea. The charts aboard only covered the coast of Nigeria. He recalls how they improvised:

❢ It took about six weeks to get mail out to Fernando Po in those days and maybe, with hindsight, we could have got charts sent out by aeroplane by special delivery or something, but that wasn't thought about. We had a chart of the Bight of Biafra and that took us about a hundred miles south of Fernando Po, and we had nothing after that, but we did have a Pilot Book – and, as any mariner will recall, the Pilot Book gives the latitude and longitude of every headland and offshore obstruction. So on some cartridge paper we drew a lattice of latitude and longitude and plotted the headlands all the way down. We drew an imaginary coastline on it and then kept at least twenty miles off that. Navigation was by star sights and dead reckoning. We had an almanac that was a year out of date, but it tells you in the back, you may recall, how to use an out-of-date almanac. We only had a sounding sextant,[17] which meant star sights morning and evening. We couldn't take any sun sight.

We then set off, aiming to go to Walvis Bay. Unfortunately the weed on the bottom meant that instead of doing ten knots we were doing eight knots but we were burning fuel for ten. We realised that we were running short, so made for Luanda. We took evening star sights and set course from them to Luanda Fairway Buoy, and the only thing that worked at this stage was the echo-sounder and the VHF. So we plodded along with the echo-sounder running and started to pick up a trace. It was a survey echo-sounder, the old round and round Kelvin Hughes style, and the trace got shallower and shallower – and when it got down to forty feet we put a lead over and found it was more than forty feet, it was in fact a secondary trace. That happened about three in the morning, and then at six in the morning

---

17. A sextant without the shades that made it safe to look at the sun.

there was the Luanda Fairway Buoy right on the nose. I always remember my sigh of relief! We managed to get a Portuguese chart in Luanda that took us down to the Cunene River and then it was blank so it was back to our homemade chart for the Dead Man's Coast and on to Walvis Bay. The navigation met the need and it worked. We obtained charts in Walvis Bay and had a refit in Cape Town. The rest of the voyage was straight-forward. **9**

Malcolm Parrott had a varied career, and latterly spent time in West Africa. His account from the 1980s shows that life could be quite exciting:

6 The ship was called *Arabella*. She was a 1,500-ton deck cargo ship. It had a complete Chinese crew apart from myself, as Master. The officers were from Hong Kong, the crew from mainland China, it was registered in Liberia, and it was a real wreck. It was running for a company called Societé Ivoire out of Abidjan. We were essentially coasting with containers – we could only carry about 150 containers. It had a big crane on it, did twelve to thirteen knots, a slow, old ship not good for fend-ing off pirates. I could not believe what had happened to me. There I was in deepest darkest Africa, with a Chinese crew, most of who could not speak English. There were no knives and forks on the ship, there were no cups, it was completely and utterly Chinese. But I have to say it was a great experience because I got to love these guys, they were so funny, and they started to teach me their language. I had to learn a lot of it. They in turn were taught naval tactics, how to defend them-selves against the pirates, which were constantly attacking us, certainly in Nigeria and off Monrovia.

We went up the New Calabar River when the oil field was being built up there and we were taking pipes and containers and general sort of things. We had two Italian engineers on board to be put ashore when we arrived. We had carried them from Port Harcourt. There are no charts for that river so you have to take a mud pilot. It is very exciting going up there. It gets more and more shallow and you go aground quite frequently, and you tie up to palm trees to discharge. We had been told that for this particular trip we were going to be attacked by insurgents, so we took a unit of the Nigerian police and, sure enough, we were attacked. They came over the side so we went to stations, but the police said no, stand back – and there was one hell of a fire fight. Quite a lot of people got killed and we were lying on the deck of the wheelhouse. The Italians were terrified, they were screaming and shouting, 'Can we speak to mamma?' So I crawled across the wheelhouse to the chartroom, these two guys following me, and I called Portishead Radio, gave them the telephone numbers in Italy and these guys babbled away to their mammas because they were both frightened that they were going to be killed. When they had finished I said, 'Please ring my wife,' and gave them the number. I got through to her and she said, 'I'm so glad you've rung. I want to talk to you about the new curtains for the hall.' I said, 'I don't think this is the best time as I am in the middle of a fire fight and there are people getting killed.' She said, 'Don't worry, but I do need to talk about the curtains.' When I finished the call the operator at Portishead said, 'Is there anything I can do to help you? Could I ring the British High Commission in Nigeria?' I said 'No, we have the Nigerian police here, they all have machine pistols, so don't worry about it, we will be all right.' 9

The role of Deputy Captain is an unusual one, not found outside the specialised niche of the luxury cruise liners. Ian Gibb recalls:

6 As Deputy Captain of the *Canberra* I sailed with the Commodore for a number of years before getting my own command. But the role of the Deputy Captain is a rather interesting one. One deputises for the Old Man in all cases. So, for example, if you have fog for any number of hours then the Deputy Captain comes up to take over, or should there be the need for some form of entertaining the passengers, then instead of the

Commodore having to go, the Deputy Captain takes his place.

But I think probably the most interesting feature of the Deputy Captain's side of things is to maintain and to be absolutely sure that the stability is correct. This was particularly interesting on the *Canberra* because quite a number of our voyages involved going to places such as in the Caribbean where we just did not know whether there was going to be any fresh water available. When *Canberra* first came into service in 1961 the passenger use of water was something in the region of 250 tons a day. By the time that I joined her in the late 1970s and the early 1980s the passenger consumption of water had gone up to something like 450 tons a day. The desalination plant that we had aboard could cope with the 250 but not with the 450, so it was essential that the places that we visited were able to provide us with a good supply of fresh water. On Caribbean cruises, however, this didn't occur because we went to places like Curaçao. First of all it was extremely expensive – the water, that is – and there wasn't a great deal of it. And if you were at anchor off some of the little islands like St Vincent or Antigua then the water had to be tendered out to you, if they had any available, and it was a considerable problem.

As you can appreciate, the stability of the ship depended on the bottom weight, and as the water and the fuel were being used so the ship was becoming more and more, if you like, top-heavy. Well, the way around this, of course, was to fill ballast tanks with salt water, but it was of particular interest to the senior staff to ensure that the metacentric height, which is the measure of stability, was positive rather than negative. So each day the First Officer used to come and see me and we used to talk through the consumption of water, the consumption of fuel, how much ballast water we had to put in to maintain a positive stability. The problem arose, of course, when going to the Caribbean. You knew you weren't going to be able to replenish stocks, and on a number of occasions I had to ask the Commodore if he would make an announcement to the passengers to say, 'Please conserve water or we will be having to cut off the water supply for certain hours of the day.' And the amusing one was always 'We would ask you to select a friend with whom you could shower so you could save the water.' But the stability on the long Caribbean cruises was always a problem, and we were always very pleased indeed when we called in to Port Everglades to get a full supply of fresh water reasonably cheaply.

Other roles of the Deputy Captain were to be the chair, if you like, of the Health and Safety Committee, when once per month each department sent a representative to discuss the health and safety of the ship and whether we could do anything about the accidents that had occurred over the previous month. **9**

In times of war the government has always chartered or requisitioned merchant ships to support the armed forces. Many famous passenger ships spent some years as troopships or hospital ships during the two world wars, and this pattern was to be repeated during the Falklands conflict in 1982. This involved the use, either by chartering or as 'ships taken up from trade' (STUFT), of nearly fifty merchant ships. This figure did not include the ships of the Royal Fleet Auxiliary, which were under naval control. The ships included cruise liners, container ships, tankers, ferries, tugs and trawlers. For the period of the charter, British crews replaced those that were not under the British flag and had foreign crews, to the disappointment of some of the original crews. From their normal use, merchant ships were converted into troopships, hospital ships, helicopter carriers, store ships, minesweepers and other assorted uses.

Michael Twomey was Master of the *Atlantic Causeway* during the Falklands War. This is his account:

6 I was on the *Atlantic Causeway* just for the three months of the Falklands War. She was converted in a most remarkable six days in Devonport dockyard from being a transatlantic roll-on roll-off container ship into what I like to think was a fairly efficient helicopter carrier, no fixed-wing aircraft unfortunately, although I did try to lure one on one day but he wouldn't come.

We had a naval party of over a hundred. We had a few portacabins stuck on for extra accommodation and the rest just doubled up. We had eight helicopter pilots in the Second Mate's cabin. They were big cabins! The rest just jammed in wherever we could put them, because the normal ship's company was something like thirty.

There was an enormous amount of very creditable work done by our shore staff, who gelled very well with the naval stores department. Our catering department did a magnificent job, in fact. The decks were flattened and anything that stuck up like ventilators and fan motors and things like that were all cut off so we had virtually a flat deck. We had to cut the container lashing boxes, and helicopter fixing points were put in their place. We had two flight decks, one on the forward deck of course, which was our major one, and another one aft of the accommodation – there were difficulties with that because of the funnel fumes and the turbulence caused by the superstructure and the fact that there was a ramp sticking up above the level of the deck by about six feet so when we were operating helicopters we had to lower the stern ramp level with the deck. There again, we used the ramp to run landing craft up on when we were there, but it wasn't considered strong enough so we had to move anchor cable so that the anchor cable supported the ramp, which were all fairly major undertakings and all done in six days.

We filled up with fuel and three thousand tons of everything the army needed. The only hiccup was our aircraft refuelling system. We used whisky containers, the tanks that were shipped across to the United States, so ACL, the container company that operated that service, gave us all their spare whisky tanks – which we then had to connect up with flexible couplings because the containers moved very slightly and this caused a bit of a problem to us because we couldn't get the flexible couplings tight. The ship was awash with avgas. At the end of the operation when we had thrown a wingding on our return to Devonport for the dockyard staff, who had done a magnificent job, I said as much to them, the yard manager said to me that everybody was involved. The flexible couplings that leaked needed O-rings, which you had asked for. We had wanted lots and lots and lots of them. He said that every plumber from

Bristol to Land's End had a policeman beating on his door in the middle of the night saying get down to your shop because we need all your O-rings. We had just sent a signal saying we need O-rings and they kept appearing – we didn't know where they had come from because we were all a bit busy.

It just shows the involvement of everybody in that conflict – it touched everyone. Normally, to get anything out of the naval stores department takes weeks and sheaves of paper. One telephone call, be on a truck with in an hour, sir, and with you in six. That was the sort of level at which it was worked. The paper went out of the window.

We went out into Mount's Bay and anchored there and all the helicopters arrived. The *Atlantic Causeway* was 800 feet long and 26,000 tons, which was bigger than a Royal Naval aircraft carrier; we were the biggest thing there.

I was a Captain RNR, which was a great help to me although I was serving as a merchant-navy captain. I did know a few of the naval officers who were there. Although we did not normally land Chinooks on board, we did occasionally, on the after deck, which does show the size of the after deck.

We were anchored in San Carlos Water. Although there were air attacks and it got very noisy we were not ourselves attacked. I acquired some ex-Argentinian rapid-firing rifles quite illicitly by swapping them with the Commodore for a helicopter. The Royal Navy had supplied us with blast protection gear in case we were attacked. We had an aircraft repair team on board, so damaged aircraft came to us for repair. As far as the weather went it was blessed – it was a normal South Atlantic weather, but on the day of surrender, winter appeared and it snowed. We brought four Argentinian Pucara aircraft back with us, which were scattered round the country, one to the Naval Museum at Yeovilton.

The *Canberra* had four thousand Argentinian prisoners on board and the Argentinian nation did not want them back because they would have been an embarrassment, so the *Canberra* sent a signal saying, 'Can support this number of souls for twenty-four more hours. Can they swim?' That did get a response.

So we came back to the UK and I came home on well-earned leave. She was restored to normal operating condition. 825 Squadron, the Sea King squadron, sent the senior pilot thereof up on the way home. 'We would like you to have a little memento of our stay on board, sir.' I said, 'That's very kind of you, old boy.' There was a chap with him, sort of staggering with something and he said, 'We thought you might stick it on the wall of the officers' lounge.' I said, 'What is it?' It was an Argentinian rocket launcher with a rocket in it. I had just received a signal to say that we were going to Belfast so I had to say that is extremely kind of you, very thoughtful, but I don't think we ought to take it to Belfast because it might have been a bit unpopular. It was ceremoniously ditched over the side. 9

Michael Twomey had another, rather special, memory of this time:

6 Whilst the *Atlantic Causeway* was anchored in San Carlos Water, the *Sir Galahad* was struck by an Argentinian Exocet missile. There were many casualties, and what were described as the 'walking wounded' were sent to my ship for treatment. All the men were from the Welsh Guards and all marched on board. Looking at them, I felt that it was only because they were the Guards that they were able to walk at all. They were taken to the officers' bar and laid out there on stretchers for treatment. When they were all safely on board I went down to make sure that everything was in order. As I walked in, in my uniform with badges of rank on my shoulders, they all tried to stand up. 9

The decline in the size of the British merchant navy since the early 1980s has called into question Britain's ability to mount another such task force, should one ever be required.

Ken Owen spent a lifetime at sea, serving under many flags as a Master of container ships, and in this extract he looks at the highs and lows of a long life at sea.

❻ From my own personal experience, it has been a fascinating life in the contrasts that you went through, from being totally humiliated by being harassed by port authorities and so forth to the very opposite, of going to very interesting places and meeting interesting people.

I was on this cruise with Princess Chichibu.[18] I used to paint, and I had painted a picture for her of the ship in the Inland Sea and we had given it to her on the voyage while she was there. The Captain had said he wanted all the officers to mix with all the VIPs from Japan, MPs, Sir John Nicholson as well as the old Shogun family. I was asked to come down off the bridge and only the ladies turned up, other than the British Ambassador, Sir Francis Rundle. So there were just the two of us there and all the ladies, in their finery, including the Princess. I wondered where everybody was, and they had in fact gone to the officers' wardroom to discuss and persuade the Japanese to start using containers. I didn't know this until years later, when Lindsay Alexander pointed it out.

On this particular voyage it was a real adventure for Princess Chichibu. We anchored at one place and they went to visit a holy island. The weather was too bad for them to come back on board, so for the first time ever she was out of range of the government – nobody knew where she was, but she thoroughly enjoyed it. They had to take a ferry across to Tamano and the ship had to go to another island in Japan to pick them up. So it was a great adventure for her. I had painted this picture, which we had given to her.

Years later I was at a reception at the Tokyo Embassy. I was telling the Ambassador about this, and he said, 'Oh, I know her, I know her personally.' And the next thing was I had an invitation up to Akasaka Palace. I was Master of the *Liverpool Bay* by then, and from that point on if Allwyne came out we were always invited up to the Palace and we became good friends. I had been Second Mate when Nicholson was having his cruise, so she knew him, and she asked me to take things back to Sir John Nicholson at his home in the Isle of Wight

18. A daughter of the Emperor of Japan.

– and sure enough, he invited us down and we became a go-between, between the Imperial family and Sir John. She had in fact stayed at the Isle of Wight and had been born in Britain and spoke perfect English. She said that she loved the English countryside and seeing the little white blobs all over the fields – which were the sheep!

But you go from that extreme to the next, where we were in Jeddah and the *Daily Telegraph* had had an advertisement for Dunlop tyres showing an Arab stabbing this tyre because it saved fuel. The Saudis took exception to this and, I am told, said 'Are there any British ships nearby?' So the next thing was I was called ashore to explain why I had been anchored in the wrong place. I got up there, and I was under arrest and I was explaining that we weren't at anchor because it was too deep, we were just hove to because there was no pilot and we had nowhere else to go. But they said. 'Why were you anchored there? There is no anchoring allowed there.' I explained that the anchor chain was only so long, it was too short to reach the bottom, I couldn't possibly anchor. 'Yes Captain we understand that, but why were you anchored?'

I was getting really worried then because they kept me there for the entire day and wouldn't let me get in touch with the ship, and then they ordered the ship to sail – so the Chief Officer, who was on his first trip, said to the Chief Engineer, 'What can we do? They have ordered us to sail and the Captain is not back.' So the Chief said, 'That's easy – the engines are not ready.' But they came along and said, 'We will tow you out.' So he was worried to death.

The agent came up and tried to get me released, but all this time I was under questioning as though I had committed a serious crime. What surprised me was that they wanted details of my wife, and what school my children went to. While I was being held there, different people were coming into the coast-guard and they were insisting that I was a guest – and I was getting the horrible coffee that they gave you. It seemed I was up for a very serious crime for being in the wrong place, and then the agent, who was Sudanese, told me that because we were the only British ship in they had been told to harass me.

They had been known to arrest people and hold them there so you could get the humiliation of that.

Then there were the Chinese and the Cultural Revolution – where you had to do exactly what you were told. I could write a book about that. But there is that from the one extreme to the other, from the indignity of having to wait outside in the cold while they search the accommodation and then take stool samples from everybody. They never did it to airline passengers. And then at the other extreme you were invited to a launching with all the top people and you were made very welcome. One day you are an ordinary seaman and the next you are considered senior management. ❾

9 · Swallowing the anchor

A significant proportion of deck officers left the sea for shore-based occupations, many soon after obtaining their Certificate of Competency as a Master Mariner. In a great number of cases the reason for the decision to leave the sea was marriage. In some cases a clean break with seafaring was made, but in others the link with the sea was maintained. Examples of subsequent careers that can be thought of as a natural sequel to the years spent at sea include marine superintendent of a shipping company, pilot, harbour superintendent, lecturer at a nautical college, and examiner for the Certificates of Competency, while yet others continued to maintain an active link with maritime life even after retirement.

It is the recollections of those Master Mariners who maintained a link with the sea that are included in this chapter: a chapter that brings into focus the shore-based infrastructure that underpinned, and still underpins, maritime trade.

Stuart Bradley recalls how his decision to leave the sea was triggered by the death of his father, who was a Master with South American Saint Line. This line, whose ships were all named after saints, traded between Europe and South America.

❦ My father, who was a Master at sea, died relatively young. He'd had a bad war, having been taken prisoner after his ship had been blown out of the water – his first command. He was only in his early thirties at the time, and he died when he was fifty-three. His sudden death had a profound effect on me. I was on a ship called the *Cannanore* coming back from Hamburg and we were just about to pick up the pilot at Spithead. I had kept the twelve-to-four watch and at five thirty in the morning there was a knock on my door. It was a cadet to say, 'The

Captain wants to see you.' I went to see the Captain, who shall be nameless, having donned full uniform as you did, with my cap under my arm. I knocked and entered his cabin and said, 'You want to see me, sir?' and he said, 'Yes, Bradley. Your father's dead.' Just like that.

He had had a cable from South America Saint Line saying that my father had died on the bridge of his ship, the *St John*, entering Beirut harbour. He keeled over just as they were picking up the pilot there. As I was only recently married his death caused me to ponder. I hardly knew my father. I had spent only three Christmases with him in my life – and it just didn't seem to make a lot of sense. Much as I loved the sea, and I really did (and, though I say it myself, I think I was an asset because it was something that I grew up with), his early death brought me up with a round turn, if you like. So I started to think. I didn't have a Master's ticket then – I did the next year, and after that I started to look for jobs ashore and left P&O four years later, when I was twenty-eight. 9

Keith Hart's career shows the determination and adaptability that were needed to pursue his profession in the post-1980s era, when British shipping companies were making huge redundancies. He sailed in various foreign-flagged ships and then on a barge in the offshore oil industry, before gaining an Extra Master's certificate and a nautical science degree. Even after that it was not easy to find satisfactory employment, although the drilling rigs and barges of the offshore oil industry needed the maritime expertise that Master Mariners possessed. However, they were also under foreign ownership. In this short extract we get a flavour of the difficulties of finding employment at this time.

6 So after I had my degree I went back onto drilling rigs. I finished my last exam on a Thursday and by the next Tuesday I was on a drilling rig, but I didn't stay for very long. I lasted about four months approximately. The reason I didn't stay was that it was an American company that I was working for, Global

Marine and Drilling, who had two lots of rigs. They had some very nice rigs and they were American flag, and they had some not very nice submersible and jack-up rigs. I wouldn't go on a jack-up, because it is on the submersibles that they need marine people. The older rigs were Panamanian flag. I could not get command of American-flag rigs because I wasn't an American national. The highest I could be was stability technician, effectively Mate, which was the job that I had – so there was no future on the nice rigs and I didn't want to work on the old rigs because they were run on a very different mentality.

So then I came ashore, although very briefly, on a freelance basis working for Shell International Marine. I had already had an interview and was awaiting a second interview with a company called London Offshore Consultants. They offered me the job and I started with them at the beginning of 1988. I did five years based in their London office and then I went out to the United Arab Emirates to open offices there. I stayed out there for three and a half years. **9**

The 1960s and 1970s were difficult years for seafarers. Change was happening, and happening very quickly, but it took time for the implications to be fully assimilated. The underlying assumption on first going to sea – that ahead of one, subject to passing the certificates of competency and performing one's duty satisfactorily, lay a career that would culminate in command – was no longer true. Cecil Smylie recalls how he came to terms with this and forged a new life:

6 I remained with P&O for twenty-six years, rising eventually to the rank of Staff Captain. In the 1970s the oil crisis meant that the steamships, mainly the passenger fleet, were no longer viable. That and the introduction of the 747 Jumbo Jet combined to decimate the Australian passenger traffic and the Far East passenger traffic. I was very concerned because by then I had decided that passenger-ship life was what I wanted to remain in, and one by one all these magnificent ships – *Iberia*, *Arcadia*, *Himalaya*, *Chusan* – one after the other they went to the scrap yard. My last voyage on *Oronsay* as Staff Captain saw her on her way to the breaker's yard in Taiwan, and that convinced me that the time had come to seek an alternative career.

I had been offered a position in Libya as a trainee pilot, and after enormous soul-searching and a personal interview with the Chief Executive of P&O, I felt that I had made the right decision and took six months leave of absence, and went out to join Occidental Oil Company at Zueitina in Libya. My two-trip training period hardly equipped me for handling some of the biggest tankers in the world, in a port without tugs, where the north-west winds were likely to blow up at a moment's notice – and I found myself in very deep water, struggling to berth them safely.

I managed to fulfil the duties without any accidents and immediately started looking for a less dangerous place to work. With the opening of Sullom Voe oil terminal in Shetland, I applied and was accepted and eventually became a licensed Sullom Voe pilot. Living in the Shetland Islands was fairly exacting. I had a home at that time in Glasgow and we didn't have a travelling remit, so it meant that I was living in Shetland with my family living in Glasgow, children at school at a critical stage, and I didn't settle as I had hoped.

Sullom Voe Pilotage was a mariner's dream – powerful tugs, state-of-the-art navigational aids, an exciting pilotage experience. Unfortunately the domestic situation overruled the professional enjoyment, and I then removed to the Middle East where I became a sea pilot with Land and Marine's affiliate Lanmaco. Once again the timing was unfortunate. I arrived, and very shortly after my arrival the Iranian revolution put paid to the embryo pilotage scheme under preparation. Shortly after its inception the Gulf Pilotage Service was discontinued.

Following the abandonment of the pilotage service I was employed in the agency division of Lanmaco at the port of Khor Fakkan in the Gulf of Oman sixty miles south of the Straits of Hormuz, which very quickly became the biggest tanker anchorage in the world. Ships were unwilling to proceed through the Straits of Hormuz with the advent of the Iran–Iraq tanker war. This caused major problems and a major interruption to the flow of oil from the Gulf loading ports to the Far East and to Europe. In conjunction with the Kuwait Oil Tanker Company I established a ship-to-ship tanker transfer facility off Khor Fakkan by locating and establishing an inventory of second-hand equipment lying unused at various UAE locations – Yokohama fenders, transfer hoses, tugs, personnel, supply craft. This was all accomplished on a Thursday afternoon, which in the Middle East would be akin to Saturday in Europe. By the most incredible stroke of luck I was able to collect suf-ficient equipment together and the first transfer took place within forty-eight hours of the idea being first promoted. At that time nobody quite realised what an asset this was going to be, since the war-risk insurance rates for ships going north from Khor Fakkan into the Gulf were to become prohibitive. Certain nationalities prohibited their flagged ships from enter-ing the Gulf and the STS facility built up, involving millions of tons of oil being transferred from ships which were prepared to run into the Gulf and attracting impressive charter rates.

There were of course numerous emergency situations involving war-damaged tonnage, loss of life and temporary repair work on vessels that were willing to undertake the dangerous Gulf transit. The Gulf transfer service continued for over three years. I can't give you the precise quantity, but it involved several millions of tons of crude oil that reached world markets without incident.[19] 9

The merchant navy was an essential part of the Task Force that recap-tured the Falklands Islands from the Argentinians in 1982. Anthony Braithwaite recalls the hectic time preparing the *Atlantic Conveyor* for sailing:

6 At the time of the Falklands War I was the Operations Manager for the Cunard cargo ships, and I was told to go up

---

19. Cecil Smylie was awarded the US Navy citation for service to the Fifth Fleet throughout 'Desert Shield' and 'Desert Storm'.

to Liverpool to board the *Atlantic Conveyor*, which was laid up. Captain Michael Layard RN, now Admiral Sir Michael Layard, was coming aboard and he was asked to bring his uniform, as was Captain Ian North who was going to command the ship. The reason for this was that I was told to make certain that we got as much publicity out of the *Atlantic Conveyor* as possible as we were trying to sell the ship to General Dynamics of America. We thought it would be a good press. And so I had a photographer visit the ship to take a photograph of the two Captains, which proved to be very useful later.

The *Atlantic Conveyor* was got ready as soon as possible and sailed round to Devonport, and in the space of some three weeks she was turned into a Harrier carrier. We had a regular Cunard crew of thirty-five and this is supplemented by well over a hundred Navy and RAF personnel. The ship was commanded by Captain Ian North and Captain Michael Layard was the Senior Naval Officer, and fortunately they got on extremely well together.

The ship sailed on a Saturday from Devonport, and because it was a Saturday I was able to go down on the Saturday morning, with my wife Jane, to see her sail. Ian said, 'Be on board, if you can at midday as I am giving a short party for the Dockyard.' When I got down there, there was frantic activity, everyone was trying to get their stuff on board before the stern door was lifted and the ship met her timetable to embark the Harriers in Devonport Sound. Ian North showed me around the ship, which was like a huge magazine – there were bombs and fuel – and it was a complete tented city. Thinking ahead, this was to accommodate the Argentine army after they had been captured. They really thought well ahead. The party was magnificent. I said to the Dockyard Manager what a wonderful job it was, and he said, 'When you see the high figures for doing surveys on naval ships, that is the premium. This is the payoff.' My wife and I were the last ones down the gangway. They lifted the gangway, the gates opened and away she went. My wife said to me, 'You would like to be on that ship,' and I said, 'I would be the galley boy.'

The rest is history. I had letters from Ian North from the

Azores, and very shortly after that she was sunk. I was the first contact with the Ministry of Defence. It was best to have one conduit only and that was me. I had gone to bed one night, fast asleep, and shortly after midnight my naval contact, the Deputy Director of Naval Operations and Trade at the MOD, rang up and said, 'Tony, they have hit your ship, and they are getting out. I cannot tell you how bad it is at the moment.' And so we put in hand a plan that we had arranged with the Missions to Seamen (now the Mission to Seafarers). We had laid out the names and addresses of next-of-kin of all the Cunard people on board and they had given this information to their honorary agents around the country, mostly the local vicar. And in several instances these good people had gone round and made themselves known to the families. About five o'clock in the morning I rang them and told them that they would shortly be active. I rang the personnel department and got them to go into the office there and then, and we went in and waited for the telegram to arrive from the Falklands. And it wasn't as bad as we expected – there were six killed or missing,[20] and so the Missions to Seamen went around and told the people that their relative, their husband, their son was safe or that they were missing. Around midday Downing Street rang up and said that Mrs Thatcher is going to name the ship in the afternoon and what was the position about the next-of-kin? And we were able to say that all the next-of-kin have been informed. **9**

Towards the end of Jeremy Carew's career in the Royal Fleet Auxiliary a very different challenge arose. He was given command of an RFA ship, the *Fort Grange*, which was being used as a stores depot in the port of Split during the Croatian war of the early 1990s. Here he became involved in Balkan diplomacy: a far cry from the normal work of a Master Mariner! In these two extracts he describes averting a potential diplomatic incident and gives an account of the convoluted nature of Balkan diplomacy.

---

20. Captain Ian North was among those who lost their lives.

❦ The agent came in one day and said, 'Captain, Captain, we've got to move the ship, because the army ship is coming in.' I told him that the *Fort Grange* had been sat there for the last two years or something and it's not going to move now. He said that it had to come in. I told him that it couldn't come in because it hadn't got 'dip clear'.[21] Some major in the 'Rickshaws Cabs and Taxis'[22] had decided to just send it in earlier. By this time we had got a very good liaison going with the Embassy and the military attaché up there, a nice chap. I rang up the Embassy and said, 'Will you tell Colonel Whatever to phone me immediately, as it is a matter of the utmost urgency.' When he rang he said, 'What's up, sir?' I told him that we were just about to have a diplomatic incident, because the 17th Port Regiment had decided to call in the RFA ship which was waiting outside, and that we were bloody lucky – for it was because, and only because, it was an RFA ship that we were talking to them. 'Dip clear' didn't start until midday, and if they had tried to bring the ship in before then there would have been all hell going on. So we had to tell the bloody pongos and they didn't like being told. I was the Commander Task Group – whenever you go somewhere there's always got to be somebody in charge, if you haven't got a real Navy ship you have a 'make do' one – so there I was, CTG. Eventually they sent a signal from the Embassy, from the Ambassador himself, to the movement side of the Army in England, saying that 'if it had not been for CTG a diplomatic incident would have occurred. All future ships movements are to be passed through CTG on *Fort Grange*.' ❧

❦ It was good out there – it was a very interesting job. The other diplomatic thing was that they had a mayor and a *zupa*. The *zupa* is a bit like a prefect, he represents the government, and the mayor represents the people. The mayor was ultra left-wing and the *zupa* was ultra right-wing, and if those two

---

21. Diplomatic clearance.
22. Royal Corps of Transport.

blokes met and spoke or even smiled at each other there would have been trouble. So whenever they actually needed to get together, I would have a luncheon party. Captain Alex would come – he had been at sea and was the Honorary Consul – and Alex would say, 'Jeremy, we need to have a lunch as the *zupa* needs to talk to the mayor.' So we'd have a lunch, a very good lunch. I would say, 'Have as many lunches as you like, Alex.' The Ambassador asked me, as well, so I told him that lunches were easy but that I didn't have an unlimited pocket – with lunch comes hooch, and I didn't have the money to pay for that. If I did that for official entertainment I had to go back to the Ministry of Defence. He said that he had some sort of fund that could deal with that. So I asked Alex, 'Your booze or mine?' and he said, 'Don't worry, I'll bring it on board, it's coming from so-and-so.' So they would be there and they would sit down, the mayor and the *zupa*. One of them would have to go to the toilet or something and the other would go up to my cabin. As well as a day room and a bedroom, there was a conference room big enough for eight to ten. So they would get in there and sort out their problems and all their business and then come back down again and be very formal with each other for the rest of the lunch. They would then be seen not talking to each other and snubbing each other as they went down the gangway. **9**

The responsibility for the lights and the buoys around the coasts of England and Wales lies with the Corporation of Trinity House. While still at sea Ian Gibb became a Younger Brother and then, following his retirement, he played an active role as an Elder Brother of Trinity House. He recalls his largely honorary responsibilities:

6 I became a Younger Brother of Trinity House in 1982 when, having got the requisite time in command, I put myself forward and was accepted as a Younger Brother. Now the Younger Brethren, of which there are approximately three hundred divided between the Royal and the merchant navy, are really just an advisory body. They don't have any specific role in Trinity

House – they are called forward if there is a specific case that requires expert attention, but, more or less, the Elder Brethren take care of the day-to-day workings of the Corporation.

It was founded in 1514, and the reason was that Henry VIII was losing more ships than he thought was necessary. They were being built in Deptford in those days. They would go out to sea and then the winter gales would cause the channels in the Thames to alter, and the ships were foundering on the way in. So a cadre of mariners was formed to ensure that the channels were buoyed, and basically that is what the Corporation does to this day – ensure that the channels around the coast are buoyed and the safety of the mariner is preserved. And this is done of course with the light vessels, the major buoyage system around the coast, and the lighthouses.

For example, there is one vessel called the *Alert* which is going round all the time, all round the English and the Welsh coasts, surveying and ensuring that the channels are deep enough for the vessels to go through in case they should be found to have altered, and I quote the spit coming into the Needles at the western end of the Solent, where it was discovered almost by accident that the spit had moved during the winter gales and therefore the channel was impossible to use by the large passenger liners.

The two ships other than the *Alert* are the *Patricia* and until quite recently the *Mermaid*. The new one is the *Galatea*, which came into service at the end of 2007, and they are going round the east and west coasts monitoring the light vessels, monitoring the lighthouses, and basically ensuring that everything is running smoothly. Should there be a wreck in the Channel then the first ship to go there would be the *Alert*, because she is very fast, and she stands by until either the *Galatea* or the *Patricia* can go along and start laying buoys to make sure that the mariner knows that there is a wreck there.

The job of the Elder Brethren – there are three paid members of the small number of mariner Elder Brethren, the Deputy Master who at the moment is an Admiral, and then there are the other two, one of whom is in charge of the navigation and the other is in charge of the administration of the organisation. Then there are several Elder Brethren, of whom I was one, who were acting in support roles, if you like, because each year the Elder Brethren make a visit to all the lighthouses and the light vessels and the buoys off the coast of England and Wales – but not Scotland, because that is looked after by the Northern Lighthouse Board. For a period of almost three weeks the Elder Brethren go round and check on the lighthouses of the east coast one year, and the west coast the following year. In addition Elder Brethren are called upon to act as assessors in the Admiralty Court, and it has been my interest and pleasure and privilege to sit with the Admiralty Court with judges on a number of cases during the course of my time as an acting, working Elder Brother.

Once you are made an Elder Brother then you are an Elder Brother until you die, and as there are only thirty-two of them, of course, it means that until one falls off his twig then another one cannot be appointed. Of the thirty-two, quite a number are actually Honoraries. For example, we have the Duke of Edinburgh, who is the Master, we have the Prince of Wales, we have the Duke of York, we have now, I am pleased to say, our first female Elder Brother in five hundred years, the Princess Royal. We also have people such as Lord Mackay of Clashfern, we have Sir Adrian Swire, Sir Brian Shaw, Lord Greenway. These are people who we feel can assist us in the event of a Bill passing through Parliament, as is the case at the moment when Lord Greenway has the interests of Trinity House to think about as well as the navigation around the coast.[23]

In my position as an Elder Brother, which I took up when retiring from P&O as Commodore, I was immediately involved in Trinity House Assessors in the Admiralty Court. I was also appointed to the Board of the Harwich Haven Authority and found myself quite unexpectedly within a matter of months the Deputy Chairman of the Harwich Haven Authority – and then, because the Chairman died, I found myself as Chairman within a year, which meant a rather larger job than I thought

---

23. This refers to the Marine and Coastal Access Bill, which was passed into law in November 2009.

because it meant running or being chair of the whole of the Stour and Orwell estuary, which was Felixstowe, Mistley, Harwich International Port and Ipswich – which took me away from home rather more than I had anticipated.

Trinity House also has a very large amount of charitable funds at its disposal from gifts that have been given to the Corporation over centuries, and I was appointed Chairman of the Grants Committee to distribute the funds of the charitable part of Trinity House, to organisations such as the Mission to Seafarers, the Apostleship of the Sea, the Royal National Missions to Deep Sea Fishermen, the RNLI, specifically for the welfare of sailors or for the safety of mariners. So it became almost a full-time job, although not paid. The only pay I got from Trinity House as an Elder Brother was when I was appointed to the Lighthouse Board. There were three members of the Corporation on the Lighthouse Board. It was very, very satisfying indeed. I still am an Elder Brother, and I involve myself in the social side and the ceremonial side when one gets dressed up in one's uniform. **9**

Masters are required to take a pilot at almost all ports anywhere in the world. The entrance to the River Thames is notoriously treacherous, with narrow channels between unstable sandbanks. From 1514 to 1987 the regulation of the Thames Pilotage was the responsibility of Trinity House, a responsibility that was then transferred to the Port of London Authority. The pilot station for ships that are outward bound is at Gravesend, and prior to 1967 there was a pilot cutter on station near the *Sunk* light vessel off Harwich for ships entering the river from the North Sea, and another stationed off Dungeness for ships entering the river from the Channel. Jim Whadcoat became a Thames pilot. He recalls:

6 Oh, I know, I saw an advert in the Telegraph, so I applied and, lo and behold, on my first application I got an interview. I was only twenty-eight then. They took applications up to the age of thirty-five, and all the pundits, including my father-in-law, who worked at Free Trade Wharf (he was the manager there), said you'll never get in, not at your age. At the interview there were pilots from the North Channel, the South Channel, all sitting round the table when I was interviewed – so as I went out I thought, this is a bit of a dull thing, opening the door and getting pushed out, that sort of thing, so I turned and said, 'Good day, gentlemen.' 'Good day,' 'Good day,' 'Good day,' they replied. One of the old pilots said later, 'I remember you, you're the only person I've ever known to do that.' To get into the pilotage, up until 1938, you had to have had sail time.

I was a pilot for thirty-two and a half years – well, actually, thirty-two years and ten months. I was a Channel pilot from Gravesend out. When I first joined, the ships outbound going southwards went to Dungeness and the ones going northwards dropped off at the cutter at the Sunk. At Dungeness we used to get onto the cutter there, and of course the ships came down on the tide – it was all tidal work – and when we arrived on the pilot cutter, the boat would come off for us, perhaps six o'clock in the morning or something like that, because we had all arrived during the night, and a fisherman used to come off and take us ashore at Dungeness, a chap by the name of Bates. Although he was a fisherman down there he was an outsider because he wasn't local. Even though there was frost on the ground he would come off in bare feet. At one time, not when I was there, one of the pilots told me the bung came out of the boat and they had to put it in pretty quickly. We would go ashore on the shingle, and then Bates used to drive us up to Gravesend. He had a little wagon there.

However, in 1967, when the large tankers started to come in, they moved back permanently to Folkestone, where we had a purpose-built tower built. It was very posh compared with what we had had before down at Dungeness. When the big tankers came in they asked for volunteer pilots to do them because nobody had any experience of them – so a few pilots volunteered, but gradually over a couple of years the younger ones came in because the older ones couldn't manage it. When those big tankers were in ballast the pilot ladder was about thirty to forty foot long. I was inducted onto them but fortunately I never had an accident on them.

One ship that I was on, when you turned it, the stern was proud of the buoy, and I had an occasion when I had to turn the ship to go out and I was doing this manoeuvre between the mooring dolphins and we had two tugs aft and two tugs forward and the line to the starboard tug broke. That was exciting. Even so I managed to achieve it without a mash-up.

The first winter that I was a pilot I had a Costa Rican ship with chain-and-rod steering gear. I had this wretched thing and the compass was out. In the river there was very often fog and you could only just about see the shore, but once you got to Gravesend it cleared somewhat. The ship only had a magnetic compass. I did have a collision then. The ship was an absolute bag of rust. Twenty years later she was still running – I couldn't believe it. There was a strike on at the time and the ships were all anchored in Gravesend Reach in line abreast, with the channel in the middle, dense fog, and as you went down you could see the lights on the anchored ships vaguely, one of them perhaps. I was totally reliant on the compass and the compass was wrong, quite a bit actually. The net result was that the first ship I came into contact with was the *Stella* something or other, a German ship with a bulbous bow. It was ebb tide so they were all heading up towards me. The barges only had one masthead light and I thought it was one of those coming in on my course but it wasn't, it was a vessel at anchor. The Chief Engineer was most annoyed because it tipped all his wardrobe into his toilet. When the collision happened, of course, I had had the wheel put hard a port to swing the ship away from her and the net result of that was that with the chain-and-rod steering it jammed. So there I was, with the wheel hard a port basically traipsing down the river. By going astern and going ahead, and going astern, I managed to go in between the two columns and eventually managed to drop the anchor. I suppose she then went into London for repairs. That was my first accident. Other than that I had one occasion when we got a rope round the propeller because they told me it was all clear and it wasn't – and once you get a rope around the propeller it winds up very quickly. From that point of view I had a very fortunate career. ❯

Edward Lloyd's coffee house in eighteenth-century London was where insurers used to meet for the latest news of marine casualties. (It is hard to imagine Starbucks or Costa playing a similar role today!) However, many ship owners have partially replaced traditional insurance with membership of one of the Protection and Indemnity Clubs. Peter Davidson recalls his time as a surveyor for the UK Club:

❠ I finished my 'official' marine career as a Ship Inspector with the UK P&I Club, the largest of all the P&I Clubs and managed by Thomas Miller. The Protection and Indemnity Clubs are all mutually owned by the ship owners, who are members of the club, and they are a very essential part of merchant shipping – and outside the shipping industry receive little credit for the excellent work they do. How many people know, for example, that a P&I Club was responsible for all the salvage work involved removing the MSC *Napoli* from the beach at Branscombe, work that lasted 924 days.

The UK Club was the only one to employ ship inspectors directly, and there were six of us. All had sailed as Master and had a variety of experience in the shipping industry. There were two ports which always had an Inspector in residence, namely Rotterdam and Houston, with the former covering not just Rotterdam but all the other Continental ports as well. Houston covered all the US Gulf ports including those in the Mississippi and generally included quite a lot of domestic flying courtesy of South West Airlines. Other parts of the world visited on a regular basis were Japan, Singapore, the US West Coast in the grain season, South Africa, the Arabian Gulf, with other parts of the world visited on request or as a result of a bad experience.

Armed with a mobile phone and a computer, we found out by various means which of the Club's ships were coming into the ports covered and submitted them to our managers, Thomas Miller, in London. Thomas Miller would then advise us which ships they would like inspecting, and would notify the owners accordingly. These lists were updated on a daily basis with a written report transmitted back to London after the ship had been visited. Rotterdam and Antwerp were comparatively simple in relation to finding ships, the Mississippi and Japan quite challenging. I remember the heavens opening coming off one ship at an anchorage in the Mississippi and getting absolutely soaked, so much so that I had to change back into my boiler suit at the launch station before getting into the car and driving to the next ship – where the Captain kindly put my wet gear to dry in the galley. Japan was the ultimate challenge, with major language problems, but surprisingly very few if any mishaps were reported – which says a lot for body language and common sense!

The time spent on board varied. Some ships had everything ready for you and officers allocated to escort you round, with others being the complete reverse. The galley was always inspected before accepting an invitation for lunch! All the Inspectors were asked to pay special attention to the human element on board, and we used to try and assess the number of hours some officers and crew were working, as fatigue was and still is a factor to be concerned about. The final question we always had to answer was, 'Would you sail in this ship?' and often by saying 'no' we did think we had a positive impact improving standards and safety on board. Whilst some owners struggled to comply with the implementation of new regulations, some, even with reduced crews, did a fantastic job and became the benchmark for the others. 9

Early on in his seagoing career, Malcolm Borland decided that he wanted to become an Examiner of Master and Mates. His early career was spent with P&O, but as soon as he had become a Master Mariner, instead of going back to sea right away, he carried on studying for a further year before obtaining his Extra Master's certificate. This was then followed by two years in command in Everards, the coastal and short sea traders. He recalls:

6 Life was pretty tough in Everards, particularly in winter, so after six months in command I applied to the Ministry, to see

what would happen. They wrote back saying, 'Thank you very much for your application, but we think that you need more time in command.' So after twelve months I applied again and got exactly the same letter back. After eighteen months I applied yet again – and I got exactly the same letter back. About that time we were in Belfast, and I vaguely knew the Examiner and Surveyor there, Ray Newbury, who I have got to know much better since. I went and had a chat with him. I knew there was an interview with the Civil Service Commissioners and asked him, 'What's the interview like?' He replied, 'Don't you worry about that. They just ask you what newspaper you read.' That kept me reasonably happy, and I didn't bother very much about the interview.

After twenty-two months in command, the Ministry wrote to me saying, 'If you are of the same mind and would like to apply, please do.' So that was a good enough sign and I left the ship, taking two years' worth of leave. Then came the interview. I wasn't too worried. Newbury said there wasn't much to worry about. I walked into the interview room. There were three people the other side of the table. One, the chairman, I found out afterwards was the Civil Service Commissioner, another I discovered was a psychologist, and the third was Captain Topley, who was then Principal Examiner of Masters and Mates. He asked nearly all the questions and started at the top end of the calculus for Extra Master. Well, after three years with Everards, I had forgotten all about that completely. I really floundered, and Topley gave me a very, very rough forty-five minutes. I went home and said to my wife, 'Well, after all of that, all that effort to get Extras, three years with Everards, and now I have blown it completely.' A week later I got a letter to say that I had passed. I nearly fell off my chair.

I was told to report to the Central Board of Examiners, at the then Ministry of Transport, St Christopher's House, Southwark. I arrived on the Monday morning. There were six examiners. Two examiners sat opposite each other at large desks. I found myself sitting opposite Captain Topley.

In the interim period since the interview he had reached sixty, retired, and had come back as an Examiner on the

Central Board in a disestablished capacity. When the coffee break arrived, I said to Topley, 'I'm very surprised to be sitting here.' He replied, 'Why is that?' I said, 'Well, at the interview you crucified me.' He laughed and said, 'We knew you would have forgotten all about any calculus you might have learnt. We wanted to see what you were like under a bit of pressure.'

A few things about the Central Board may be of interest. How we operated, how we worked. There were six Examiners, and two Senior Examiners, one who supervised the Central Board, and the other who worked in the area of the equivalence of academic qualifications to certificates of competency. In overall charge were the Deputy Principal Examiner and the Principal Examiner. We ran some ten different examinations: Second Mate, Mate, Master Foreign-going; Master and Mate, Home Trade; Compass Adjuster; Yacht Master Coastal; Yacht Master Ocean; Second Hand Fisherman, Skipper Fisherman; plus three Extra Master examinations a year. Some of the larger ports – London, Liverpool, Southampton – had the examinations for the main grades twice a month. The smaller ports were once a month. There was a continuous stream. It was rather like an examination factory, setting and marking papers. For all the exams, other than Extra Master, we had a stack of some 120 papers for each subject. We would use the same paper more than once, perhaps eighteen months apart. But every year we would be replacing some old papers with new. There were occasions, however, when something happened such as the Admiralty changing the layout of the Nautical Almanac or the presentation of the tide tables. That would make us have to replace all the relevant questions because they had to be in the same format as current Admiralty publications. That could cause us a lot of work. We ran examinations four weeks in every month. If we had five Mondays in the month, then we had a week free of marking. We would prepare new papers or work on Extra Masters.

Candidates would start on the Monday morning and expect the results, except in very busy weeks, on the Friday. The way we achieved that is quite different from the way I suspect academic examinations are marked today. You did not get marks for what you got right, you got marks deducted for what you got wrong. Take navigation, for example – if you made an error in principle, say by applying the correction for Venus the wrong way, you lost 50% of the marks, while an arithmetical error lost 10% of the marks. And the pass mark for both navigation and chart work (chart work was marked in the ports, not by the Central Board) was 70%. The overall mark for the exam was also 70%. For other papers the pass mark was 50%, but you had to get 70% overall to pass. The Monday morning examination was Navigation – let's take Second Mate's as an example. If you did not get 60% in Navigation you failed. We did not mark the rest of your papers. They were never looked at. If you got between 60 and 70% you were marked as a 'ringer' and we carried on marking your papers – but three ringers and you were out.

At the end of the week, if you had a few marks less than 700 plus a ringer or two, we would go back and invariably find another few marks to pass you. The only way we were able to cope with the numbers is by that quite drastic method of marking. I think few people realised that a lot of their papers were not even looked at. But there were frequent exams. People who failed could go up again the next fortnight. If you failed twice, I think, you had to wait a month or so. But you could have any number of attempts. The record, I think was someone who actually did pass after twenty-three attempts for Second Mate.

That is how we managed the marking, which in some respects was quite tough. But what we were interested in was the correct answer. For a question containing two star sights, for example, we wanted the correct position. If you got that you got 100%. If you made a couple of errors of principle – say you applied the index error the wrong way or plotted the intercept 'towards' when it should be 'away' – no marks at all. In the area of navigation and chart work what mattered was getting the correct position. I was about seven years on the Central Board, in two separate spells, and never had a single candidate appeal against failing in that time. Today when you see GCSE 'O' or 'A' level results published I read that thousands of people appeal. We never had a single appeal in the seven years when I was there. Perhaps that is an indication that people knew and accepted it when they had failed – a different culture in those days.

For Extra Master new papers were prepared for each examination, three exams a year. The exams were moderated externally. On my first spell on the Central Board I set the navigation and nautical astronomy paper. The external moderator was a Professor William Smart, Professor of Astronomy at Glasgow University. He was at one stage the author or editor of the *Admiralty Manual of Navigation*. I never met him, but we used to correspond a lot, and as the 'mad professor' he always used to write his comments on the back of a laundry or shopping list or something like that. He was a rather an eccentric character, but extremely clever in the area of navigation and nautical astronomy.

Looking back, there is one story that is worth retelling, At times, particularly just before the summer holidays or before Christmas, we would have a lot of candidates in London, possibly seventy or eighty. Examiners were pulled from the Survey Office and the Central Board to do orals. So we could have four or five examiners doing the orals simultaneously. The Senior Examiner in Dock Street was a Captain Lewis, and he used to draw up the list of examiners and candidates showing the time of the orals. He used to give this list to the porter, whose job was to pin it up in the waiting room. Candidates would arrive to see which examiner they had and the time of their orals. What this porter was doing when we were very busy, and there were several examiners on the go, was not pinning up the list – so the candidate would have to go up to him and ask him which examiner he had. Let us imagine for a moment this candidate had Captain Smith. Now there was one examiner, Captain Wallace, who was rather unpopular. Actually a very competent examiner, but he was somewhat gruff, and candidates tried to avoid Wallace if they possibly could. So a candidate coming up to the porter would ask him, 'Who've I got?' The porter would take out the list from his pocket and say, 'Oh, you've got Wallace.' Now the candidate didn't have Wallace at all. He had Smith. And he would say, 'Oh that's terrible, terrible. Can't you do anything about it?' And the porter would say, 'Well, for a small consideration I'll see if I can switch you.' And he was pocketing a fiver or so each time. The candidate always had Smith. So the porter wasn't changing anything. If however the candidate did actually have Wallace the porter would say, 'Well, I can't do anything about that, it is cast in stone. You've got Wallace.' But he was making a tidy little profit, certainly on busy weeks when there were several examiners on the go. Anyway it all came to light in the end and he got the sack. But it just shows you mankind's ingenuity! **9**

Malcolm Borland then transferred to the Administrative Branch of the Civil Service, but found that his involvement with seafarers was not over.

6 After my second spell on the Central Board of Examiners as the Senior Examiner, I then moved to the administrative side of the Civil Service where you tend to change jobs every three or four years – the qualification for being an administrator is to be thrown in at the deep end. But it so happened that I had two posts as an administrator which actually did bring me back into contact with ships and seafarers. The first of those was when I headed a section in the Department that looked after employment matters concerning seafarers. I was in that post for three years which coincided with two ILO conferences in Geneva. The ILO is the International Labour Organization, somewhat equivalent to IMO but on the labour, rather than the safety side. There are specific ILO Conventions and Recommendations concerning seafarers. That is probably because seafarers are in many senses vulnerable. They are taken all over the world, they sometimes fall sick, they sometimes miss their ship. The history of the treatment of seafarers is not particularly good. Even today you get cases where the owner has gone bust and the crew, often of mixed nationality, are abandoned with no food or wages.

While I was in this post there were these two ILO conferences. Now, why two conferences within three years? Well, there was the preliminary conference and then the main conference. I always wondered why it was necessary to have two conferences on the same subject matter. The alleged reason was that the first conference was supposed to be preparing the ground for the second conference. I think all it did really was to add to delegates' air miles, but that's the way these international organisations work at times.

The ILO is what they call a tripartite body. You have governments in the middle, the unions on one side, and the employers on the other. Most of the preparatory work for these conferences fell to me, which kept me quite busy. There were four subjects on the agenda: one was a Recommendation about young seafarers but the main item was a Convention about labour issues on flag-of-convenience ships. After adoption of this Convention I understand it was combined with the IMO Convention on substandard ships, which brought the two aspects, safety and labour issues, together.

In addition to all of that, during my time we redrafted the Repatriation Regulations, which are quite interesting and complicated because when seamen get left abroad, who pays to bring them home? It is quite often a bone of contention. We also reviewed the voting arrangements for seafarers. But there was a lot of casework as well. Quite amusing times but also sometimes rather tragic – Jolly Jack abroad can get himself into a few difficulties. I will mention a few cases.

First, a not very pleasant one. There was a British ship in Jeddah, Saudi Arabia, and there was a fight on the ship between two seamen, one of whom was British and the other Arab. In the course of this fight the Arab seafarer dropped dead. The Saudi police came aboard and arrested the British seaman. An autopsy was conducted in Saudi on the dead man, which concluded that he had died as a direct result of the fight. The British seaman was jailed and charged with murder. The British Embassy in Saudi were concerned on two grounds – firstly, there were some doubts about the accuracy of the Saudi autopsy, and secondly, of course, the penalty for murder in Saudi was chopping your head off, or something equally drastic, which wouldn't have gone down very well in the UK.

So, at much expense, we arranged for a leading UK pathologist to go out to Saudi Arabia, where they had kept the body on ice, to conduct another autopsy. He came to the conclusion that the man didn't die from the blows he had received in the fight, but he had some inherent weakness. I can't remember the medical details now, but his conclusion was that the fight was not the direct cause of death. There was a trial, and we sent the UK pathologist out again to give evidence and had to employ counsel. The British seaman was acquitted. The Embassy provided him with his airline ticket home. He was arriving at Heathrow on a Sunday afternoon. So I arranged for one of my staff to go to Heathrow to provide him with a rail ticket to where he lived, I think it was somewhere on the north-east coast, and a cash advance to tide him over till he got home. On the Monday morning I went into work and said to the fellow who had gone to Heathrow, 'How did you get on?' 'Absolutely terrible,' he said. 'This chap arrived, steaming drunk, abusive, violent, all sorts of hassle. After all our efforts to get him acquitted it's destroyed my faith in mankind.'

A more amusing case concerned a Parliamentary Question (PQ). One of the tasks of being an Administrator is that you have to deal with PQs. Those for a written answer are not usually much of a problem, but PQs for oral answer can be. The question itself is often quite innocuous, but the MP who asks the question then has the right of asking a supplementary. And the sting is always in the supplementary. The job of the civil servant is to try to ascertain what underlies the question – what the supplementary is likely to be – and to arrange a range of possible supplementaries, with answers, for the Minister.

Parliamentary Questions in those days used to come in a bright yellow folder, and I came back from lunch one day to find this bright yellow folder on my desk. A Parliamentary Question for oral answer had been put down by Clement Freud, the MP for Ely.

The question was, How many British seamen on British ships had been convicted under Section – I can't remember the number, let's say 28 – of the Sexual Offences Act of 19... – again I can't remember the date, so let's say 1967.[24] Well, I

---

24. The Act in question was indeed the Sexual Offences Act 1967.

didn't know that I had any responsibility whatsoever for that Act, and I had no idea at all what the question was about or what was underlying it. My first thought was to go down to file registry, back a good few years, and see if we had any old files about the Act in question. Well, file registry managed to come up with quite a stack of files. Delving into these – some quite interesting reading, actually – I started to discover something of what the PQ was all about.

The Sexual Offences Act had started life as a Private Member's Bill put down by Leo Abse, who was a Labour MP for a South Wales constituency. It was all about making homosexual acts between consenting adults, in private, no longer a criminal offence. This Private Member's Bill was taken up by the government and it eventually became law. However, there was an exception in the Act, whereby such acts would remain criminal offences for seafarers aboard British ships. That was to protect young cabin boys and the like.

So I now knew the background, but I was still quite in the dark as to why Clement Freud had put down this question and what lay behind it. I still had no idea what the supplementary was likely to be, let alone possible answers. There used to be about ten or twelve days notice of PQs coming up for answer, and I was several days trying to ascertain, without any success, what it was all about. And then I had an almighty stroke of luck. We used to get the Order Paper for PQs circulated well in advance. Your Minister would be on about once a fortnight, but you could see on the Order Paper the questions down for other Ministers. And I saw there that the day after our Minister was due to answer his PQ, the Secretary of State for Defence had virtually the same question from Clement Freud, asking how many members of the armed forces had been convicted under another section of the Sexual Offences Act. When you looked at that section, there was virtually the same exemption there for the armed services as there was for the merchant service.

So the route to solving my problems appeared to be to get in touch with the Ministry of Defence to find out who was responsible for homosexual matters and answering their question. That resulted in an amusing three-quarters of an hour on the telephone with lots of giggling from the telephonists, but I eventually found the right chap and I explained I had discovered that, like me, he had this PQ to answer. 'Do you know what it is all about?' I asked. 'Oh, yes, it's all about CHE,' he replied. All I could think of was Che Guevara. 'No, no, nothing to do with Che Guevara,' he said. 'It's all about CHE. CHE, you know what CHE is?' 'No,' I replied. 'It's the Campaign for Homosexual Equality,' he explained, 'that's what it is.' So I said, 'What is it all about?' 'Well,' he said, 'I am most certain that we have no cases where our exception has been used to convict people. The CHE argument is, "If you are not using the section, why do you want to keep it?" They want to get rid of the exception altogether. That's what it is all about. They've been on to us and now they have woken up to you.' 'Oh, have they asked this question before?' I enquired. 'Oh, yes,' he said, 'they ask it every six months. It comes up regularly.' In the expectation that all my problems were about to be resolved, I asked, 'What answers do you give?' 'Oh, it's quite simple,' he replied, 'we just tell them to bugger off.'[25] 9

The Honourable Company of Master Mariners is one of the 108 livery companies of the City of London. Many of the livery companies trace their history back over six hundred years. In the Middle Ages they controlled entry and training to a trade or craft, set the standards, and looked after the interests of their members. A number of the original companies still perform some of these functions. For example, the Fishmongers still have regulatory responsibilities at Billingsgate fish market.

However, the history of the Honourable Company of Master Mariners goes back less than a hundred years. The initiative for the formation of the Company came from Mr Robert Chadwick (later Sir

---

25. Contrary to contemporary practice in the armed services, there was no discrimination against homosexuals in the merchant navy. During the war gay crew members of the merchant navy served as gallantly and died as bravely as their straight counterparts.

Robert Chadwick-Burton), the Member of Parliament for Wallasey, who suggested that Master Mariners were entitled to form a Guild or Company very much on the lines of the City of London livery companies. His vision was realised on 25 June 1926 with the formation of the Company of Master Mariners. In 1932 the Court of Aldermen of the City of London conferred the status of Livery on the Company, so enabling the Company to participate in the corporate life of the City. This, the first new livery company for 240 years, became the seventy-eighth in order of precedence.

Uniquely among the city livery companies, the Master Mariners is entitled to use the prefix 'Honourable', the others being 'Worshipful' (a title originating in the Middle Ages meaning 'deserving of respect'). His Majesty King George V had been very moved by the great loss of life that resulted from the sinking of so many merchant ships during the First World War, and in recognition of the sacrifices made at that time he accorded the Company the right to use the title 'Honourable'.

The core function of this modern livery company is as a professional institution, looking after the interests of Master Mariners in particular and seafarers in general.

Anthony Davis was Master for the year 2008/09, and here he gives an outline of what was involved:

❝ This last bit is more about the Honourable Company of Master Mariners and my role as Master in 2008/09. After I left the sea I joined the Honourable Company mainly to maintain my connection with my seagoing past, having gone off and become an accountant by that stage. I took an interest in the affairs and in due course I became a Warden – and then Master in 2008 to 2009. Being Master is a fairly heavy job, heavy in the sense that it is more or less a full-time occupation for twelve months. It's not just wining and dining around the City, although there is plenty of that. There is a range of other bits and pieces that come with it.

The Honourable Company is a livery company of the City of London, and livery halls are supposed to be within the City. The *Wellington* only just qualifies, as technically we are in Westminster, but our rear anchors cross the boundary into the City, and there is an old tradition that if your footings are within the City, you qualify. So our anchors are our footings in a marine sense. It is also a professional body, it's a curious mix of both, and it's in the latter role that some interesting bits and pieces come up.

We are very interested in technical matters relating to the sea, safety at sea, ships and Master Mariners in particular. And one of the things that struck me in recent years was the criminalisation of seafarers in general and Masters in particular. There was the incident off the north-west coast of Spain where a ship was denied shelter with the result that there was oil pollution – almost certainly generated by lack of shelter – and the Master was then charged with the criminal offence of polluting.

A similar case came up during my year as Master with a ship called the *Hebe Spirit*. This was a ship which was at anchor in a recognised anchorage off a port in South Korea. Within this anchorage there was a crane barge, being towed by a tug. The tug lost control of its tow, which hit the anchored ship causing damage both to the *Hebe Spirit* and to the crane. The Master of the *Hebe Spirit* was subsequently arrested for causing an accident. Now it struck me that because he was at anchor, he was basically charged with not getting out of the way fast enough. Bearing in mind that he was at a reasonably exposed anchorage, and the tug and tow at one moment appeared to be passing him reasonably safely and the next moment it was veering

Anthony Davis's 'Master's Ticket'.

off course and, even if he had been able to work the miracle of shifting his ship out of the way ... It struck me as almost bizarre that a man whose ship is at anchor could achieve this. Anyway in due course, the Captain, who I think was an Indian national, was duly arrested. He was refused bail and held in jail for, I think, a period in excess of eighteen months. His lawyers were trying (a) to get him out on bail and (b) to garner support. Anyway, I received a letter from the lawyers and it struck me that this was exactly the sort of thing we should get involved with, so I wrote a fairly strong letter of support. Eventually he was released on bail and in the end he was acquitted. But the man had several years taken out of his life for what seemed to be almost ... I found it difficult to believe that he could be guilty in the first place, and even if he was, in the circumstances the blame, if any, must be substantially towards the tug and its barge, who were local anyway, so must have known the waters much better than him. Anyway, that was one of the interesting technical bits, if you like.

Dealing with other matters, there were two events which struck me in particular. On one evening I had to go to a church service and a reception held by the Imperial Society of Knights Bachelor at St Paul's with the Queen and the Duke of Edinburgh. A very grand occasion where you were mixing with the cream of society. Two days later we went to a concert at Queen Victoria Seamen's Rest down in Poplar. Those of you who, like me, did their Second Mate's at King Ted's will know the Queen Vic. It's about as far removed from St Paul's and a reception with the Queen as you could get. But you get these contrasting things where you go to some very grand occasions and a couple of days later you move to the absolute opposite extreme. But the Queen Victoria, it's much less grand – in my day it was a Seamen's Home. Often, mainly for ships visiting the Pool, where you paid off, seamen might stay there for a week or, if you were doing a course at King Ted's you might stay there for two or three months. But it was basically a home from home for seamen. These days the maritime content is down to about twenty or twenty-five per cent. It's more dealing with local social problems in the area – but then the docks are no longer, they are now docklands rather than docks, and so they have a first-class site but it's now in the wrong place for dealing with ships and seamen. You get these very sharp contrasts between the top end and the bottom end. **9**

With just a few exceptions, all the contributors to this book are members of the Honourable Company of Master Mariners.

10 • Those left behind

By the time he had obtained his Master's certificate, the young deck officer would be around twenty-seven years old. He might also be married.

This chapter gives an opportunity for the wives, and they generally were wives in those far-off days, to tell something of what it was like to be married to a merchant seaman. The memories so far have been those of the deck officer, from the time that he went to sea right through to the years in command and beyond, but the experiences of the deck officers' wives would have been little different from those of the wives of other members of the crews of the ships on which their husbands were sailing.

In the early part of the period covered by these chronicles few, if any, shipping companies allowed wives to sail with their husbands. However, over the succeeding years the climate gradually changed. The first tentative steps were to allow an officer's wife to stay on board when her husband was on duty in a home port. This was then followed by permitting wives to accompany their husbands when the ship was on passage in coastal waters, until, around the 1960s, it became quite usual for wives to make ocean passages, at least for part of the year.

For those married to men serving in the passenger and cargo liner companies there was always the advantage that the likely length of the round voyage would be known and could be measured in months rather than years. But with both tramps and tankers the length of the voyage would usually be uncertain, and it could be as long as two years. There were areas around the main ports where seafaring communities were to be found, and here there was often support from both family and a wider social network, but nevertheless many wives, especially those with children, had to accept responsibility very early. Six of these wives tell their stories in this chapter.

When ships were loading or discharging in a home port, often with a relief crew, they normally relied on their auxiliary engines for the generation of electricity. However, there were, inevitably, times when the ship was in port but not working cargo. When this occurred, owners often reduced the manning level, and shore power was connected to supply the very much reduced needs of the idle ship. At a time (the early 1950s) when, in the majority of companies, wives were not welcomed aboard, Peter Richards-Jones took advantage of this relatively quiet period and obtained permission to invite his young wife to spend the night aboard. It didn't work out quite as he had planned, as Mary Richards-Jones recalls:

❦ Now I was very keen to go on board a ship, but Peter said, 'No, only the Captains' wives are allowed on board ships to stay the night.' And I said, 'Why can't I go?' and he said, 'Well, there might be some opportunity.' Then, soon afterwards, he went into the King George V Dock in London, and he phoned me up and said, 'Would you like to come up to the ship and stay the night? And then I'll come home for the weekend.' So I said, 'Oh, can I?' and he said, 'Yes, I tell you what, you get the Tube and I'll come and meet you there, and then we'll go on board.'

And we met up and we must have gone on a bus, but we got there and it was very cold. Must have been winter time, because I know there was a very strong wind and it's all open

Peter and Mary Richards-Jones

there. And he said, 'Come on, we'll go aboard,' and we got on and he took me down to his cabin and I told him, 'What a miserable place,' and he said, 'Well, we've got a fire, there's an electric fire there.' It began to warm up in a while, so I said, 'What are we going to do to eat?' 'Oh, you can't eat on board,' he said, 'there's no means of eating. They've got biscuits and maybe the odd sandwich or something, but you won't get anything else.' So I said, 'Well, I haven't had any tea or anything. I must have something.' So he said, 'I'll tell you what we'll do. We'll go ashore and we'll find a little café and we'll have sausage, egg and chips, or something like that'. So I said, 'That's fine,' and we certainly went ashore and I can't remember what we had, but had a meal, and when we walked back it was perishing. So we got on board and he said, 'Are you still cold?' and I said, 'Blooming cold,' and he said, 'I'll go and get you some extra blankets.' So he went down, I don't know where he got them from, some other cabin or something, but he brought me these blankets and he said, 'Wrap yourself up, because I've got to go up on the bridge, we are going to have to move the ship.'

So he disappeared and left me with these blankets and then, presently, the electric fire went out, and then the lights went out, and the only lights that I could see were coming in through the porthole. So I thought, 'What is it?' and of course we were moving. He was moving the ship. I wasn't involved in that, but by the time he came back to me, I was really fed up. I said, 'I'm sat here, and I'm wrapped up in these blankets and I'm still frozen.' 'It was only four hours,' he said. 'Well,' I said, 'four hours is too long.' So – I can't remember now, but we must have crawled in together into the bed.

I can't remember then, whether we left in the morning or sometime the next day. He would remember what he was actually doing, but I was only on the receiving end of it, sitting down in the cabin waiting for him to come down. This excitement of being on board, you know, the romance, it all fizzled out, and I think we went home the next morning to our flat at my mum's. 9

Anne Jewell married Terry in the late 1950s, when company regulations regarding wives on ships in the British merchant navy were very
much more stringent than in later years – and in stark contrast to the
more relaxed rules on some foreign-flagged ships. Her account high-
lights the more restricted lifestyle of the period. She recalls:

❦ We met when Terry was fifteen and he was going to the
Plymouth School of Navigation, and I was going to school
and we went on the same bus – so that was how we met, and
we developed a friendship and went out together a lot in the
summer holidays, and then, on Terry's sixteenth birthday, he
signed his indentures. He went to sea very soon after that,
two or three weeks I guess – he went away and he was away
for thirteen months. I wasn't terribly impressed, but we cor-
responded and he came home on leave and came to see me
and was full of what a wonderful life it was and it was what
he wanted to do for ever. I felt there is not much joy here, so
I didn't actually write to him so much after that, and when he
came back the next time he said to me, 'You didn't write to me
very much.' I told him that I couldn't see that we were going
to go anywhere with this friendship, but anyway every time he
came home we went out and we had good fun and in time it
became quite clear that we were going to stick together. I must
have been twenty when we got engaged, which was after he
had completed his apprenticeship and got his Second Mate's.
He was home for quite a time because he had to sit it more
than once, so I guess that was when we got engaged, and we
got married eighteen months later.

I could go and stay with him while the ship was in port, but
I couldn't even do a coastal trip. It was against the company
rules. I went, even after I had Beverley I went and stayed with
him, and he made up a cot in his cabin, and the chippy boarded it in. She was only three months old and I had gone out to
Holland to meet him because he didn't think that the ship was
going to come home to the UK, and so it was the only chance I
would have had to see him.

He had seen Beverley when she was just born and was a
few days old, and then he went away, so he was keen to see
her. So I went out – I went with another wife. She had travelled

Anne Jewell

Terry Jewell

before and had been round the Continent. I don't know whether I would have gone on my own, because in those days you didn't travel quite so much. My father certainly didn't think I should be going, anyway, with the baby, but I did. She was fine. It was a wonderful time because they all made such a fuss, particularly of the baby. The Captain and his wife would baby-sit so that we could go ashore for an evening.

I can't remember what the crew was, but the officers were all British. They were a nice bunch of people and I enjoyed it. We joined the ship in Rotterdam and they had to go to Amsterdam, and the Captain said, 'I'm sorry I can't let you do this.' It wasn't very far, and he said, 'I could close my eyes to you being on board but I can't take a risk with the baby.' So they put me on the train to Amsterdam, and the agent picked me up and took me to a B&B where I stayed until the next morning when he arrived to fetch me with a rose – and then we went down to the ship, which had arrived. I loved Amsterdam. We had a lovely time there. After that I went to places like Birkenhead, which is not as nice as Amsterdam!

We lived in Plymouth. We had all four children while we were still living in Plymouth. Eighteen months after the first baby I had the next one, and nineteen months after that I had another. That wasn't quite what we had planned at the time. So there we were, and still young, with three children. That was quite hard work. We lived then in an upstairs converted flat, so all the time I was up and down the stairs with the babies. It wasn't ideal. It was then that I started to say, 'Could you consider coming ashore?' It had become impossible to go and see him, even in the UK, with three children. 9

Eunice Elphick was living in Singapore when she met her husband. After a whirlwind romance she had an unusual honeymoon in Japan before finding herself the only woman aboard a cargo ship trading on the China coast.

❦ The naval base, where my mother and father lived, was adjacent to the causeway that led to Malaya so I got a job in the police station there and I used to walk across the causeway, which was about half a mile long. It seemed a long way at the time, but looking back I was wearing high heels and a skirt so I don't think it was really very far. I worked looking after the confidential files in the police station there. I didn't stay there very long because I had to work weekends because it was a Muslim country, so I finally left because all my friends were having a whale of a time.

It was difficult to get a job, so I went back to Hong Kong and lived with a girlfriend of mine and her family for about two or three months. Then I went back to Singapore and almost immediately met Peter. In fact it was the first weekend that I was back. I contacted a friend and she said 'I'm pleased you're back, come and have a weekend with us – we are all going to the beach and we shall have a lovely time. This guy has got a little motorboat and he is going to take us all across to this little island.' That happened to be Peter, and we never looked back after that. We married very, very quickly because my mother and father were due to go back to England and my mother said, 'Well, I'm not leaving you out here unmarried.'

Just before Peter had met me he had decided to leave the sea and take a job with the Singapore Harbour Board, so he was just about to leave anyway – but then the people who employed him, as one of their ships had broken its crankshaft in Japan and the captain had died, wanted Peter to go there and supervise the repairs and stand by until the ship was seaworthy again and bring her back . So I went with him. We had a wonderful honeymoon. We stayed in a lovely hotel because we couldn't stay on the ship because it was in dry dock. We stayed there for three months, and it was really lovely. Then we came back via China.

I loved being on the ship – I was the only woman on board. On the ship coming back there was one thing that was quite funny. We were all sitting round and somebody came charging up and said, 'There's a fire in the hold.' Everybody was climbing out, but Peter, being the Captain I suppose, thinking that it was his responsibility, climbed into the hold and I remember standing thinking, 'Oh gosh, I've only just got married to this man and he's going to go and fight this fire in the hold.' Anyway he put it out quite quickly – and it probably wasn't quite as bad as they thought – and it was all OK.

We came back via some ports on the Chinese coast, including Tianjin. The Communists of course were very prominent then and we had Red Guards on board the ship. When we did go ashore we went into a sort of club place and all round the walls it said 'Down With American Imperialists.' You really had to be very careful because it wasn't a nice place to be. I remember once, Peter must have been on the bridge or something and I was sitting in the day cabin – it must have been in the summer because it was quite hot and I had the curtain drawn across. I could hear somebody arguing, so I peeped through the crack and there was a Red Guard arguing with the Chief Officer. As I watched, all of a sudden the Chief Officer, whose name was Henry by the way, put his hand on the shoulder of the Red Guard to emphasise his point and immediately the Red Guard said 'You hit me!' They arrested Henry and took him ashore. I said to Peter, 'But he didn't hit him. I was watching. They didn't know I was watching.' 'Don't tell anybody, they wouldn't want a witness,' said Peter. He

Eunice Elphick

Peter Elphick

went ashore and was able to get him back, but we all had to go into the public room there, on the ship, and the Chief Officer had to make a public apology to the Red Guard. That wasn't very nice at all. It was a horrible thing to have to do.

Then we went on from there and stopped in Hong Kong and then on to Singapore again. I almost didn't get off at Singapore, because my passport was in my maiden name and my parents had left so I had to stay on board while Peter went ashore to sort out my passport. **9**

The attitude of shipping companies towards having wives aboard ship had changed dramatically by the time that Ann Gibb experienced life aboard ship as the wife of the Master of a large cruise liner.

6 I'm Ann Gibb and I am the wife of Ian Gibb who was the Master of the *Canberra* when we got married, so my story is probably not typical of many wives – because by the time we married I was already independent. I was forty and my life was a little bit different, because I wasn't even used to having a hus-band at home, so being separated, although we missed each other, perhaps wasn't quite the same. In those days – and we are talking 1978/79 – wives had only just been allowed to go to

Anne and Ian Gibb

sea on the large passenger ships, certainly with P&O, and it was only the wives of the senior officers, and we were allowed to go for one month each year. This gradually changed over the years until all spouses were allowed to accompany their husband or wife at sea and the time is much less restricted.

At that time children couldn't go to sea. But I think it was very important that a wife could go to sea and see what life was like for her husband. Admittedly as a Captain of a passenger ship it was a luxurious life, and when the husbands came home what they wanted to do was relax, stay at home and eat cauliflower cheese or sausage and mash, and I think particularly some of the younger wives, who had been longing for their husband's leave, longing to go out dancing, to films, out to meals, could find it very frustrating that that was not what their husbands wanted to do the minute they came home on leave.

It was also quite difficult to organise what you did when your husband came home on leave. When we were first married and Ian went off to sea lots of people in the village – I live in a village in Wiltshire – would say to me, 'Oh, you must come to dinner when your husband comes home,' or 'Oh, you must come to lunch when your husband comes home,' and after a while I tactfully suggested that I did eat even when my husband was away, and that perhaps it would be quite good if they invited me on my own for a meal – and they were very, very generous, but it is just an automatic reaction that you wait until you've got both husband and wife.

And then children come along, and I think the men at sea are quite ambivalent because they want a wife that they can safely leave who will cope with anything that happens, but as soon as they come home they want to be master of their own house, their own destiny, so it is quite a difficult line to be competent enough but not too competent, and I can remember when our girls were quite small, Ian getting into the car and one of the girls saying, 'That's Mummy's seat.' In other words, the driving seat was Mummy's – and we had to point out that it was Daddy's as well.

Having two young children and very elderly grannies and lots of local commitments, you either count the days until your husband comes home on leave or you get involved in the local community, which I did. I didn't find it very easy to find enough time, actually, to go to sea with Ian, but I did go at least once a year for a two-week cruise, and this was usually decided by force of circumstances. It was easier to go in term time when the children could stay with friends, so it wasn't really because of the destination, it was really just because the time was right to be away.

And I love watching people at work and I found it absolutely fascinating. When I think my friends and family at home thought that I was having a luxurious life, that was not exactly the case. I was very well looked after, and we did have delicious food, but our normal day at sea – Ian's day – began at seven in the morning. He had a 'boy' who would come in and tidy up, and I never liked to lie in bed when it was delaying the activity so I, too, would get up soon after seven. We would meet for breakfast at eight and then Ian would go off to conference and I would be on my own for the whole morning doing whatever I wanted to do – there was plenty to do on the ship – and then if we were lucky we would meet at lunchtime, but Ian always liked to lunch with the passengers so that would be in the cafeteria, where we would share a table with some of the passengers. And possibly after that we might have had half an hour when we went back to the cabin or sunbathed, then we would meet up again in the evening, showering ready for the first-sitting party which started at the awful hour of half past five or six o'clock, just when it would have been nice to be on deck, get into all one's finery and go and drink Perrier water until one was drowning in Perrier water, and then the second-sitting pre-dinner parties, smiling at everybody, and then dinner and then walk around the ship and by that time it would be eleven o'clock at night, half past eleven at night, and time for bed

So although I had a great experience, I didn't necessarily see very much of Ian. People's reaction to the Captain's wife are quite interesting. In particular I found the Americans slightly trying, but I suppose I shouldn't be racist. I can remember one occasion when nobody knew who I was and there wasn't really room for me to sit down, or anything else, at the table they were at when somebody said, 'Gee, that's the Captain's wife' – and immediately I was very, very welcome – and I find that very difficult to cope with. That's not the way I am. But it was lovely, and I did visit some extremely interesting places, met some very interesting people. **9**

Towards the end of the period dealt with in this book many shipping companies allowed wives to accompany their husbands, although in practice the opportunities were often limited by family and career responsibilities. Mary Procter tells how things went badly wrong on one voyage:

6 One really dramatic story from my point of view was that I managed to contract malaria. We hadn't been taking malaria tablets because we weren't in a malaria area. We were actually off Libya, anchored about twelve miles offshore, so it must have been a rogue mosquito that had somehow reached me Anyway, that's where we think I contracted it. By the time we arrived at Bonny[26] I was feeling terrible and my husband told me I was delirious. The local doctor attended the ship. He was a big guy and was called Dr Steven Jumbo. He told us he had been to the UK to do his training but had failed to qualify. He looked down my throat and said, 'Oh, you've had your tonsils out.' I replied, 'No, they're still there' – so that did not inspire me with much confidence.

Anyway, after a bit he came to the conclusion that I had malaria, so he said, 'Oh, I had a chap on a ship last week who had malaria and I gave him an injection, but he died unfortunately.' Of course as you can imagine this was quite a cause for concern. It was decided that I had to be taken to hospital and then be repatriated. Fortunately I was airlifted by helicopter to the Shell clinic at Port Harcourt. We had only been married a few months at that stage, and my husband said goodbye to me on the ship and thought that he was never going to see me again. I spent a week in the clinic in Port Harcourt and there

---

26. In Nigeria.

Mary and Jeremy Procter

they discovered that I also had paratyphoid as well as malaria. I think the paratyphoid was contracted from water that the ship had taken on at Trieste, as it transpired later that several of the people on the ship had stomach problems. After a week in Port Harcourt I was flown in a tiny plane to Lagos. We had to land on a very narrow strip in the jungle to refuel, and fortunately the pilot said I could stay on board because of my illness. From Lagos I took a scheduled flight home.

Shell were extremely helpful whilst I was in the Port Harcourt clinic and kept my husband informed of my progress by passing the info to a Shell tanker based at Bonny whose Radio Officer then transmitted the news to the Radio Officer on my husband's ship.

It's at times like this that you realise how important it is to have good insurance, because I dread to think of the cost of my flights, treatment and hospital accommodation. However, none of this put me off travel, and I have taken further voyages at sea with my husband.

As a footnote to this story, when my husband eventually left the ship in Yugoslavia he had with him a lot of my clothing and effects that I had left on the ship. When crossing the Italian border, the customs asked him to open some cases and gave him some very strange looks when they encountered my clothing! **9**

And finally, Colette Davidson talks about her married life:

❢ I was a farmer's daughter and from a young age always wanted to be a veterinary surgeon or possibly was expected to marry a farmer – but I met Peter, and meeting him changed my whole life.

I never had any doubts about taking on a seafarer. In the area where we lived a lot of other seafaring families were also resident, so it was easy to support each other. When Peter was away I would have friends call or telephone, and many of the older more experienced wives were very supportive. I was also of an independent nature, and having lost my mother as a child I found looking after a home, managing money and all those practical things came as second nature. However, I was always ready to hand over the reins the moment Peter came home.

I can honestly say I was never lonely, because he was such a good communicator and wrote regularly in the early days, and latterly telephoned more or less daily. We always felt very close. I was very happy and very proud of him. I thought he looked wonderful in his uniform! The life suited me, as I had many interests and my own career. I was a teacher and thoroughly enjoyed my work. Peter's days at sea gave us a lot of scope for conversations, anecdotes and laughs about where he had been and the scrapes he had got into when he was younger.

Peter and Collette Davidson

He sailed with some great colleagues who were his 'family' then and are friends to this day. We have had brilliant holidays as a result of places he saw as he was going round the world and wanted to take me to share the enjoyment. We've many friends all over the world, and our Christmas list is enormous – Australia, Singapore, Hong Kong, Malaysia, Philippines, Sri Lanka and many places in America. We have people visiting who Peter met during his seafaring days or during his work with the P&I Club. So many memories. Being a seafarer's wife has been a privilege, and I am very glad that Peter enjoyed his time at sea and he knew everything was alright at home. That's the main thing. **9**

And here are Peter and Colette Davidson in the only double interview in the book. If this were to be published in the style of *Hansard*, every exchange would be followed by '(Laughter)'.

6 C. Do you remember the time, shortly after we were married, when you came into Liverpool late, at the end of one trip, and you found out you weren't going to be relieved there, you were going to have to go up to Glasgow the next day, then what did you do?

P. I remember it very well, because I decided to come home, albeit it was half past one in the morning, and I arrived home and the house was in total darkness, and I knocked at the door and no reply. I threw about half a ton of earth against the bedroom window and no reply, and I remembered that the catch on the back bedroom wasn't working, so I got the ladders out of the garage and came in through the back bedroom window, opened the bedroom door and found two figures in bed.

C. Did you realise then who the other person was?

P. No. Not initially, no. It was only when you put the light on. And I said, 'Move over and I'll jump in the middle.'

C. My sister, who had been staying the night – and in those days we only had one bed. She had to leap up and put a dressing gown on and sleep on the rocking chair for the rest of the night. **9**

Epilogue

Collecting these reminiscences has meant that one or other of the authors interviewed all the contributors, many in their own homes. Even if we had known nothing about the background of those whom we visited, it would nearly always have been obvious that at least a period of their lives had been spent at sea. Pictures of ships on the walls of a study, photographs of slim young men in uniform on the bridges of ships, framed Certificates of Competency as Master Mariner, these all indicated that not only had time been spent at sea, but that there was a desire to keep the memory of this time alive. Perhaps this extract from the interview with Christopher Laycock catches the feelings of most of those whom the two authors were privileged to meet:

❢ Moving on to the emotions of life at sea, they were many, varied and very, very pronounced on occasions. At the beginning of the voyage there was the excitement of perhaps visiting a new place that you had imagined, but you wanted to see for yourself. There were the inevitable goodbyes, which were never easy, but they were compensated for later by the big hellos and the big reunions at the end of a voyage.

From the outset I always had a great respect for the sea. I wasn't frightened of it, but I knew it needed to be respected, and sometimes when I looked at it in its more angry moments I definitely realised that this was not a force to be messed with, and was one that had to be tempered and used as best one possibly could to give yourself the easiest and safest passage.

Other emotions were visual. I remember my first sighting of Table Mountain above Cape Town. This appeared as a very clear silhouette across the horizon on my very first trip to sea, such that the famous outline was depicted very clearly just above the horizon – and it is an image that will remain with me for ever. There are those nights at sea when it is almost daylight because of the moon, when you can see for ever. There are also those disconcerting experiences of being in fog where you cannot see a horizon to relate to, such that you sometimes get a feeling of actually sailing uphill or downhill because your sense of balance has gone.

Fortunately I was never ever seasick, so heavy weather was not a problem. I did enjoy heavy weather, particularly in my younger days when I didn't have the responsibility of making sure the deck cargo was not going to disappear overboard with me being held responsible at the end of the day. I remember some of the monumental waves that you came across – you got into a trough and you looked at the crest and you thought that the ship would never get to the top of this one, but somehow you do and you come down the other side, and it is very awe-inspiring.

Another emotion or sense that is very memorable is that of sound. The sound of a howling gale, the repetitive cycle of a motor ship and its engine running twenty-four hours a day, such that when you first leave a port you can't sleep because of the noise. However, when you get into port after a ten- or twelve-day passage, and this noise is not there any more, you can't sleep for the silence. Perhaps one of the sights of nature that inspired me more than anything else at sea was watching the albatrosses in the South Atlantic. When I had spare time to watch, there would invariably be one following the ship. We all know how it manages to stay at sea for months and months on end, seemingly without moving its wings, and this was something that I could watch and watch and watch.

So there were many emotions about actually being at sea, and for one reason and another my seagoing days ended in 1979. My last appointment was as Master of one of the P&O Jetfoils running on a passenger service between St Katharine Dock in London direct to Ostend. From then on, to date, I had never actually been on a ship under way even as a passenger on a cross-channel ferry, to the best of my recollection. However, towards the end of 2007 I was offered the opportunity to join HMS *Sutherland*, our affiliated Type 23 frigate. I did wonder about the significance of the name of this vessel – the name of my first ship being the *Clan Sutherland* and the last being HMS *Sutherland* seemed a remarkable coincidence.[27]

Having left the sea in 1979, I have always remained connected with ships and the sea through commercial aspects of shipping, either through marine surveying or operating worldwide commercial interests for equipment for ships and the like, and I had never thought about missing the sea. However, HMS *Sutherland* was due to go to refit in Rosyth and the assistant clerk[28] and myself were fortunate in being able to join the ship on its delivery passage from Plymouth round to Rosyth, via the Dover Straits. We left Plymouth on a beautiful sunny day in October in the middle of the afternoon, and I have to say that I did feel some emotion upon departure while proceeding through Plymouth Sound. It came to me very quickly and very forcefully that whilst I had told myself that I did not miss being at sea, I had in fact missed the sensation of being on board a large vessel and all that goes with it more than I had been prepared to admit to myself – to the extent that I experienced a slight moistening in the corner of one eye as we were moving down Plymouth Sound. **9**

---

27. HMS *Sutherland* is affiliated to the Honourable Company of Master Mariners.

28. Of the Honourable Company of Master Mariners.

Contributors

An asterisk denotes contributors who are past Masters of the Honourable Company of Master Mariners.

Peter Adams

Born 1943. Started his seagoing career as Mate on a river barge on the River Trent, and then worked on deck before acquiring his Second Mate's certificate in 1966. He worked on coastal tankers with Ellerman and Papayanni Line, sailing to the Mediterranean, and with Tor Line and North Sea Ferries across the North Sea. He qualified as a North Sea Pilot, and worked as a pilot for five years. After a spell on the Thames with the Thames Water Authority ships, he became a Master with Ugland car carriers. Since coming ashore he has become a marine artist. He has provided all the line drawings and the cover painting for this book.

William Allen

Born 1928. He went to sea in the last year of the war as an apprentice with the British Tanker Company, but joined Clan Line in 1951 as Second Mate, after gaining his First Mate's certificate. His last ship was the *Clan Urquhart*, which he left in June 1955 when he came ashore to Milford Haven. Here he became Director of the Port Health Authority, in which post he remained until he retired.

Sir Robert Atkinson, DSC and two bars, RD

Born 1916. Apprenticed to Lambert Brothers in 1932. Joined the Royal Naval Reserve in 1938 and saw wartime service in command of corvettes and frigates in the Mediterranean, the North Atlantic and the Arctic. After the war he returned to the merchant navy in command before leaving the sea to read mathematics and mechanical engineering at London University. His subsequent career was in the steel industry, culminating with his appointment as Chairman and Chief Executive of British Shipbuilders in 1980. He was knighted in 1984 for services to shipbuilding.

Eric Beetham

Born 1939. Following pre-sea training at Warsash, he served his apprenticeship with the New Zealand Shipping Company. He then joined Shell Tankers until passing his First Mate's certificate, and then sailed in a variety of ships, under foreign flags, gaining his first command at the age of twenty-seven. Coming ashore in 1985, he became a consultant, undertaking surveys and expert witness work, and he has written and given some sixty papers for many maritime organisations. He is a Nautical Assessor for the Lord Chancellor, a past President of the Nautical Institute, a Younger Brother of Trinity House and a Fellow of the Royal Institute of Navigation, the Nautical Institute and the Royal Society of Arts. He was awarded the Merchant Navy Medal in 2009.

Malcolm Borland

Born 1934. *Worcester* cadet. Joined P&O, reached Chief Officer, Extra Master. Joined Everards, serving as Chief Officer and Master trading to the Baltic. Subsequently Nautical Surveyor and Examiner on the Central Board of Examiners and in Aberdeen, then Senior Examiner running the Central Board. Transferred to Administrative Class of the Civil Service, and worked in a variety of posts including harmonisation of company law within the EC, the accounting aspects of the Companies Acts, on loan to NATO as Head of Secretariat NATO Planning Board for Ocean Shipping, and Head of Mergers Secretariat, Office of Fair Trading. After leaving the Civil Service he became Deputy Director of the Securities and Investments Board, responsible for the regulation of the collective investment scheme product industry (unit trusts).

Stuart Bradley, CBE

Born 1936. Spent a year at the School of Navigation, Warsash, before joining the Peninsular and Oriental Steam Navigation Company as an apprentice in 1952. He remained with P&O, serving in both cargo and passenger liners, obtaining his Master's certificate in 1961, until coming ashore in 1964 to join the British Transport Docks Board in the South Wales ports as an Assistant Dockmaster. Various positions in port management in the UK culminated in his becoming Managing Director of Associated British Ports in 1988. From 1989 to 2001 he was Chairman of the Red Funnel Group. In 1990 he was awarded the CBE for services to British ports.

Anthony Braithwaite, OBE, RD *

Born 1936. HMS *Conway*, 1947/49. Apprenticed to Port Line, serving in all ranks up to Master (1966) and Assistant Marine Superintendent (1967). Port Operations, Blue Star Port Line, 1968. From 1970 he served with Cunard as Assistant Marine Adviser, setting up the Cargo Handling department and serving as Operations Manager and Fleet Personnel Manager from 1976 until early retirement in 1991. He joined the Royal Naval Reserve in 1953, being promoted to Captain in 1971 and serving as ADC to Her Majesty the Queen in 1979/80. Founder member and Fellow of the Nautical Institute. Younger Brother of Trinity House. Sometime Deputy Chairman KGFS/Seafarers UK, Vice-Chairman of the Royal Alfred Seafarers' Society, and a Director of the Merchant Navy Welfare Board.

Jeremy Carew, OBE

Born 1941. Apprenticed to the Royal Fleet Auxiliary after training at HMS *Worcester*. He joined RFA in 1960 and served with them for his entire career at sea, seeing service in various conflict zones including the Falklands in 1982 and Croatia in the 1990s. He was promoted to Master in 1984, and retired in 2001.

Simon Culshaw *

Born 1939. After training at Aberdovey Outward Bound Centre, he joined Alfred Holt and Company in 1956 for his apprenticeship. He then sailed with the Jamaica Banana Producers Association Ltd. After passing his First Mate's certificate he sailed on ships of the British Antarctic Survey for twelve years. Since coming ashore he has obtained BSc and MPhil degrees and specialises in offshore and environmental consultancy throughout the world. He is a Fellow of the Royal Institution of Chartered Surveyors, the Royal Geographical Society and the Royal Institute of Navigation.

Christopher St J H Daniel *

Born 1933. Joined the National Maritime Museum in 1964, after a career at sea, becoming Head of the Department of Museum Services. In 1974, he was given leave to serve as second-in-command of the reproduction of Sir Francis Drake's famous ship the *Golden Hinde*, crossing the Atlantic and sailing to San Francisco via Panama, using copies of period Tudor navigation instruments. In 1986 he left the Museum to pursue his current career as a sundial designer. His works include the 'dolphin' sundial at Greenwich, marking the Queen's Silver Jubilee, and the Sir Francis Drake commemorative stained-glass sundial in Buckland Abbey. He is Chairman of the British Sundial Society, wrote the Shire book *Sundials*, and is the regular author of 'the sundial page' in *Clocks* magazine.

Colette Davidson

Born 1940. Colette Blundell was the eldest child of a farming family from Lancashire. She trained as a teacher and worked as a PE specialist before marrying Peter Davidson in 1963. During the next decade their daughters were born and she resumed her career in stages as the family moved to Lincolnshire and finally to Bristol with Peter's work. She studied for a BEd at Bristol whilst teaching full-time as a special needs coordinator at a local school. Now retired, she is an instructor with a riding-for-the-disabled group, a school governor and a parish councillor.

Peter Davidson

Born 1935. Born near Bolton, the second son of a policeman, and moved around various locations in Lancashire, finally ending up in Formby. Served with Moss Hutchison Line of Liverpool from 1951 to 1967, reaching the rank of Master before coming ashore in 1967. Worked as Superintendent Stevedore with Ocean Ports Liverpool, from 1967 to 1970, and then with Tor Line/Exxtor, a subsidiary of the Swedish Company Salen, from 1970 to 1991, initially as Operations Manager of a ferry terminal and finally as a Divisional Director for South East Asia, based in Singapore, always connected with the development of ro-ro ships and terminals. Ship Inspector with the UK P&I Club, 1991 to 1997. Consultancy work, mainly in the ports and ro-ro sector, from 1998 to 2006.

Anthony Davis *

Born 1931. HMS *Conway*, 1947/48. Apprenticed to the British Tanker Company (now BP Shipping) and served up to Second Mate on tankers up to 42,000 tons (in those days, a supertanker). Obtained his Master's certificate in 1957, and moved ashore to the Marine Training Department of BP. Subsequently qualified as an accountant and became Company Secretary of National Provident Institution, a major insurance company in the City. Set up unit trusts, involved with investment operations, promoted an Act of Parliament and chaired the insurance industry tax committee. On retirement, he became a tax consultant.

Eunice Elphick

Daughter of a Royal Naval officer. At the age of twelve she sailed on the *Carthage* to join her father in Ceylon (Sri Lanka) for three years. She subsequently lived as a girl in Hong Kong and Singapore, where she met and married Peter, after a whirlwind courtship. She sailed with him, and when he subsequently came ashore they lived in Singapore, Kuching, Jeddah and Rotterdam.

Peter Elphick

Born 1930. After pre-sea training he joined Harrison's as a cadet in 1946, staying with them until 1955, when he joined the Atlantic Steam Navigation Company, sailing on former landing ships at the start of the ro-ro ferry concept. In 1957 he was promoted Master in the Cathay Shipping Company of Singapore. He subsequently joined the Singapore Harbour Board, after which he worked in Sarawak, London, Liverpool, Felixstowe, Jeddah and Shuabai (Kuwait), managing and setting up container-port installations. His last post was as a consultant in The Hague, following which he retired in 1984. He has since become a successful writer, with seven books published to date.

Ann Gibb

Born 1938. Trained as a nurse at Guy's Hospital and the Hospital for Sick Children, Great Ormond Street. She worked for twenty-two years as a nurse, ward sister, tutor and examiner. In 1978 she married Ian Gibb and exchanged life in Brixton for a Wiltshire village. They have two daughters. Ann is involved in many local activities including the village school, the church, the Women's Institute, a Brendoncare Home and the Royal Alfred Seafarers' Society.

Ian Gibb

Born 1936. Joined P&O as an apprentice after a year at the School of Navigation, Warsash. Served in all ranks to Commodore of the fleet, having obtained his Master's certificate in 1962. In command of many ships of the P&O/Princess fleet including *Royal Princess, Sea Princess, Canberra* and *Oriana,* from which he retired in 1996. An Elder Brother of Trinity House from 1996, serving on the Lighthouse Board, as an Assessor in Admiralty Court and Board member and sometime Chairman of Harwich Haven Authority. Now active in several maritime charities (e.g. Marine Society and Sea Cadets, Royal Alfred Seafarer's Society, RNLI), and acts as an advisor to the Greenwich Maritime Institute.

John Gray *

Born 1937. Joined Thos and Jno Brocklebank Ltd as an apprentice in 1953. Saw officer service in the same company until 1965, when he joined the Decca Navigator Company as Master and Hydrographic Surveyor. Extra Master 1964. Mate and Master with Offshore Marine Ltd, 1968/69. From 1975 to 1986 he worked on marine operations for the construction and installation of the Ninian Central gravity platform and the Maureen platform deck. Conceived *Tog Mor*, the Howard Doris derrick barge which lifted the *Mary Rose*. From 1986 to 1988 he worked as an independent marine consultant, and he joined Trinity House Pilotage and Marine Services in 1988. From 1990 he was Managing Director of Eidesvik Shipping Ltd. He is a Fellow of the Nautical Institute.

Richard Goss

Born 1933. He served his apprenticeship with Prince Line. He then became interested in economics and passed 'A' level examinations at sea after following a correspondence course. He gained a scholarship to Cambridge, passing his Master's certificate during his first term as an undergraduate. He subsequently became an economic adviser to the Board of Trade and was the Economic Adviser to the Committee of Inquiry into Shipping in 1970. He moved from there to academia and was a professor in the Department of Maritime Studies and International Transport at the University of Cardiff. He has published many articles and books. He has MA and PhD degrees and is a Fellow of the Nautical Institute, the Royal Institute of Naval Architects and the Royal Society of Arts.

Keith Hart *

Born 1957. He joined Sir William Reardon Smith and Sons Ltd after leaving school in 1973. He stayed with them, leaving to serve on foreign-flagged ships before becoming involved in the offshore oil business. He is a Director of Aquarius

International Consultants Ltd. He has an Extra Master's certificate, and a BSc (Hons) degree. He is a Fellow of the Royal Institute of Navigation and of the Nautical Institute, and is a Captain in the Royal Naval Reserve.

Roy Jenkins

He joined Runcimans as an apprentice in 1947, where he was promoted to Chief Officer after obtaining his Master's certificate, staying with them until joining Silver Lines as a Chief Officer. He was promoted Master in 1967 and was made redundant in 1983 when the manning policy of the company changed.

Anne Jewell

Born 1934. A Plymouth girl, she met Terence Jewell in 1949. They married in 1956. She and Terence have four daughters. After living in Plymouth, when he left the sea they moved around the country, settling in their present home 32 years ago.

Terence Jewell

Born 1934. Spent a year at Plymouth School of Navigation before joining the Hain Steamship Company as an apprentice in 1951. He then had a short period with Clan Line before rejoining Hain's. He was with them until 1960, by which time he had reached the rank of Chief Officer. After he had obtained his Master's certificate he spent four years ashore in the family engineering firm. He had another spell at sea in the ocean tugs of the Royal Fleet Auxiliary, and then came ashore to work in a managerial capacity in the oil industry in the UK, Nigeria and Ghana, before retiring at the age of fifty-five. He is a Fellow of the Energy Institute and a Member of the Nautical Institute.

John Johnson-Allen

Born 1944. Went to sea in 1961 as an apprentice with the BP Tanker Company, staying with them until 1969, leaving as Second Mate with a First Mate's certificate. He subsequently qualified as a Chartered Surveyor, spent two years lecturing at Lowestoft College in the Maritime Studies Department and taught RYA evening classes for twenty-two years. Retiring from full-time employment as a surveyor in 2004, he was awarded an MA degree in maritime history at the Greenwich Maritime Institute, part of Greenwich University, in 2008. He is a Fellow of the Royal Institute of Navigation and the Royal Institution of Chartered Surveyors, and is currently Chairman of the Institute of Seamanship.

Herbert Jones

Born 1933. Starting as an apprentice with Eagle Oil in 1951, he stayed with that company for nine years before taking his Master's certificate and moving to MacAndrews, trading to the Mediterranean, including service on wine tankers. After leaving MacAndrews he became a Trinity House pilot on the North Channel for ten years, and then for Harwich port for a further eleven years until retirement.

Michael Keat

Born 1942. Joined the New Zealand Shipping Company as an apprentice in October 1958, aged sixteen years and two months, directly from grammar school. He stayed with NZSC until 1971, having gained a Master's certificate in 1968. He joined Overseas Containers Limited (OCL) in 1972 as part of a large ex-seafaring workforce helping to develop all the technologies of containerisation, specialising in the carriage of un-containerised cargo and livestock on container ships. After these days of R&D, he moved into the Commercial Documentation department of what was then P&O Nedlloyd. Advancing technology finally won, and early retirement was imposed in 2000.

Peter King

Born 1943. Went straight from school to the BP Tanker Company as an apprentice, from 1957 to 1961. He then joined New Zealand Shipping for the next seven years. In 1968 he was appointed Master in an inter-island ship in the Gilbert and Ellice Islands at the age of twenty-eight. He has since had a very varied career, and is now a marine surveyor and consultant, an Elder Brother of Trinity House, and until 2009 a council member of the Shipwrecked Mariners' Benevolent Society.

Sir Robin Knox-Johnston, CBE, RD and bar

Born 1939. He served as an apprentice in British India and stayed with them until he left the company as Chief Officer. He built *Suhaili* in India and, on his way, sailing her back to the UK, stopped in Durban, where he was in command of a coastal ship for three months. After coming ashore, his career is well documented. He has been President of the Sail Training Association, is a Trustee of the National Maritime Museum Falmouth, a Council member of the Society for Nautical Research, and a Fellow of the Royal Institute of Navigation. He holds records for various sailing achievements, is an author, and is currently chairman of Clipper Ventures plc.

Christopher Laycock

Born 1948. Joined British and Commonwealth Lines as a direct-entry cadet in 1966. Officer service in passenger ships, general cargo and container vessels. Certificate of Competency as Master Mariner in 1977. He then joined P&O Jet Ferries and served as Master in Jetfoils on the London to Ostend service. From 1981 to 2001 he held management posts in maritime-related industries both in the UK and in the Far East. In 2001 he acquired the 140-year-old Allchorn Pleasure Boats business, based in Eastbourne, and was instrumental in the company's vessels being entered onto the National Register of Historic Vessels.

Ramsey McLaren

Born 1926. Started his seagoing career as an apprentice with R Chapman and Sons of Newcastle in 1942. After his Second Mate's certificate he joined Sutherlands, also of Newcastle. He sat his First Mate's certificate in Singapore, having joined Shell Tankers, with whom he stayed for some years until joining Common Brothers, sailing on Border Tankers. In 1959 he became a Trinity House Pilot, based in Harwich. Died 2008.

Kenneth Owen

Born 1934. Joined Blue Funnel Lines as a midshipman and served with them, including sixteen years as Chief Officer, until the container revolution happened. After obtaining command he sailed with many companies under various flags, including OCL and Maersk. In that time he has worked out that he has carried over one million containers. He was still in command at the age of sixty-eight, and in 2004 he was Shipmaster of the Year.

Malcolm Parrott *

Born 1941. Joined the New Zealand Shipping Company as an apprentice in 1958, his first ship being the *Otaio*. He remained with that company whilst completing his apprenticeship and attaining his Second Mate's and First Mate's certificates. In 1969 he joined the Royal Fleet Auxiliary as Second Officer and remained with them until 1977, serving on various ships and obtaining his Master's certificate. In 1977 he joined Sea Containers Ltd and sailed as a Master on various ships until 1985. He then came ashore and held senior management positions with that company. He is currently a Director of the Maritime Group (Europe). He is a Fellow of the Royal Institute of Navigation, the Institute of Logistics and Transport and the Nautical Institute.

Jeremy Procter

Born 1942. Joined BP Tankers in 1960 and spent sixteen years with the company, gaining his Master's certificate in 1970. This was followed by a further seventeen years with BP International and BP Exploration, involving a variety of posts including moving exploration rigs in the UK Continental Shelf area, Marine Superintendent at BP's Rotterdam refinery, managing supply and standby vessel operations in the UKCS, and Marine and Offsites Superintendent at Sullom Voe terminal. In 1992 he spent two years as a marine consultant based in Maracaibo, on loan from BP to the Venezuelan petrochemical subsidiary of PDVSA. In 1994 he took early retirement and set up a consultancy specialising in marine and port services for the oil industry. A past Chairman of the North of Scotland branch of the Nautical Institute, he was also a member of Aberdeen Harbour Board from 2003 to 2007.

Mary Procter

Born 1944. Trained as a nurse at St Bartholomew's Hospital in London, 1963–67, then returning to Dorset to work for a local GP. Married Jeremy Procter in 1970, and went away to sea with him for nearly three years until the birth of a son. Two years later a daughter was born, and at the end of 1976 her husband gave up his seagoing days. Based in Aberdeen since 1979, but has also lived in the Netherlands, Shetland and Venezuela. Since returning to Aberdeen, she has been involved with both the Citizen's Advice Bureau and Victim Support.

John Redman

Born 1956. Joined Shell Tankers (UK) Ltd in 1971 as a Navigating Cadet. He was awarded the Shell Cadet of the Year prize in 1975 and gained promotion to Third Officer the same year. Promotion to Second Officer followed in 1978 and, after gaining his Master's certificate, he was promoted to Chief Officer in 1982. His sea experience includes service on tankers and bulk carriers ranging from 18,000 to 350,000 tons. He came ashore in 1984 and studied for a BSc in nautical studies at Plymouth Polytechnic, graduating in 1987. He is a shareholder and Director of W K Webster & Co Ltd, a company specialising in managing marine and transit insurance claims.

Mary Richards-Jones

Born 1929. A native of Streatham, London, and educated at St Helens, a private school, where she achieved her Oxford School Certificate. Her ambition was to go on the stage but her father disagreed. And so she went to work in the city, having first obtained her RSA in shorthand and typing. Eventually she became personal assistant to the editor of *Civil Engineering*, and later PA to a heating and ventilating consultant. During this time her love of the stage continued and she passed her LGSM in speech and drama. This led to amateur dramatic competitions, wherein she won Performer of the Week in the Croydon One Act Festival at the Fairfield Halls. She married Second Officer Peter Richards-Jones in 1954, and they have two sons.

Peter Richards-Jones

Born 1930. Served his apprenticeship with J & C Harrison's, a London-based tramp-ship company, and then saw officer service with Port Line. After gaining his Master's certificate he came ashore and initially became a shipside surveyor, specialising in frozen meats and obtaining the Diploma in Meat Technology. He then spent some years with Walford Lines as their Marine Superintendent before becoming a lecturer specialising in astronomy and nautical studies.

Oliver Signorini

Born 1937. Joined Stag Line Ltd as Deck Apprentice in 1953, serving on tramp ships. Officer service in all ranks with Caltex, LOF and Trident Tankers (P&O Bulk Shipping Division). Obtained Master's certificate in 1962. Master with P&O Bulk

Shipping Division on product tankers – crude carriers and very large OBOs. 1972-1980 Harbour Master of Peterhead, 1972 to 1980, a joint appointment by the Scottish Office and Peterhead Harbour Board. During his term of office, the port developed into the second largest oil support base in Scotland, and the largest fishing port in Europe. Worked for Texaco North Sea as Marine Services Coordinator between 1980 and 1994. In 1996, formed SOS Consultancy Services Ltd, providing project marine/safety consultancy to all North Sea operators until retirement in 2007.

David Sims

Born 1939. He joined British India Steam Navigation at the age of seventeen and stayed with them for his entire career at sea. He sailed with Robin Knox-Johnston on one ship, where they both built canoes in their spare time. After coming ashore he became a cargo superintendent until retirement. Since retiring he has studied and obtained an MA in landscape history. He is a member of the Royal Institute of Navigation and of the Nautical Institute.

David Smith

Born 1931. Spent a year at the School of Navigation, Warsash, before joining the Pacific Steam Navigation Company as an apprentice in 1948, serving on cargo liners, a troopship and a passenger liner before obtaining his Second Mate's certificate in 1952. He then spent six months on molasses tankers with Athel Line before joining Royal Mail Lines, where once again he served on cargo liners, a troopship and a passenger liner. He obtained his Master's certificate in 1957 and left the sea in 1958. He then qualified as a dental surgeon, and subsequently became professor of dental radiology at King's College, London, and a Fellow of the Royal College of Radiologists. He died on 15 February 2010, just after this book was completed.

Cecil Smylie

Born 1934. Following two years at HMS *Worcester*, he joined P&O as a cadet in 1951 and remained with the company until 1977. On leaving P&O he spent four years in various pilotage assignments including Libya, Sullom Voe and the Arabian Gulf. From 1981 until retirement in 1995 he held senior management positions with shipping agency majors in the United Arab Emirates. This particular period encompassed the unsettled operational difficulties experienced in the course of the Iran–Iraq conflict, with its toll on Gulf shipping and the consequential effects of 'Desert Shield' and eventually 'Desert Storm'. On retirement, he returned to London as Managing Director of the Greek-owned Fairdeal Group operation. Awarded the US Navy citation for service to the Fifth Fleet throughout 'Desert Shield' and 'Desert Storm'.

Alan Storey

Born 1937. Went to South Shields Marine College for pre-sea training, subsequently serving his apprenticeship with the Temple Steamship Company, of Newcastle, from 1954 to 1958. Three years later, after gaining his First Mate's certificate, he joined Stevenson Clark, on coasting colliers, principally on the east coast of England. He stayed with that company until he joined Trinity House in 1969 as a North Channel pilot, where he stayed until he retired.

Ian Tew

Born 1943. Went to Pangbourne College from 1956 to 1960 for pre-sea training, then joining British India Steam Navigation as an apprentice until 1963. He was aboard the *Dara* when she was sunk by a bomb on board in 1961. He subsequently joined Ellermans, and then went to the Far East, joining Jardines in 1966. In 1974 he became a salvage master and has had a successful career including working in the Persian Gulf during the Iran–Iraq war. Since retiring he has published an account of his experiences in *Salvage: a Personal Odyssey* (Seafarer Books, 2007).

Eric Tinney

Born 1934. After a short pre-sea training course in Greenock, he served his apprenticeship in Glasgow-based tramp ships. After obtaining his Second Mate's certificate, he sailed with Shell Tankers and then with J & J Denholm Ship Management, becoming Chief Officer in 1963. In 1964 he moved to foreign-flagged ships, sailing, amongst others, with ZIM Line of Israel, for six years, being promoted Master in 1967. He became a Marine Superintendent in 1972.

Michael Twomey RD

Born 1931. From pre-sea training at King Edward VII Nautical College in London, he joined Port Line in 1949 as an apprentice. He then stayed with them throughout a career at sea spanning thirty-seven years. He was promoted Master in 1968, and was in command of the *Atlantic Causeway* during her deployment as a helicopter carrier in the Falklands War in 1982. He also held a commission in the Royal Naval Reserve, rising to the rank of Captain.

Jim Whadcoat

Born 1925. Joined Union Castle Line in 1941, straight from school, and served as apprentice and uncertificated Fourth Officer until 1945, when he took his Second Mate's certificate. He returned to Union Castle, leaving after promotion to Chief Officer. He worked on the Thames Water Board ships until becoming a Trinity House Pilot on the South Channel in 1953. He retired in 1985.

Adrian White

Born 1939. Undertook pre-sea training at TS *Mercury* from 1952 to 1955. He served his apprenticeship with Trinder Anderson and Company, before joining Ellerman Line, with whom he stayed until taking his Master's certificate. He then came ashore and after various appointments had a career in the marine electronics industry, spending some fifteen years working in Russia and Eastern Europe in the Communist era. He ended his career as a Director of Decca Navigators.

John Williams

Born 1947. Joined the Bibby Line in 1964, sailing on *Yorkshire* and then general ships and bulk carriers before taking his Second Mate's certificate in 1968. He obtained his Master's certificate in 1974 and became Chief Officer of several Bibby Line vessels. He left the sea in 1977 to join the UK deep-sea fishing industry and became a partner in a Grimsby-based company, leaving in 1998 to become General Manager of the Hull company, Boyd Line. He has served extensively overseas, including the Falkland Islands, the Balkans, West Africa and the Middle East. He retired in 2007, only to qualify as an ISM Auditor and work independently as a specialist in marine health and safety for the oil exploration industry and the renewable energy sector.

Roger Woodcock

Born 1937. Following three months pre-sea training at King Edward VII Nautical College in London, in the autumn of 1954, he joined the BP Tanker Company as an apprentice until the end of 1959, when he returned to the same college for his Second Mate's certificate. Returning to BP, he stayed with them for the remainder of his career at sea, being promoted Master in 1973. On coming ashore in 1974 he became a Marine Superintendent with BP until he took retirement and became an independent consultant.

Richard Woodman

Born 1943. Went to sea in a sail-training race before joining the Blue Funnel Line as a midshipman in 1960 to serve a full four-year apprenticeship. After two years as a junior officer with Alfred Holt & Company he spent a winter in Ocean Weather Ships in the North Atlantic before joining Trinity House. He was promoted Commander in 1980 and commanded several Trinity House vessels, coming ashore into Operational Management from THV *Patricia* in 1991. Heavily involved with the automation of the lighthouse service and caught up in the inevitable downsizing that went with it, he took early retirement in 1997 to further his literary career and sail. He served for several years on the National Historic Ships Committee, including as Chairman, was elected a Younger Brother of Trinity House in 2000 and an Elder Brother in 2006. Remains active with Trinity House, and is currently writing a history of the British merchant navy in five volumes.

Acknowledgments

Frist and foremost, we would like to thank all those members of the Honourable Company of Master Mariners who so willingly gave up their time to share their experiences with us. We like to think that most of them enjoyed it. We certainly did! Our experience has been richer than the transcription of the interviews would suggest. We have individual memories from the interviews: hospitality and laughter at homes around the country, a huge bowl of mussels and a bottle of wine at a creek-side pub in Faversham, with yet more mussels in a restaurant in Aberdeen, and a lunch at the Baltic Exchange of a type that the City Fathers try to pretend is a thing of the past. Interviews have been conducted in unlikely places, such as the sail locker of a racing yacht. Others have had a certain poignancy: the oxygen bottle in the corner of one room and a walking frame in another, while we knew that we were just a hazy blur to one contributor.

David Smith thanks Ruth and Jim Yeeles for their patience when help was needed with computing, Patrick Jones for help with the origins of the London Nautical Training School, and Elaine Webster and Melanie Calver for reading and commenting on an early draft.

John Johnson-Allen thanks Dr Phil Belcher, who gave him the idea for a book, and Professor Sarah Palmer, for her support and encouragement.

It has been a real pleasure working with our publisher, Patricia Eve of Seafarer Books, Hugh Brazier, the editor, and Louis Mackay, the graphic designer. Theirs is a personal and old-fashioned approach that made preparing our manuscript for publication a delight.

Peter Adams, another contributor, catches the mood of the book perfectly with his atmospheric artwork.

The dedication at the front of the book is our way of thanking our wives for their support and encouragement.

This is a work of history made possible by the individual memories of each of the contributors, and it should, perhaps, be remembered that the stories they tell are of events that in many cases happened over half a century ago. The authors do not necessarily share the sentiments and opinions expressed by the individual contributors, but are responsible for, and apologise for, any errors in the connecting text.

We would like to finish by making a possibly unprecedented and undoubtedly solipsistic acknowledgment of each other. This book was not a joint effort from the beginning, as we had both started separately on similar projects. When we decided to collaborate, rather than compete, we could not take it for granted that we would work together for over two years in harmony and friendship.

David Smith and John Johnson-Allen
January 2010

The Wellington Trust

The authors have assigned their royalties from the sale of this book for the benefit of the Wellington Trust. The Wellington Trust is a registered charity that owns the HQS *Wellington.* Moored in the Thames, off Temple Stairs in London, she is the floating livery hall of the Honourable Company of Master Mariners. The primary aims of the Trust are the restoration, maintenance and preservation for the public benefit of the sloop HQS *Wellington* as part of the nation's heritage, and the education of the public in the history and traditions of the British merchant navy.

THE WELLINGTON TRUST